I0010793

Microsoft Office 2019 Beginner

M.L. HUMPHREY

Copyright © 2021 M.L. Humphrey

All Rights Reserved.

ISBN: 978-1-63744-049-0

SELECT TITLES BY M.L. HUMPHREY

EXCEL ESSENTIALS 2019

Excel 2019 Beginner

Excel 2019 Intermediate

Excel 2019 Formulas & Functions

Excel 2019 Formulas and Functions Study Guide

WORD ESSENTIALS 2019

Word 2019 Beginner

Word 2019 Intermediate

POWERPOINT ESSENTIALS 2019

PowerPoint 2019 Beginner

PowerPoint 2019 Intermediate

ACCESS ESSENTIALS 2019

Access 2019 Beginner

Access 2019 Intermediate

CONTENTS

Word 2019 Beginner

WORD ESSENTIALS 2019 BOOK 1

M.L. HUMPHREY

CONTENTS

Copyright © 2021 M.L. Humphrey

All Rights Reserved.

ISBN: 978-1-63744-033-9

Introduction

The purpose of this guide is to introduce you to the basics of using Microsoft Word 2019. While there are a number of other word processing programs out there, Word is still the gold-standard go-to program in use in large portions of the corporate world, so if you're going to be involved in a white collar job (and even some blue collar jobs), being familiar with Word will be a significant advantage for you. And essential for many jobs. (The days of having an assistant who could do those things for you are gone.)

Word at its most basic is incredibly simple to use. You open a new file, type in your text, save, and done.

But chances are you'll want control over the appearance of what you type. Maybe you need to use a different font or font size. Maybe you want to indent your paragraphs. Or include a bulleted or numbered list.

That's where this guide comes in. First I will walk you through the absolute basics (open, save, delete) but then most of this guide will be focused on what to do with your text once it's been typed into your document.

Having said that I'm not going to cover everything you can do in Word. The goal of this guide is to get you up to speed and comfortable with what you'll need for probably 98% of what you'll use Word for on a daily basis.

Some of the exceptions to that are if you're working in an environment where you need to use track changes with a group of users or you need to create something like tables or complex multilevel lists. Those are more advanced topics that are covered in *Word 2019 Intermediate*.

The goal here is to give you a solid foundation that you can work from.

As noted in the title and above, this book is written using Word 2019. I previously wrote a book, *Word for Beginners*, that was written using Word 2013 and was written to be generic enough that any user of Word could learn the basics from it. But this guide is written specifically for Word 2019, so I'm not going to mention what wasn't possible in older version of Word, for example.

As a beginner it probably won't matter. Where it becomes more relevant is at the intermediate level. But just so you know. The focus in this guide is Word 2019.

Alright then. Let's get started with some basic terminology.

Basic Terminology

Before we get started, I want to make sure that we're on the same page in terms of terminology.

Tab

I refer to the menu choices at the top of the screen (File, Home, Insert, Design, Layout, References, Mailings, Review, View, and Help) as tabs. If you click on one you'll see that the way it's highlighted sort of looks like an old-time filing system like below with the Home tab.

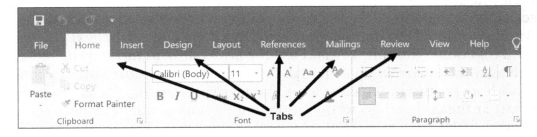

Each tab you select will show you different options.

For example, in the image above, I have the Home tab selected and you can do various tasks such as cut/copy/paste, format paint, change the font, change the formatting of a paragraph, apply a style to your text, find/replace words in your document, or select the text in your document. Other tabs give other options.

Click

If I tell you to click on something, that means to use your mouse (or trackpad) to move the arrow on the screen over to a specific location and left-click or right-click on the option. (See the next definition for the difference between left-click and right-click).

If you left-click, this generally selects an item. If you right-click, this generally creates a dropdown list of options to choose from. If I don't tell you which to do, left- or right-click, then left-click.

Left-Click/Right-Click

If you look at your mouse or your trackpad, you generally have two flat buttons to press. One is on the left side, one is on the right. If I say left-click that means to press down on the button on the left. If I say right-click that means press down on the button on the right.

Not all track pads have left- and right-hand buttons. In that case, you'll basically want to press on either the bottom left-hand side of the track pad or the bottom right-hand side of the trackpad. Since you're working blind it may take a little trial and error to get the option you want.

Select or Highlight

If I tell you to select text, that means to left-click at the end of the text you want to select, hold that left-click, and move your cursor to the other end of the text.

Another option is to use the Shift key. Go to one end of the text you want to select. Hold down the shift key and use the arrow keys to move to the other end of the text. If you arrow up or down, that will select an entire row at a time.

With both methods, which side of the text you start on doesn't matter. You can start at the end and go to the beginning or start at the beginning and go to the end. Just be sure to start at one end or the other. You cannot start in the middle

The text you've selected will then be highlighted in gray. Like the words "sample text" in this image:

This is sample text so you can see what I'm talking about.

If you need to select text that isn't touching you can do this by selecting your first section of text and then holding down the Ctrl key and selecting your second section of text using your mouse. (You can't arrow to the second section of text or you'll lose your already selected text.)

Dropdown Menu

If you right-click in a Word document, you will see what I'm going to refer to as a dropdown menu. (Sometimes it will actually drop upward if you're towards the bottom of the document.)

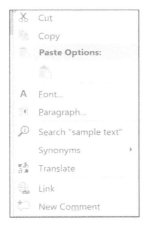

A dropdown menu provides you a list of choices to select from.

There are also dropdown menus available for some of the options listed under the tabs at the top of the screen.

For example, if you go to the Paragraph section of the Home tab, you will see arrows next to the options for bulleted lists, numbered lists, multi-level lists, line and paragraph spacing, shading, and borders.

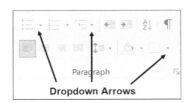

If you click on any of those arrows you'll see a list of additional choices.

Expansion Arrows

I don't know the official word for these, but you'll also notice at the bottom right corner of most of the sections in each tab that there are little arrows. If you hold your mouse over the arrow you will see a brief description of what clicking on the expansion arrow will do like below with Paragraph Settings.

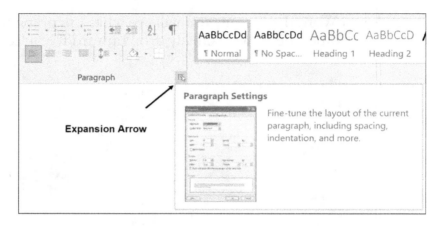

In general, clicking on that arrow will then open a dialogue box although sometimes a task pane will open instead.

Dialogue Box

Dialogue boxes, such as this one for Find and Replace, are pop-up boxes that cover specialized settings.

As just mentioned, if you click on an expansion arrow, it will often open a dialogue box that contains more choices than are visible in that section.

When you right-click in a Word document and choose Font, Paragraph, or Hyperlink from the dropdown menu that also opens a dialogue box

Some of the menu options will do so as well. For example, clicking on Replace in the Editing section of the Home tab will bring up the Find and Replace dialogue box. (As will using Ctrl + H, which is a control shortcut. We'll define those momentarily.)

Dialogue boxes often allow the most granular level of control over an option so if you can't find what you want in the menu section tabs at the top, try opening the relevant dialogue box.

Also, be aware that if you have more than one Word document open and open a dialogue box in one of those documents, you may not be able to move to the other documents you have open until you close the dialogue box.

Task Pane

Sometimes instead of opening a dialogue box, Excel will open what I refer to as a task pane. These are separate panes that appear to the right, left, or bottom of your main workspace. (As opposed to a dialogue box which generally appears as a separate item on top of your workspace.)

I believe the Navigation pane is open on the left-hand side by default for any new document for new users of Word. It will show headings if you use those in your document and is also the default location if you try to use Find in your document.

Task panes can be closed by clicking on the X in the top right corner. If you close the Navigation pane and want it back, Ctrl + F, which is for Find, will open it again.

Clicking on the expansion arrow for the Clipboard section of the Home tab also opens a task pane.

Scroll Bar

This is more useful in Excel than in Word, but on the right-hand side of the screen and sometimes at the bottom of the screen you may see a scroll bar which will allow you to see the rest of your document if it's too large or too long to be fully visible on the screen.

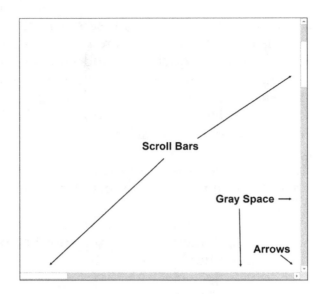

You can click in the gray space around the bar to move up or down a small amount. Or you can left-click on the bar, hold the left-click, and drag the bar to move through the document more quickly.

You can also use the arrows at the ends to move through your document.

The scroll bar isn't always visible in Word. If you don't see it, move your mouse over to the side of the screen and it should appear.

Also, by default you normally won't see a scroll bar at the bottom of the screen, but it is possible to see one, usually when you have your document or screen zoomed in.

Arrow

If I ever tell you to arrow to the left or right or up or down, that just means use your arrow keys. This will move your cursor to the left one space, to the right one space, up one line, or down one line. If you're at the end of a line and arrow to the right, it will take you to the beginning of the next line. If you're at the beginning of a line and arrow to the left, it will take you to the end of the last line.

Cursor

There are two possible meanings for cursor. One is the one I just used. In your Word document, you will see that there is a blinking line. This indicates where you are in the document. If you type text, each letter will appear where the cursor was at the time you typed it. The cursor will move (at least in the U.S. and I'd assume most European versions) to the right as you type. This version of the cursor should be visible at all times unless you have text selected.

The other type of cursor is the one that's tied to the movement of your mouse or trackpad. When you're typing, it will not be visible. But stop typing and move your mouse or trackpad, and you'll see it.

If the cursor is positioned over your text, it will look somewhat like a tall skinny capital I. If you move it up to the menu options or off to the sides, it becomes a white arrow. (Except for when you position it over any option under the tabs that can be typed in such as Font Size or Font where it will once again look like a skinny capital I.)

Usually I won't refer to your cursor, I'll just say, "click" or "select" or whatever action you need to take with it. Moving the cursor to that location will be implied.

I may also sometimes refer to this as moving your mouse or holding your mouse over something instead of moving your cursor or holding your cursor over an item.

Quick Access Toolbar

In the very top left corner of Word is something called the Quick Access Toolbar. By default it contains icons that let you save, undo, and redo. Bur you can customize your options for tasks that you use often by clicking on that arrow at the end and choosing from the dropdown menu it will bring up.

For example, I will usually customize mine to include inserting section breaks because those are listed on a different tab than the text formatting options I also need to be using at the same time. This saves me having to move back and forth between the two.

Control Shortcuts

What I refer to as control shortcuts are easy and quick ways to complete common tasks by using the Ctrl key paired with, generally, a letter.

I mentioned the Find control shortcut, Ctrl + F, above as well as the Replace shortcut, Ctrl + H. So, for example, by typing Ctrl and the letter H at the same time you can open the Replace dialogue box that allows you to replace text in your document with different text.

When I refer to a control shortcut, I write the letter as a capital letter, but you don't actually have to use the capitalized version of the letter. It just means hold down the control key and that letter at the same time.

There is a list of control shortcuts at the back of this book. It is not a comprehensive list, but I highly recommend that you memorize the ones that are there. They will save you a tremendous amount of time over the years.

Absolute Basics

Before we do anything else, there are a few absolute basics that we should cover.

Starting a New Word File

To start a brand new Word file, click on Word from your applications menu or, if you have one, the shortcut on your computer's taskbar. Either choice will bring up a welcome screen with a list of various options or templates, including the first one which is for a "Blank document". Ninety-nine percent of the time that's the one you'll want. To use it, left-click on the image.

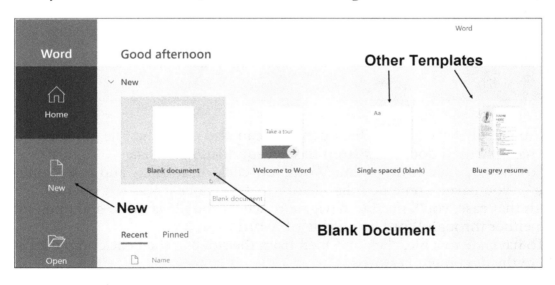

If you're already in Word and want to start a new Word file, go to the File tab and choose New from the left-hand menu. It will again show various choices. This time the Blank Document choice will be at the top and other templates will be shown below.

You can also the control shortcut Ctrl +N while in an existing document and a new blank document will immediately open.

Opening an Existing Word File

To open an existing Word file you can either go to the folder where the file is saved and double-click on the file name. Or, if the file is one you used recently, you can instead open Word and choose the file from the list of Recent documents. (If it's a file you've pinned even if it hasn't been used recently, you can still choose it from the list of Pinned documents.)

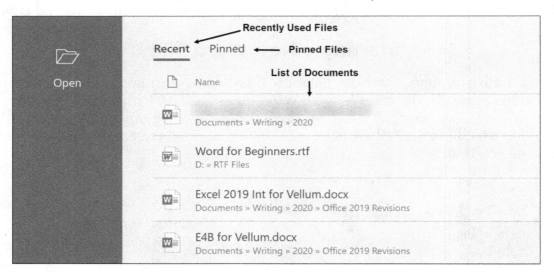

If you already have a Word file open, you can also go to the File tab and choose any recently used document from the Recent documents list.

To choose a file from within Word, left-click on it once, and it will open as long as you haven't renamed the file or moved it since it was last opened.

(In that case, you'll need to navigate to where the file is saved and open it that way, either through Word or outside of Word.)

To navigate to a file, click on Open from the sidebar, then click on the location where the document is stored.

If you use OneDrive click on that. I don't, so I click on Browse to open a standard Windows dialogue box. Mine defaults to the Documents folder on This PC. I can then navigate through my folders or shortcuts from there and click on the file I need.

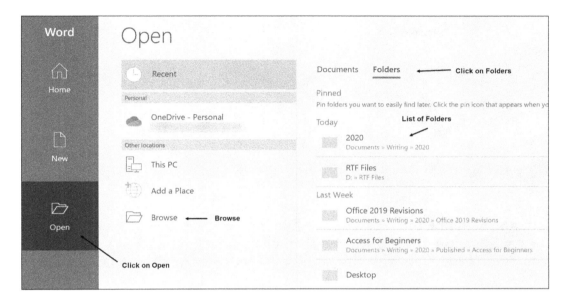

You can also click on Folders on the right-hand side to display a list of folders that contain files you've recently used. Click on one of the folder names to bring up a list of the files and folders that are in that folder.

It will show the files and folders within the Word workspace. Only documents that can be opened in Word will be listed.

Saving a Word File

If you want to keep the changes you made to a document, you need to save it. To do so quickly, you can use Ctrl + S or click on the small image of a floppy disk in the Quick Access Toolbar in the top left corner of the screen above File.

For a document you've already saved, that will overwrite the prior version of the document with the current version while keeping the file name, file type, and file location the same.

If you try to save a file that has never been saved before, Word will automatically default to the Save As option and open a Save This File dialogue box which asks for the file name you want to use and a location to save the file in.

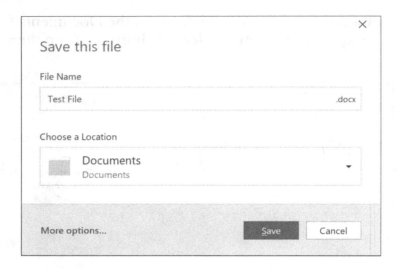

Type your file name into the box for File Name, choose your location from the Choose a Location dropdown, and then click Save.

The default file type with this option is .docx which should be fine for most purposes.

If you are working with someone who has a version of Word that dates prior to 2007, you'll need to save the file as a .doc file. To do so, click on the More Options choice at the bottom of the dialogue box.

This will take you to the Save As option on the File tab screen. From there you can double-click on a location to save your file and this will open a Save As dialogue box which lets you choose your file type as well.

Even for an existing document there will still be times when you need to use the Save As option to change the location of a file, the name of a file, or the file type.

(With respect to file type, I often need to save a .doc file as a .pdf file or a .docx file or to save a .docx file as a .doc file, for example.)

You can reach the Save As option while working with an existing file by clicking on the File tab and then the Save As option on the left-hand side.

From there double-click on your location and make whatever necessary changes you need to make in the dialogue box that opens. (If the location is not listed, you can get the dialogue box to open and then navigate to your preferred location using the left-hand side options.)

To rename a file, it's actually best to close the file and then go to where the file is currently saved and rename it that way rather than using the Save As option within Word.

This is because if you use Save As, Word will keep the original version of the file with the old name as well as create a version with the new name. That's great when you want version control, but not when you just wanted to rename your file and now can't remember which version is the most current one.

(This is a good opportunity to point out that using something like YYYYMMDD or V1, V2, etc. in your file names can really help with keeping version control. If I have a file named Great Report 20201220 and one named Great Report 20201101, I can easily tell which is the most current version. They will also sort in order if you use YYYYMMDD format for the dates in the file name and place the date in the exact same spot in the name each time.)

Renaming a Word File

As discussed above, you can use Save As to give an existing file a new name, but that approach will leave you with two versions of the file, one with the old name and one with the new name. If you just want to change the name of the existing file, close it and then navigate to where you've saved it.

Click on the file name once to select it, click on it a second time to highlight the name, and then type in the new name you want to use, replacing the old one.

If you rename the file this way outside of Word, there will only be one version of the file left, the one with the new name you wanted.

Just be aware that if you rename a file by navigating to where it's located and changing the name that you then won't be able to access the file from the Recent Workbooks listing under Open file, since that listing will still list the old name which no longer exists.

(This actually applies for any file that is moved, renamed, or in a location that is no longer available. If you look at that file listing above, my file Word for Beginners was in a location D: which was a removable thumb drive. I don't have that thumb drive attached to my computer at the moment, so if I tried to click on that file name right now I would see an error telling me that the directory name isn't valid. I personally run into this issue more with moved files than I do with renamed ones, but it's something to be aware of.)

Deleting a Word File

You can't delete a Word file from within Word. You need to close the file you want to delete and then navigate to where the file is stored and delete the file there without opening it. Once you've located the file, click on the file name. (Only enough to select it. Make sure you haven't double-clicked and highlighted the name which will delete the file name but not the file.) Next, choose Delete from the menu at the top of the screen, or right-click and choose Delete from the dropdown menu.

Closing a Word File

To close a Word file click on the X in the top right corner. You can also go to File and then choose Close which will keep Word open if that was your last Word file.

(You can also use Ctrl + W, but I never have. That also closes the file but leaves Word open.)

If no changes were made to the document since you saved it last, the document will just close.

If changes have been made, Word will ask you if you want to save those changes. Your choices are to Save, Don't Save, or Cancel. For a brand new document you need to provide a file name and choose a location. For an existing one, Word will assume the file name and location are going to stay the same.

If you cancel, the document remains open. If you save, it will overwrite the prior version of the document with any changes you've made. If you choose don't save, then the version of the document that remains will be the one that existed last time you saved. Or, in the case of a new document, that document will be lost.

I almost always default to saving any changes. If I'm in doubt about whether I'd be overwriting something important, I cancel and choose to Save As and save the current file as a later version of the document just in case (e.g., Great Book v2).

If right before you closed the document you copied an image or a large block of text, you may also see a dialogue box asking if you want to keep that image or text on the clipboard to paste elsewhere Usually the answer for me is no, but if you had planned on pasting that image or text somewhere else and hadn't yet done so, you can say to keep it on the clipboard.

Basic Tasks

At its most basic, adding text into a Word document is incredibly simple. Just open a new blank document and start typing. When you're done, save the document.

But you probably want to do more with your text than that.

We'll cover all the formatting, which is the majority of what you'll want to do, in the next section. First, I want to cover a few basic tasks in Word that will make your life easier as you enter your text and then edit it.

Undo

Undo lets you take the last thing (or few things) you did, and undo it. That means you don't have to be afraid to try something that you're not sure will work, because you can always reverse it.

To undo something, simply type Ctrl + Z. If you did a few things you didn't like you can keep typing Ctrl + Z until they're all gone.

Your other option is to use the undo arrow in the Quick Access Toolbar. It's the left-pointing arrow and will only be an option to click on when there's something that can be undone.

When there are multiple actions that can be undone the Quick Access Toolbar option will also include a dropdown arrow. You can click on it to see a full listing of what actions can be undone.

Keep in mind that Word undoes things in order. So if you highlighted text, bolded that text, and then underlined it and you want to undo the highlight, you'll have to undo the bolding and underline as well.

You can't pick and choose.

When there are multiple steps to undo the Quick Access Toolbar option is the better choice because you can simply choose the last item on the list that you wanted to undo and it as well as all of the actions that were taken after it will be undone.

Redo

If you take it too far and undo too much and want something back, then you can choose to redo. That's done by typing Ctrl + Y.

There is also a Redo option on the Quick Access Toolbar. It's the right-pointing arrow.

It works much like the Undo option since it's only available when there is something that can be redone, but it will only redo one action at a time. So in my example above where I could undo three actions at once, to put them back in place I had to do each one individually.

Delete

Another basic task you need to master is how to delete text. There are a few ways to do this. If you're trying to delete something that you just typed, use the backspace key to delete the letters one at a time.

You can also click into your text to place the cursor next to the text you want to delete and then use the backspace or delete keys depending on where the cursor is relative to the text you're trying to delete.

If your cursor is on the left-hand side of text, use the delete key. If it's on the right-hand side, use the backspace key. (And if you get it wrong, remember that you have Ctrl + Z to undo what you just did.)

If you want to delete a large chunk of text at one time, select the text first and then use the delete OR backspace key.

Select All

The other basic task that you should know about before we start talking formatting is how to select all of the text in your document.

Select All is very useful for applying a format to your entire document or for copying text from one document to another or another program.

I tend to write in the default font that Word uses and then change the font once I'm done, for example.

The easiest way to select all of your text is to use Ctrl + A. You can also go to the Editing section of the Home tab, click on the arrow next to Select, and choose Select All from the dropdown menu.

I have also added Select All as one of my Quick Access Toolbar options in the past.

If you ever choose all of the text in a document and then decide you didn't want to, just click somewhere in the document and the selection will go away. (You can also arrow up or down, but that will take you to the top or the bottom of the document and you may not want that.)

Copying, Cutting, and Pasting

Copy and Cut are similar. They're both a way to move text from one location to another. Copy leaves the text where it was and creates a copy of that text to move to the new location. Cut removes the text from where it was and puts the text on a "clipboard" (that's usually not visible to you) for movement to a new location.

Paste is how you tell Word where that new location is regardless of whether you copied or cut the text.

The first step in copying or cutting text is to select all of the text you want to move.

As discussed before, to select text you can left-click at one end of the text, hold down that left-click and move your mouse or trackpad until all of the text you want is highlighted. Or you can click at one end of the text and use the shift key and the arrow keys. Your selected text will be highlighted in gray.

Once your text is selected, to copy it type Ctrl + C or to cut it type Ctrl + X.

If you don't want to use the control shortcuts, you can also go to the Clipboard section of the Home tab and choose Copy or Cut from there. Or you can right-click and choose Copy or Cut from the dropdown menu.

I recommend using the control shortcuts, because it's the easiest and fastest option and doesn't require using your mouse or trackpad.

If you copy text, it remains visible in the location you copied it from. Behind the scenes Word has taken a copy of that text and placed it on a "clipboard" for use elsewhere.

If you cut text, the text is immediately removed from the document. It too is placed on a "clipboard" for use elsewhere. (This also means that cutting text, if you choose not to paste it elsewhere, deletes it.)

If you want to collect multiple selections of text to eventually paste elsewhere, click on the expansion arrow for the Clipboard section of the Home tab. This will open the clipboard. You can then select different sections of your document and copy or cut them and they should appear on the clipboard for your use.

(It looks like it should also work even if you don't have the clipboard open at the time you're copying or cutting multiple selections, but best practice would be to have it visible so you know that the items your are copying or cutting are being captured properly.) Here I've selected three snippets of text. Two were copied, one was cut, but there's no difference in how they appear on the clipboard.

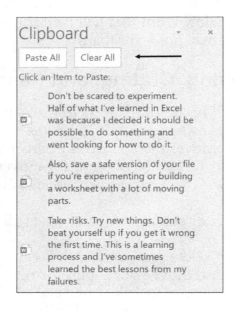

If you ever copy or cut items to your clipboard and decide you don't want them, just choose Clear All. Otherwise click on where you want to paste an individual item in your document and then click on the item in the clipboard to paste it.

The Paste All option will paste all of your copied or cut selections into that one location.

Items remain on the clipboard after they are pasted which means you can technically paste something into your document multiple times using the clipboard option.

If all you want to do is just copy or cut one thing and paste it one time, then using the paste control shortcut is going to be easier. To paste use Ctrl + V. So highlight your selection, copy (Ctrl + C) or cut (Ctrl +X) it, go to where you want to place it and click into the document, use Ctrl + V to paste it, and you're done.

Rather than use Ctrl + V to paste you can also go to the Clipboard section of the Home tab and click on Paste from there or right-click in your document and choose one of the Paste options from the dropdown menu.

The reason to use one of those options instead of just Ctrl + V is because it gives you control over the formatting of the text when you paste it, so let's talk about those options now.

Paste Options

If you use Ctrl + V to paste text, you'll be pasting not only the text you copied or cut, but its formatting as well. Usually, that's fine and you'll probably be able to use Ctrl + V ninety-five percent of the time.

(Even if you ultimately don't want to keep the formatting, there's a trick I'll show you later—using the Format Painter—that you can use to quickly correct formatting after you paste the text into its new location. All the Format Painter requires is that you have some text that's already formatted the way you want so you can copy its formatting.)

But in case you do want control over how you paste in your text, that's where the Paste Options can be used. There are four paste options: Keep Source Formatting, Merge Formatting, Picture, and Keep Text Only.

As you can see here, when you hold your cursor over each option it will tell you which option that one is. I have my cursor over the first option which is Keep Source Formatting and that description is shown directly below the option as I hold my cursor there.

The best way to figure out what each of these options does is to just experiment with them. That's what I've done below.

I took the word TEST and I formatted it in a larger font, a different font, bolded it, colored the text red, and highlighted the text in yellow. (You may not see all of that in print, but I can describe it for you.) I then copied that text and pasted it into each of my sample sentences using the different paste methods above.

The first paste option was just using Ctrl + V and that pasted the text in with all of the formatting I'd applied still in place.

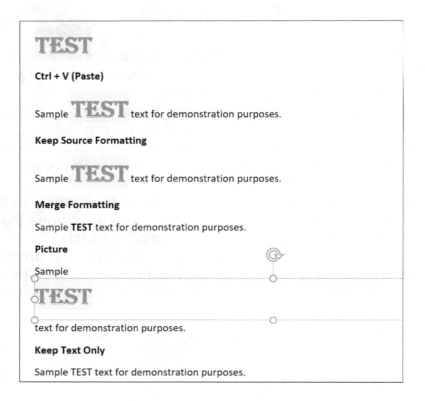

The second option, Keep Formatting, also kept everything. The third option, Merge Formatting, lost the different font size, different font, font color, and highlight. But it kept the bolding.

The fourth option, Picture, actually pasted the copied text in as a picture in a picture box.

And the final option, Keep Text Only stripped way all of the formatting I'd applied, including the bolding.

Interesting, but my recommendation is to stick to Ctrl + V and use the Format Painter when and if needed.

Okay. On to text formatting. If you remember anything from what we just walked through, remember this:

Ctrl + C to copy.

Ctrl + X to cut.

Ctrl + V to paste.

Text Formatting

Now that you know how to create a file, enter the text you want, and save your work, it's time to actually format that text. Let's start with font.

Fonts

Choosing a Font – General Thoughts

Word 2019 uses Calibri font as the default, but there are hundreds of fonts you can choose from and the font you use will govern the general appearance of the text in your document. Here is a sample of a few of those choices written in each font:

Sans-Serif Font Examples:

Calibri

Arial

Gill Sans MT

Serif Font Examples:

Times New Roman

Garamond

Palatino Linotype

The first three samples are sans-serif fonts. (That just means they don't have little feet at the bottom of the letters.) The second three samples are serif fonts. (They do have those little feet at the bottom of each letter.)

All of these fonts are the same size, but you can see that the different fonts have a different appearance and take up different amounts of space on the page. Arial is darker and taller than Calibri, for example.

Many corporations have a standard font they want you to use to be consistent with their brand and places like literary magazines will often specify which font to use for submitting stories. If that doesn't happen I'd suggest using a serifed font like Garamond or Times New Roman for main body text since a serifed font is supposed to be easier to read. Sans-serif fonts are good for headers or titles or for display text.

Also, unless you're working on a creative project, I'd recommend that you don't get too fancy with your fonts. Certain fonts, like Comic Sans, are so well-known for misuse that they are an immediate indicator that someone doesn't know design or isn't "professional."

The six fonts listed above are ones I'd generally consider safe.

Remember, at the end of the day, the goal is to communicate effectively, which means that a font like Algerian as main body text is not a good idea because readers will focus on the font and not the words.

Font Selection

Okay. So how do you change the font used in your document?

There are a few options.

But before we discuss those, let me point out that if you already know you want to use a different font, it's easier to change the font before you start typing. Once you do so, any new text will be in the new font.

Otherwise you'll need to select all of the text you want to change and then choose your font, which can be tricky if you're using different fonts for your headers and main body text

(A situation like that's also a good time to use Styles which is an intermediate-level topic covered in *Word 2019 Intermediate*.)

The first way to change the font is through the Font section of the Home tab. Click on the arrow to the right of the current font and choose a new one from the dropdown menu.

The first section of the dropdown menu lists the fonts for the theme you're using. Usually that'll be the defaults for Word, in this case, Calibri and Calibri Light.

Next you'll see Recently Used Fonts. (Most of the time there will only be one or two fonts there, but I had used a number recently.)

Finally, below those sections will be an alphabetical listing of all available fonts. If you know the font you want, you can start typing in its name rather than scroll through the entire list. Otherwise, use the scroll bar on the right-hand side or the up and down arrows to move through the list.

Each font is written using that font to give you an idea what it will look like. See for example the difference between Algerian and Garamond above.

The next way to change your font is to right-click and choose Font from the dropdown menu. This will bring up the Font dialogue box. In the top left corner you can choose the font you want.

There's a third option for changing the font, something I'm going to call the mini formatting menu. If you highlight your text it will appear on the screen when you let up on the left-click.

It will also appear above or below the dropdown menu if you right-click in your Word document.

As you can see, one of the options that you can change in the mini formatting menu is the font. In the example above, the current font is Arial, but I could click on the arrow on the right-hand side and change that. The dropdown menu looks the exact same as the one from the Font section of the Home tab we saw above.

Regardless of where you choose to change the font, if the font listing is blank that's because you have selected text that contains more than one font.

Font Size

Font size dictates how large the text will be. Here are some examples of different font sizes in Garamond font:

8 point 12 point 16 point

As you can see, the larger the font size, the larger the text for that specific font. Most documents are written in a ten, eleven, or twelve point font size. Often footnotes or endnotes will use eight or nine point size. Chapter headings or title pages will use the larger font sizes.

Whatever font size you do use, try to be consistent between different sections of your document. So all main body text should use just one font size. Same for chapter or section headings.

Changing the font size works much the same way as changing the font. You have the same three options: You can go to the Font section of the Home tab, bring up the mini formatting menu by right-clicking or selecting your text, or bring up the Font dialogue box by right-clicking and choosing Font from the dropdown menu.

If you want to change existing text, you need to select the text first. Otherwise, change the font size before you start typing.

For all three options the current font size is listed to the right of the current font name in the Font section of the Home tab.

If you use the Home tab or the mini formatting menu there is a dropdown list of font sizes to choose from that you can see by clicking on the arrow next to the current font size. In the Font dialogue box that list of choices is already visible in a box under the current value.

If the font size you want isn't one of the choices listed you can type in the value you want instead by clicking into the box that shows the current font size and changing that number to the size you want just like you would with text in the main document.

With the Home tab and the mini formatting menu you can also increase your font size one listed value at a time by using the increase and decrease font options directly to the right of the font size.

These are depicted as the letter A with a small arrow above it that points either upward or downward. The one on the left with the arrow that points upward will increase the font size. The one on the right with the arrow that points downward will decrease the font size.

The values available with that option are the ones in the font size dropdown menu, so you can increase from 14 point to 16 point but not to 15 point using this option.

Font Color

Changing your font color works the same as changing your font or font size. Select the text you want to change and then either go to the Font section of the Home tab, pull up the mini formatting menu, or right-click and choose Font from the dropdown menu to bring up the Font dialogue box.

This time you want to click on the arrow next to the A with the solid colored line under it in the bottom right corner of the Font section:

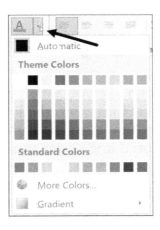

That line is red by default but will change as you use the tool and will stay the mostly recently selected color until you close the document.

Clicking on the dropdown arrow will give you a dropdown menu with seventy different colors to choose from. Simply click on the color you want and it will change your selected text to that color.

If those seventy choices are not enough, you can click on More Colors at the bottom of the dropdown box to bring up the Colors dialogue box where you can choose from even more colors on the Standard tab or specify a color in the Custom tab using RGB or HSL values.

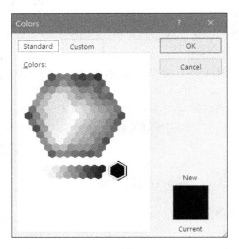

Once you select a font color any new text will be in that color. To go back to the default color choose Automatic from the dropdown menu.

Other Text Formatting

Highlight Text

You can also highlight text much like you might do with a highlighter using the Text Highlighter option which is located to the left of the Font Color option in the Font section of the Home tab or in the mini formatting menu. It has the letters ab and a pen with a colored line underneath.

By default the line is bright yellow but that changes as the tool is used.

To apply highlighting, select the text you want to highlight, and then either click on that option to highlight the text in the currently-displayed color or click on the dropdown arrow and choose from one of the fifteen color choices shown there.

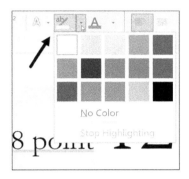

To remove a highlight select the highlighted text, go to the highlight dropdown, and choose the No Color option. Once used, a highlight wil/ *not* be applied to new text.

Bold Text

This is one you will probably use often. At least I do. As you can see with the headers in this chapter.

The easiest way to bold text is to use Ctrl + B.

You can use it before you start typing the text you want to bold or on a selection of text that you've chosen.

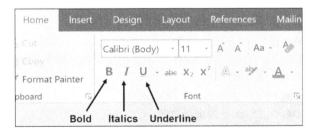

If you don't want to use the control keys, you can also go to the Font Section of the Home tab and click on the B on the left-hand side.

The final option is to select your text, right-click, choose Font from the dropdown menu, and then choose Bold in the Font Style section of the Font dialogue box.

(If you want to both bold and italicize text, you would choose Bold Italic.)

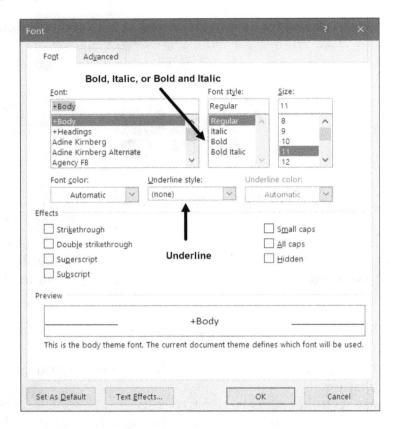

Italicize Text

To place text into italics—that means to have it sloped to the side like the subsection headers in this section for Italicize Text and Underline Text—the easiest way is to use Ctrl + I.

It works the exact same way as bolding text. You can do it before you type the letters or select the text and then use it.

Another option is to click on the slanted capital I in the Font section of the Home tab.

Or if you use the Font dialogue box select Italic under Font Styles. Or Bold Italic to have both italicized and bolded text.

Underline Text

Underlining text works much the same way as bolding or italicizing text.

The simplest way is to use Ctrl + U.

Or in the Font section of the Home tab you can click on the underlined U in the bottom row of the Font section.

There is also an Underline Style dropdown in the Font dialogue box.

Underline is different from italics and bold, however, because there are multiple underline options to choose from.

Using Ctrl + U will provide a single line underline of your text. So will just clicking on the U in the Font section of the Home tab. But if you click on the arrow next to the U in the Font section, you will see seven additional underline options to choose from including dotted and wavy lines.

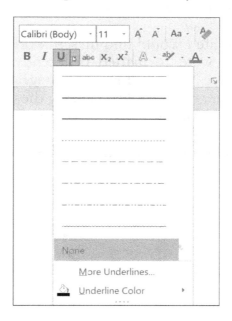

Choosing More Underlines at the bottom of that list of options will open the Font dialogue box where you have a total of sixteen underline styles to choose from.

Remove Bolding, Underlining, or Italics

If you have bolded, underlined, or italicized text and you want to remove that formatting, you can simply select the text and use the command in question to remove that formatting.

So Ctrl + B, I, or U. Or you can click on the letter in the Font section of the Home tab or go to the Font dialogue box and remove the formatting from there.

If you select text that is partially formatted one way and partially formatted another—so say half of it is bolded and half is not—you will need to use the command twice. The first time will apply the formatting to all of the selected text, the second time will remove it from all of the selected text.

Also, with specialty underlining using Ctrl + U will initially revert the type of underlining to the basic single underline. To remove the underline altogether, you'll need to use Ctrl + U a second time.

Copy Formatting

Now for a text formatting trick that has saved me more times than I can count, the Format Painter.

Often in my corporate life I would find myself working on a group document where different sections were formatted differently. Usually it was a subtle difference such as the space between lines in a paragraph. Rather than guess and poke around trying to figure out what was causing the difference, I would use the Format Painter to copy the formatting from a "good" section to the rest of the document.

The Format Painter is located in the Clipboard section of the Home tab.

You can also access it in the mini formatting menu.

What it does is it takes all of the formatting from your selected text and applies it to the text you choose. This means color, font, font size, paragraph spacing, etc. All of it changes.

To use it, select the text with the formatting you want to copy (generally I select a whole paragraph or more), then click on Format Painter, then select the text you want to transfer the formatting to.

You need to use the mouse or trackpad to select the text you want to transfer your formatting to because using the arrow keys or the arrow and shift keys won't work

You'll know that the format painter is ready to transfer the format when you see a little paintbrush next to your cursor as you hover over your document. Format Painter in the Home tab will also be highlighted gray.

To turn it off without using it, use Esc.

If you double-click on the Format Painter it will remain available for use on multiple selections until you hit Esc or start typing in your document or click on it again.

A few more tips:

The format painter can be unreliable if there are different formats in the sample you're taking the formatting from. For example, if part of the text is red and part of the text is bolded and I format sweep from that sample to new text, only the formatting of the first letter in the sample will transfer.

Another issue worth mentioning. Sometimes with paragraph or numbered list formatting, I have to select the paragraph from the bottom instead of from the top in order to get the format painter to carry over the paragraph formatting I want. (This is also why I sometimes select multiple paragraphs.)

It's also possible to sweep formatting that's in one document to another document.

Last but not least, when you copy formatting over, *all* of the formatting in your target text will be removed. This can be an issue if you've used italics or bolding within a paragraph, for example.

That means you may have to go back and put the bold and italic formatting in manually, but sometimes Format Painter is the only way to get paragraphs formatted the same even when they appear to have the exact same settings in place.

Okay, then. On now to a discussion of paragraph formatting.

Paragraph Formatting

What we just discussed was basic text formatting. Now it's time to cover paragraph formatting which includes text alignment, line spacing, the space between paragraphs, indents, etc.

Here we're just going to discuss how to change the formatting of a specific paragraph but once you're comfortable enough in Word, I'd advise that you also learn to use Styles which will let you format one paragraph the way you want it, create a style from that paragraph, and then apply that Style to all other paragraphs that you want to have the same formatting. (It's covered in *Word 2019 Intermediate* or you can learn about it through Word's help function.)

Alright then. Let's talk about how to format a paragraph one element at a time.

Paragraphs

Alignment

There are four choices for paragraph alignment. Left, Center, Right, and Justified. The easiest way to choose your paragraph formatting option is via the Paragraph section of the Home tab. All four options are shown in the bottom row and are formatted to show the alignment they represent.

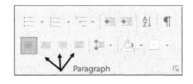

M.L. Humphrey

In the image below I've taken the same three-line paragraph and applied each alignment style to it to show the difference between all four using real paragraphs of text:

This paragraph is **left-aligned**. And now I need to write enough additional text so that you can see what happens when a paragraph falls across multiple lines of text since that can be one of the most significant differences between the choices.

This paragraph is **center-aligned**. And now I need to write enough additional text so that you can see what happens when a paragraph falls across multiple lines of text since that can be one of the most significant differences between the choices.

This paragraph is **right-aligned**. And now I need to write enough additional text so that you can see what happens when a paragraph falls across multiple lines of text since that can be one of the most significant differences between the choices.

This paragraph is **justified**. And now I need to write enough additional text so that you can see what happens when a paragraph falls across multiple lines of text since that can be one of the most significant differences between the choices.

Left-aligned, the first example, is how you'll often see text in documents. The text of each line is lined up along the left-hand side of the page and allowed to end in a jagged line on the right-hand side of the page.

Justified, the last example, is the other common way for text to be presented. Text is still aligned along the left-hand side, but instead of leaving the right-hand side ragged, Word adjusts the spacing between words so that all lines are also aligned along the right-hand side. (That's how the paragraphs in the print version of this book are formatted.)

Centered, the second example, is rarely used for full paragraphs of text like above, but is often used for section headers or titles or quotes. When text is centered the ends of each line are equally distant from the center of the line. You can end up with jagged left and right margins as a result and a final line, like above, may be substantially away from the edges.

Right-aligned, the third example above, is rare for paragraphs, at least in the U.S. and other countries where text goes from left to right. It aligns each line of text along the right-hand side and leaves the left-hand side ragged.

I have seen right-alignment used for text in side margins of non-fiction books and would expect to see it used for languages that read right to left.

So that's the difference between the choices. Like I said, I use Styles or the Home tab to change my paragraph alignment, but there are also control shortcuts that you can use. Ctrl + L will left-align, Ctrl + E will center your text,

Ctrl + R will right-align, and Ctrl + J will justify it. The only one I use enough to have memorized is Ctrl + E.

The third way to change your paragraph alignment is to select your text, right-click, and choose Paragraph from the dropdown menu to bring up the Paragraph dialogue box. The first option within that box is a dropdown where you can choose the alignment type you want. It has the exact same four formatting types that are available in the Home tab.

Spacing of a Single Paragraph

If you've ever attended school in the United States, you've probably been told at some point to submit a five-page paper that's double-spaced with one inch margins. Or if you've ever submitted a short story you were told to use a specific line spacing. In Word this is referred to as Line Spacing. So how do you do it?

As with the other formatting options, you can either do this before you start typing or by selecting the paragraphs you want to change after they've been entered into the document.

Once you're ready, go to the Paragraph section of the Home tab and locate the Line and Paragraph Spacing option. It's to the right of the paragraph alignment options and looks like five lines of text with two big blue up and down arrows on the left-hand side.

Click on the small black arrow to the right of the image to bring up the dropdown menu.

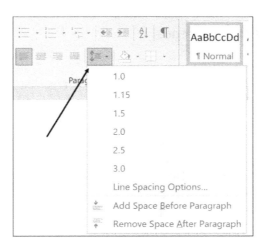

You have a choice of single-spaced (1.0) double-spaced (2.0), or triple-spaced (3.0) as well as 1.15, 1.5, and 2.5 spacing.

Below are examples of single, double, and triple-spaced paragraphs, Note how the amount of space between each row of text increases as you move from single-spaced up to triple-spaced:

This is a sample paragraph to show you the difference between line spacing. This is a **single-spaced** (1.0) paragraph. I'm going to keep typing so there are three lines of text to help you see the difference.

This is a sample paragraph to show you the difference between line spacing. This

is a **double-spaced** (2.0) paragraph. I'm going to keep typing so there are three

lines of text to help you see the difference.

This is a sample paragraph to show you the difference between line spacing. This

is a **triple-spaced** (1.0) paragraph. I'm going to keep typing so there are three lines

of text to help you see the difference.

If you want a different spacing than one of the dropdown options, then click on Line Spacing Options at the bottom of the list to bring up the Paragraph dialogue box.

You can go straight to the Paragraph dialogue box (shown in the next section) by right-clicking and choosing Paragraph from the dropdown menu. This setting is shown under the heading Line Spacing in the third section of the dialogue box which is labeled Spacing. It is on the right-hand side.

The dropdown menu gives you the choice of Single, 1.5, and Double as well as At Least, Exactly, and Multiple. Multiple lets you enter any value (such as 3 for triple-spacing). At Least and Exactly base the line spacing off of the number of points. So if you have 12 pt text, you can make the line spacing Exactly 12 point as well.

(This is often where I find that in corporate settings someone has tweaked the line spacing on a paragraph so that it doesn't match the rest of the paragraphs in the document. I usually fix it with the Format Painter, but if you don't want to use that, this is another setting to check.)

Okay. On to the spacing between paragraphs.

Spacing Between Paragraphs

There are basically two accepted ways to format paragraphs for most writing. One is what you see in the print version of this book where there are paragraphs without spacing between them but each new paragraph in a section after the first is indented to show that a new paragraph has begun. (Sometimes the first paragraph will also be indented.)

The second option is to start every paragraph on the left-hand side, but to add space between the lines to separate the paragraphs.

By default Word will add spacing between your paragraphs, but you can change the settings so that that does not happen or you can adjust the amount of space that Word adds.

Also, for items like titles or section headers (like you see on this page), it is better to add spacing to separate your text rather than use an extra blank line, because as your document adjusts to new text that extra line here or there can impact the appearance of the document. You may suddenly end up with a blank line on the top of the page that you never wanted there, for example.

And, please, for the love of everything, do not add lines between paragraphs by using enter unless the document is just for you or will only be seen by someone else in a printed format. That's about as bad as using the tab key to indent your paragraphs. (Don't do that either. Use indenting which we'll talk about next.)

Okay, so where do you go to adjust the spacing between your paragraphs? If all you want to do is remove any existing spacing, you can do that in the same dropdown we looked at above. It's the Remove Space After Paragraph option.

If someone has already removed the space after a paragraph and all you want to do is add it back in, you can also use that dropdown and select Add Space After Paragraph. (It's not listed above because there was already a space for the paragraph I was working with, but if your paragraph does not have a space after it, that will be an option you can choose.)

Be careful with the dropdown because it also, as you can see above, can have an Add Space Before Paragraph option. That will put the space above your paragraph as opposed to below it.

For this one, though, I tend to work in the Paragraph dialogue box which you can access by choosing Line Spacing Options in the dropdown or by right-clicking and choosing Paragraph from the dropdown menu in the main workspace:

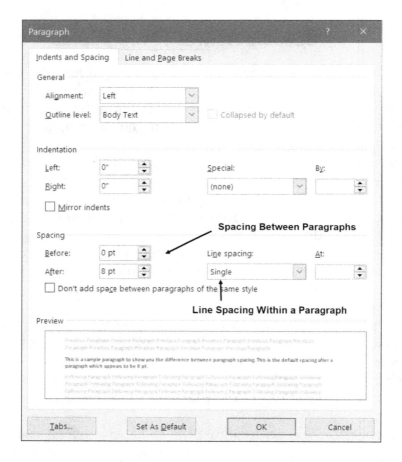

The spacing between paragraphs options are in the third section of the dialogue box, which is labeled Spacing, and on the left-hand side. There is a box for Before and one for After.

If you set your paragraphs to have spacing both before and after, the space between two paragraphs will be the higher of those two values not the combination of them. (So if you say 12 point before and 6 point after, the spacing between them will be 12 point not 18 point.)

If you just wanted spacing at the top of a section of paragraphs or at the bottom of a section of paragraphs but not between them, you can click the box to say don't add spacing to paragraphs of the same style Another option is to just add paragraph spacing to that top-most or bottom-most paragraph (although if you're working with Styles I wouldn't recommend that because you can accidentally override it.)

Below are examples of different paragraph spacing after paragraphs. I have no spacing, the default space that you get from the dropdown which is 8 pt, and 14 pt spacing just to show a visual difference. Because this is a screenshot they may not in fact be 8 and 14 pt spaces, but you can see the relative difference in appearance between each one.

This is a sample paragraph to show you the difference between paragraph spacing. There is **no spacing** after this paragraph.
This is a sample paragraph to show you the difference between paragraph spacing. This is the **default spacing** after a paragraph which appears to be 8 pt.

This is another sample paragraph to show you the difference between paragraph spacing. This time I'm going to put a **14 pt space** after this paragraph.

And this is final paragraph so you can see the spacing above.

Usually if I set a spacing I don't go above the font point size. The above font was 11 point in the document I was using, so in that case my spacing would normally be no more than 11 pt. (If I was writing a large-print document that might not be the case, so know your audience and the standards for that audience.)

Okay. So that was spacing within paragraphs and then spacing between paragraphs. As I mentioned above, if you have no spacing between paragraphs, the standard for indicating a new paragraphs is to add an indent to the first line of each new paragraph. Let's discuss how to do that now.

Indenting

Word provides two indenting options in the Paragraph section of the Home tab, but neither one will not give the first-line indent we need. They move the entire paragraph in or out.

For indenting a single line you need to use the Paragraph dialogue box which can be opened by right-clicking within your document and choosing Paragraph from the dropdown menu.

The second section of the dialogue box is labeled Indentation and covers whole paragraph and single line indents.

The whole paragraph indent options are on the left-hand side. The single-line or hanging indent option (which indents all but the first line of a paragraph) options are on the right-hand side.

Here I have settings for a paragraph with a first line indent:

And here are examples of the various indenting choices:

> This is a paragraph with **no indentation**. I am now going to make it long enough so that you can see what happens with the second line as well.
>
> This is a paragraph with a **left indent of .2"**. I am now going to make it long enough so that you can see what happens with the second line.
>
> This is a paragraph with a **right indent of .2"**. I am now going to make it long enough so that you can see what happens with the second line.
>
> This is a paragraph where the **first line has an indent of .2"** but the rest of the paragraph has no indent added.
>
> This is a paragraph where the indent is a **hanging indent of .2"** but the rest of the paragraph has no indent added.

The first example above has no paragraph indent.

The second and third show indents from the left and right-hand sides, respectively. Each is indented by .2" and you can see that on the side where it's indented it either starts or ends earlier than the non-indented paragraph.

(I formatted the paragraphs as Justified so that they'd fit the entire line and make that difference more obvious.)

The fourth example has the first line indented, but the remaining lines would not be. So you can see that "added" on the second line is as far left as the unindented paragraph at the top.

The final example is of a hanging indent where the first line is not indented, but the second and any subsequent lines would be.

To indent an entire paragraph, change the value for Left or Right on the left-hand side of the Indentation section.

To indent just the first line of a paragraph, choose First Line from the dropdown menu under Special on the right-hand side of the Indentation section and then specify by how much in the By box.

To create a hanging indent, choose Hanging from the Special dropdown and then specify the amount in the By box.

Remember to either do this in advance or to select the existing paragraphs you want to change before you start making your changes.

As I mentioned above, there are increase and decrease indent options in the Paragraph section of the Home tab. They're on the top row and show a series of lines with blue arrows pointing either to the left (to decrease an indent) or the right (to increase an indent).

They allow you to increase or decrease the indent for a paragraph or an entire selection of text from the left-hand side.

In my version of Word it indents by .5" the first time, then to a 1" indent the second time, and then to a 1.5" indent the third time.

If there are other indented paragraphs in the document, such as the ones I added before that had a .2" indent, then it will indent to those points as well.

When you decrease the indent it should follow the same stopping points on the way back to zero.

I will often use these quick indent options when dealing with a bulleted or numbered list that I want to visually separate from the main text of my document.

Lists

Bulleted

A bulleted list is just what it sounds like, a list of items where each line starts with some sort of marker or bullet on the left-hand side. The most common bullet choice is probably a small dark black circle that's filled in, but Word has additional options you can choose from such as an open circle, a filled-in square, and a checkmark. (See image below.)

You can either start a bulleted list before you have your items ready or you can take a list of items, highlight them, and then apply a bulleted list.

With either option, the way to do this is to go to the Paragraph section of the Home tab and click on the arrow next to the bulleted list option to bring up a dropdown menu where you can select the type of bullet you want.

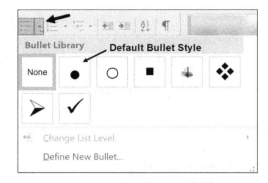

If you simply click on the image of the bulleted list instead of using the dropdown menu, your bullet will be a solid black circle.

Here are samples of each of the bullet choices shown above. (I had to create this by going into each line and choosing a different bullet type for that line. The default with bulleted lists is that once you choose a bullet that will be the bullet used for every line.)

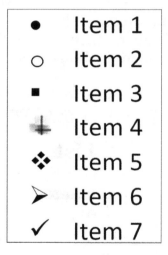

When you choose to insert a bulleted list, if you don't have any text selected already then a single bullet will appear on the page where your cursor was, waiting for you to type in your first entry.

If you do have items selected, each paragraph will be indented and the bullet type you chose will be added at the beginning of each of the paragraphs.

The mini formatting menu also has the bulleted list option available in the middle of the bottom row, so that's another option for applying or removing a bulleted list.

Once you've started a bulleted list each time you hit enter at the end of the text for a bulleted entry a new bullet will appear on the next line for you to add your next item.

Hit enter twice to return to normal paragraph indenting with no bullet. If you add a new bulleted list and then don't type any text before you hit enter again that will also revert back to no bullet.

(The double enter trick works for the first level of bullets. If you have a list with multiple levels of bullets, which we're about to cover, then you will need to hit enter until Word works its way through the levels of bullets and back to a blank option.)

You can create a bulleted list with multiple levels by using the Tab key to indent any line you want to the next level. Like so:

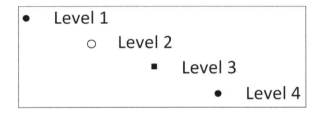

Here I've created three levels of indented text. I started with my first bullet and typed my text, then hit enter after Level 1. Next I used the tab to move that solid bullet in one level and create a second-level bullet. I then typed my text for that level and hit enter. And then repeated the process of tab, type, enter to create the other levels.

By default, when you hit enter from an existing line of a bulleted list the next line will be indented at that same level and will use the bullet mark for that level of indent.

To decrease an indent one level you can use Shift- + Tab.

When using Tab or Shift + Tab, if that line already has text in it be sure to place your cursor before any text. In the examples above, that would mean place it to the left of the first L in Level.

When you create a multi-level bulleted list, Word assigns a different bullet type for each indented level.

From what I can tell it uses the open circle for the first indented bullet, the black square for the second one, and then the black circle for the third one regardless of which option you chose for your first bullet. (See above.)

It then starts over again with the open circle for the next-level indent.

To change the bullet style for any level in your list, click on that line and go to the bulleted list options and choose a new bullet type.

That will apply that new bullet type to all lines in your list that are indented at that level. So, for example, all second-level indents will have the same bullet type and if you change that type for one line it will change it for *all* second-level indents in your list even if they are not listed together.

To remove bullets from a list, select the list, and then click on the bulleted list option in the Home tab or mini formatting menu. Your bullets will be removed, but the text will remain indented.

Another option for removing a bullet is to go to the beginning of the text for that line and backspace. Once will remove the bullet but keep the text where it is. Twice will move the text to the beginning of the line.

(You can also use the Format Painter to apply bullets to a list of entries or to remove them.)

With bulleted lists, Word will automatically indent your bullet and text when it adds the bullet for the first level. If you don't want that, you can use the Decrease Indent option to move the bullet back to the left-hand side of the page but keep the bullets.

If you decrease the indent for the first level of a multi-level bulleted list, this moves all levels back one indent.

The same works for increasing the indent using the Home tab option. If you increase the indent for the first level, it will increase the indent for all levels.

(For levels below that first level using Decrease Indent or Increase Indent just moves that specific line forward or backward one indent.)

You can also use the Paragraph dialogue box to have more control over how much each line is indented and whether each bulleted line should be treated as a hanging paragraph or not.

Another option you can use for indenting is the Adjust List Indents option from the dropdown menu on the main workspace. That will bring up the Adjust List Indents dialogue box.

This dialogue box allows you to choose the indent amount for the bullet. (It also is available for numbered lists, which we'll talk about next.)

The first choice is how much to indent the bullet or number.

The second choice is how much to indent the associated text.

The third choice is what type of separator to use between the bullet or number and the text. The default is a tab but you can also choose to use a space or nothing.

The choices you make here are probably more finicky for numbered lists than they are for bulleted lists since the bullet size remains constant no matter how many entries you have in your list. With numbered lists you have to move from 1 through 9 to 10 to 99 and then to 100 on which requires different amounts of space so each change can create a difference in the appearance of the list.

One more thing to note and then we'll move on to numbered lists.

I often will use the Paragraph dialogue box to add extra line spacing between bulleted list entries since sometimes I think entries in a list look better with a little more spacing between them than is used in a normal paragraph.

Numbered

A numbered list is similar to a bulleted list except the entries are either labeled with numbers or letters. If you've ever had to provide an outline of a paper for school, I'm sure you've run across a numbered list before.

One easy way to create a numbered list is to simply type the first number you want to use, the separator mark you want, and then a space.

So, for example, if I type a capital A and then a period and then a space that will give me the first entry in a numbered list that uses A, B, C, D, etc.

When I do that, Word automatically indents that text and turns it into the first entry in a numbered list so that when I type in my text and then hit enter the next line will be "numbered" in sequence and indented as well.

(If Word ever does that to you and you don't want it to indent and start creating a list, just use Ctrl + X to Undo. You can also click on the little AutoCorrect dropdown that appears to the left-hand side of the entry and choose to undo from there.)

The other option, especially if you already have your text entered and just need to convert it to a numbered list, is to select the lines you want to number, go to the Paragraph section of the Home tab, click on the arrow next to the Numbering option, and choose the numbered list option you want from there.

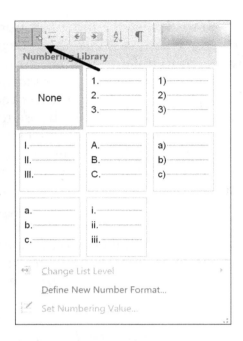

As you can see, you have the option to choose between lists that use

1, 2, 3

i, ii, iii

I, II, III

A, B, C

a, b, c

and then between using a period (.) or a paren( )) as the separator.

For a basic list, that should be all you really need. The default numbering choice if you just click on the image instead of using the dropdown is 1, 2, 3 separated with a period.

(In addition to the Home tab, the mini formatting menu also has the numbered list option.)

As with bulleted lists, you can create a multi-level list by using the tab key to indent a line or paragraph in your numbered list, but there appears to be that same pre-defined order for what will be used for each of the indented levels.

For the first indent Word uses the lower-case letters (a, b, c). For the second indent it uses lower-case Roman numerals (i, ii, iii). For the third indent it uses regular numbers (1, 2, 3). And then it cycles through again starting with the fourth-level indent. Like so:

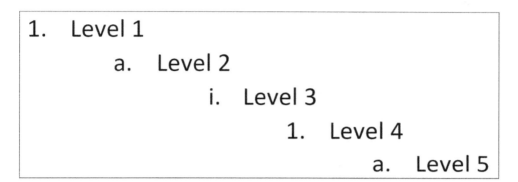

This generally results in a multi-level list that doesn't fit what I was taught in school which was I, A, 1, a, i for the numbering order for different levels.

To create a list with customized numbering in each level, you'd need to use the Multilevel List option which we are not covering here because it has given me more problems over the years than probably anything else I've ever worked with in Word.

(It's the option to the right of the number list option in the Paragraph section if you want to experiment with it and I do reluctantly cover it in *Word 2019 Intermediate.*)

For now, back to basic numbered lists.

If you had a numbered list earlier in your document and want that numbering to continue with additional numbered items later in your document, you can do that. Likewise if Word continued the numbering and you didn't want it to, you can change the settings to restart the numbering.

In either case, create your numbered list and then right-click on the number for the line you want to change.

Depending on what else is in your document and which entry you click on, you will see different options in the dropdown menu.

Restart at 1 or Restart at A will change the number of the entry to 1 or A or whatever the first value would be for that numbering type. All you have to do is click on this one for it to be applied.

Continue Numbering is also applied immediately. Click on it to continue the numbering from the last time that numbering type was used. So if you have a list in your document that has the "numbers" A, B, C and another list that has numbering of 1 and 2 and the numbering style on your current line is the A, B, C style then when you choose to continue numbering your next entry will be D even if the 1 and 2 values are closer to that line in the document.

(If it sounds confusing, just play around with it in Word and you'll see what I'm talking about.)

The final option you'll see is Set Numbering Value which will bring up the Set Numbering Value dialogue box when you choose it.

This gives you the most control over what happens with your list numbering. You can restart the list, continue numbering, continue numbering with skipped numbers, or start numbering at any value you want.

If you do set the numbering at a random value, just be aware that your choices are based upon the list type for that line. So if it's a level that's numbered with Roman numerals then you'd have to use X for 10, you couldn't type in 10.

Be a little careful with all of this because a change to the numbering style of one entry will change all other linked lines which is great when that's what you want but can be dangerous if you're working with a very large document and don't realize that the list on page fifty is somehow tied into the list on page ten.

Always if you're working with numbered lists be sure to go back through your entire document at the end to make sure that a change you made towards the end of the document didn't change something at the beginning of the document.

(This actually goes for page or section breaks as well. Best practice is to always do one last read through or scan of a document after all changes have been made and to restart that scan from the beginning if you end up making more changes.)

Okay. A few final points. As with bulleted lists you can change the indent and format of your numbered list using the Paragraph dialogue box or the Adjust List Indents option on the dropdown menu.

Also, I mentioned it above, but one thing to be careful of with numbered lists that go into the double-digits or triple-digits is that you can end up with a situation where the text is lined up for values of 1 through 9 but then not aligned once you reach a value of 10 or more.

This can happen, for example, when you use a space instead of a tab to follow the number, but I want to say that I've also seen it happen with tabs if the tabs were set in such a way that it changed which tab stop was used for 1 through 9 versus 10.

Also, it won't be an issue most times, but if you hold your mouse over the numbered list options that Word gives you by default some are right-aligned and some are left-aligned. As you move into larger and large values for your numbered list this may impact the appearance of your list.

To fix this, you'll need to create a New Number Format where you can customize the alignment. That option is at the bottom of the dropdown menu under Define New Number Format. (See screenshot on next page.)

Click on that and it will bring up the Define New Number Format dialogue box where you can choose the number style, number format (whether to use a period or paren or something else even), and the number alignment.

So, for example, the default for 1,2,3 is left-aligned. But you could use this option to make it right-aligned or centered. Here are what those three options look like for numbered values of 9 and 10:

9.	Level 1 Left-Aligned
10.	Level 2 Left-Aligned
9.	Level 1 Centered
10.	Level 2 Centered
9.	Level 1 Right-Aligned
10.	Level 2 Right-Aligned

The only change I made here is in the alignment of the numbers. You can see in the first example that the 9 lines up with the 1 in 10. In the second sample it lines up with the center of the 10. And in the third example it lines up with the 0 in the 10. Personally I prefer the right-aligned version. But the default is left-aligned, so the only way to get this is to create your own number format using Define New Number Format.

One nice thing in Word is that once you've used a number format in a document that format is available for you to select again in the Document Number Formats section in the Numbering dropdown menu of the Home tab or the mini formatting menu.

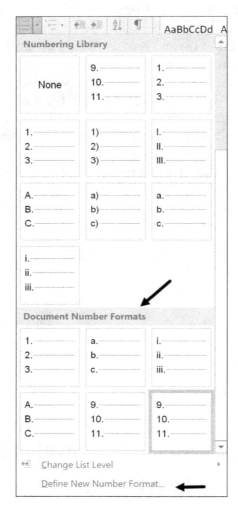

Although one weird thing about that section is that it will show formats you've used at one point but are no longer using. For example, in this screenshot I only have numbered lists in my document right now but it's showing lists with a, b, c, and A, B, C, and I, II, III even though they're not currently in use anywhere in the document.

(One of the reasons I'm careful with playing around with lists in a working document.)

In the case above where I had three different number formats for the 1, 2, 3 numbering you can't tell which is which just from looking. You have to hold your mouse over each one to figure out which one has each alignment.

You could also click on a line that already has that format and see which one of the formats in the dropdown is then surrounded by a dark gray border.

Or you could just use the Format Painter to copy the number formatting over, which is probably what I would actually do instead.

Other Tips & Tricks

Alright. We've talked about how to enter text into Word and how to format that text once you've entered it and how to format your paragraphs. But there are a few more basics we need to cover that don't really have anything to do with entering or formatting your text, although they may lead to changes in your text.

Let's start with Find and Replace.

Find and Replace

Find

If you ever want to find a particular word or phrase in a Word document and you don't want to scan through the whole document, you'll need to use Find. It's very easy to use on the surface, but can also be incredibly powerful if you get into the specialty search options.

For a basic search in Word you can use Ctrl + F or just go to the Navigation task pane on the left-hand side of the workspace. If the Navigation pane is already open then using Ctrl + F will seem like it did nothing, but what it will actually do is place your cursor in the Search Document box in the Results section of the Navigation pane.

(In older versions of Word using Ctrl + F opened the Find and Replace dialogue box so this one throws me every single time.)

If all you're looking for is a simple word or phrase, type it into the search box. You don't even need to hit enter, all instances of the search term will be listed immediately right below the search box. Like so:

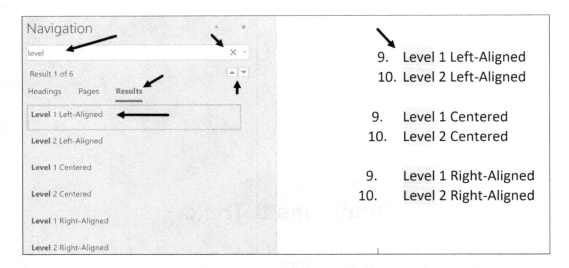

The gray area on the left-hand side is the Navigation pane where I entered "level" as my search term. Immediately below that are the six search results for the document. It bolds the location of the text and provides some of the text around that to make it easy to determine which search result you want.

On the right-hand side is the document itself. Each instance of the search term is highlighted in yellow.

For a larger document where all of the search results are not on the same page, you can simply click on the search result in the list that you want to see and Word will take you to that page. You can also use the up and down arrows just below the far end of the search box (in the same row as the number of search results) to move through your search results one-by-one.

Click on the X at the end of the search box to clear the search result.

Right next to that X is a small dropdown arrow with a list of additional search options. Click on the arrow and one of the first choices is "Advanced Find".

The dropdown is available even if you haven't searched for anything. In that case the X is replaced with a magnifying glass.

Clicking on that Advanced Find option will open the Find and Replace dialogue box which lets you search for far more than just a word or phrase.

I usually get to the same place by using Ctrl + H (which is the control shortcut for replace) and then clicking over to the Find portion of the dialogue box. Either way what you will then see is this:

Type your search phrase into the Find What search bar and then click on Find Next to walk your way through the entire document and look at each instance of your search term.

For a basic search the Navigation pane is the far better choice.

But click on that More button in the bottom left corner of the Find dialogue box and you get this:

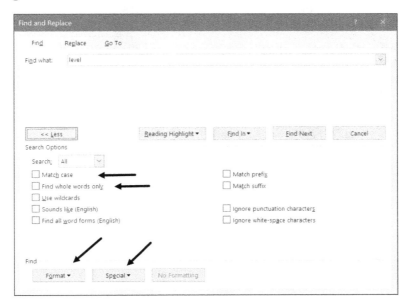

There are a ton of additional search options you can use, but I want to focus on four of them right now.

First, is Match Case. Which is in the Search options section in the middle.

Match Case will look at the search term you enter and only find words with the same capitalization. So if you search for "CAT" and you check this box it will only locate "CAT" for you not "cat" or "Category".

(For my old job something like that would be useful since CAT stood for consolidated audit trail.)

When searching for a proper name or an abbreviation like that, I recommend always checking this box. (This becomes even more important if you're going to use Replace. You wouldn't want to try to replace CAT with some other term and accidentally also replace the cat portion of category with that same term, for example.)

The next option I want to point out is Find Whole Words Only.

Find Whole Words Only will only search for the entire word you enter. So again, with the example of "CAT", if you just searched Word normally it would return any word that has "cat" in it. So "category" and "implication" would be returned along with "CAT" and "cat."

By using Find Whole Words Only the search results would be limited to "CAT" and "cat". You can also combine these two and then your only result would be the one for CAT.

So those are great. And I've saved myself a lot of time over the years by using them.

But a few that I only started using in recent years may be even more powerful than that when they're needed.

At the bottom of the dialogue box are Format and Special dropdown options. Here's what the Format one gives you for choices if you click on it:

A little hard to see maybe, but the options are Font, Paragraph, Tabs, Language, Frame, Style, and Highlight.

Using these options you can search your document for pretty much any format, paragraph style, text style, or highlight that you want. Here's what comes up when you choose Font for example:

Look at all those options.

Now, that may not sound exciting to you, but let me give you a weird example of where I've needed to use this:

For large-print books they don't use italics, they use bolded text instead. I recently published a seven-hundred-page book in large print. Manually going through that book to find each instance of italics would've been a nightmare. But I was able to easily use find (and replace) to change all of my italics over to bolded text in the space of a minute.

Another time I've needed this is when I've been working on a report and someone decided that all uses of a specific term needed to be in italics or not in italics.Using Format I could search for instances of the term that were not formatted properly. Far easier than looking at every single use of the term one-by-one.

If you know your control shortcuts, you can skip the dropdown and use them directly in the search box.

Just click into the search box and use, for example, Ctrl + I. The first time the search will change to search for that formatting. The second time it will change to search for text that does not have that formatting. The third time it will go back to a neutral search. Which state you're in will show directly below the search box.

To find all text in a document with a specific format, like italics, just leave the search box blank. Don't enter any text. But do use the Ctrl + I or whatever shortcut it is to specify that format. When you click on search Word will show you all of the the text with that specific format.

Also, be careful when using the formatting search options that you don't forget to change your search back to neutral because next time you search you may end up missing a search result. It doesn't happen often, but it has happened to me in the past at least in older versions of Word.

The final one I wanted to point out is right next to the Format option and that is the Special option.

The Special search dropdown allows you to search for specific formatting marks in your document such as paragraph marks, em dashes, en dashes, etc.

This can be a lifesaver if someone gives you a document where they used Enter multiple times instead of using a page break or used tabs to indent paragraphs instead of formatting the paragraph properly.

Maybe most people won't run into needing these options, but if you've ever been the one stuck with a group report that has to be fixed to make everything work properly chances are there's something in this section that will make your life easier.

Replace

Okay. So that's Find which is helpful, but where the real power of Find comes into play is when you pair it with Replace. So not only do you find that italicized text, but you replace it with bolded text at the same time.

Same with fixing two spaces after a period. I was raised to type two spaces after a period but there are members of the younger generation (and even some of my own) who think that using two spaces after a period makes you an archaic fool stuck in the typewriter age. Rather than engage in heated debate about something that really no one should care about, I just used Find and Replace to find all instances of two spaces after a period and replace them with one space.

Easy.

(And I will add that I finally converted from two spaces to one space when I started publishing printed books because when you use justified paragraphs like I am in the print version of this book that extra space after a sentence can created some ugly white space on the page. But honestly, even though I've converted I think it's one of those silly issues people use to distinguish those who are "in the know" from those who are not and I hate that kind of thing with a burning passion. But I digress.)

Back to find and replace. It is fantastic and powerful and will save you so much time. But it's easy to mess up and create horrible and strangely embarrassing errors.

So before you replace every instance of something in your document in one step, make sure that you've thought through what that means.

Let's say I want to replace CAT with SEC CAT. I know I'm not using "cat" in the report I've written, but what about implication, category, catastrophe, etc. If I don't realize that replacing "cat" with "SEC CAT" can affect those words, too, I might be tempted to not constrain my replacements to match the case and to whole words only. In which case I will have SEC CATastrophe in my document somewhere and impliSEC CATion.

Not what you want, so always think it through first.

Okay. So the basics of find and replace:

Use either use Ctrl + H or go to the Editing section of the Home tab and click on Replace to bring up the Find and Replace dialogue box, which will open onto the Replace tab.

The Find What box is the exact same as before and you can click on the More option in the bottom right corner to specify Match Case, Whole Words Only, any formatting, etc. for what you want to find.

There will now be a Replace With box below that where you type what you want to replace that text with. So if CAT needs to become SEC CAT I would type CAT in the Find What box and SEC CAT in the Replace With box. (And be sure to check the whole word and match case boxes as well.)

Another example: If I were replacing two spaces with one I'd type two spaces in the Find What box and one space in the Replace With box.

You then have two choices for how to replace text. You can replace the instances of your search term one one at time by using Find Next and then clicking on Replace once you confirm that you want to use replace. Or you can use Replace All to replace all instances of your search term with your Replace With term at once.

(I recommend double-checking you got it right if you do use Replace All.)

As mentioned above, you can find one type of formatting and replace it with another type of formatting. So I can find italics and replace it with bold, for example. To do this, click into the search and replace boxes and use the relevant control shortcuts for the formatting you want to find and the formatting you want to replace it with.

One other item to note. When Word finds and replaces, it will sometimes do so only from where you are in the document forward. When this happens it tells you how many items it found and replaced and then asks if you want to continue searching from the beginning. To be sure that you've found all instances, say yes.

This means you can also do find and replace on just a highlighted section of text, too, which is sometime very useful. In that instance when it asks if you want it to continue with the rest of the document, say no.

Spelling and Grammar Check

Unless you've done something to your settings or are working in a document that's already hundreds of pages long, you'll notice little red squiggly lines or blue double-underlines appear under some words as you type.

This is Word's real-time spelling and grammar check at work.

> To be fair, she wasn't actually trying to pee on her toy, but in Fancyworld there wasn't a good cause and effect connection in place. So it always went: smell something interesting, drop toy to smell it better, step forward to pee on something interesting while forgetting that the toy that was just dropped is right there, too.
>
> I tell ya, that girl keeps me on my toes.

It may be a little hard to see, but in the screenshot above Word flagged Fancyworld and ya as spelling mistakes by placing a squiggly red line under each word and the use of So as a grammar error by placing a double blue line under it.

For spelling errors, right-click and Word will suggest possible spellings at the top of the dropdown menu.

Here, for example, Word suggested using yam, yak, yaw, a, and yet instead of ya. Which actually highlights a key point with using the spelling and grammar check. Word can't always tell what you were trying to do. So in this case "ya" is slang usage for "you" but that never even made the list of suggestions.

The dictionary that Word works from does not contain slang, but when writing fiction, for example, you may find yourself using lots of slang, especially in dialogue. So spellcheck is great and you should use it for every single document you ever give to anyone else, but it has its limits. Do not blindly follow the recommendations.

Not even the grammar recommendations. I have seen the grammar check suggest using its when it's was actually the correct usage. It is not infallible.

But it is helpful.

More so for business or school writing than fiction or casual writing, although you can at least customize your dictionary if you want. In the dropdown shown above you can see that there is an option to Add To Dictionary which if you choose it will add that word to your Word dictionary so that it is never flagged as a misspelling again. (In business settings I will often add my first name to the dictionary because Word flags it every time and wants to change it to something that would not be good in a business setting.)

In general, though, I don't add words to the dictionary. I would rather in each document use the Ignore All choice.

This is mostly because I can't think through every possible usage of a word to make sure there wouldn't be times when it was in fact a misspelling of some other word. For example, what if I had a document that used the word yam in it and I really did misspell it once as ya. I'd miss that if I had added ya to the dictionary.

Bottom line: Don't do something permanent unless you're sure of what you're doing.

A few more things to know about spellcheck:

Sometimes it flags a word as misspelled when it isn't. I've found that I have one or two words in each novel I write that it flags that are genuine words but aren't listed in the default dictionary. I verify the word is spelled and used correctly with a quick internet search before I ignore the error.

Also, if you're not close enough to the right spelling Word can't help you. I used to consistently spell bureaucracy in such a way that it had no idea what word I was trying to write.

For grammar errors, Word will also suggest an immediate fix. I usually leave those until the end when I can run the Spelling and Grammar check on the entire document at once.

And again, sometimes the suggestions it makes aren't the actual problem. For example, above with "so" its suggestion was to keep the so but put a comma after it which to me is simply a different pacing for that sentence that I don't like as much. What it should actually suggest is that I not use so so many times.

(See what I did there? Haha.)

Unless Word has flagged a blatant spelling error I tend not to worry about any of this until I'm done with the entire document and then I run through it all at once. Stopping every single time Word flags a potential issue would bring me out of my writing flow and make me far less efficient. (For those who cannot continue if they know there's an error in what they've already written those lines can be very useful, though.)

Of course, if your document is long enough you will eventually get a message that it had to stop real-time tracking of spelling and grammar errors. I want to say this happens somewhere around one hundred pages.

Okay, then. For those who want to wait until the end and do it all at once, you do not have to scroll through your document and try to find every one of these.

You can use the Spelling & Grammar option which is in the Proofing section of the Review tab on the left-hand side.

Once you click on that option, Word will open a Proofing pane on the right-hand side of your workspace and will show the next grammar or spelling error in the document. (It doesn't automatically start at the top. If you had a selection of text highlighted it will focus on that selected text. If you're clicked somewhere in the document it will work from there forward.)

Here is the result for the grammar error for "so" that we discussed before:

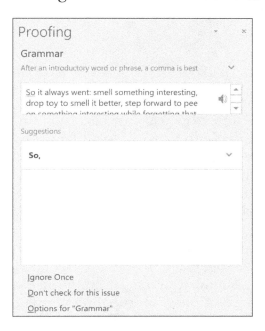

At the top it describes the issue, then it displays a snippet of text around the word or usage that was flagged, and then below that in the Suggestions section shows suggested fixes for the error.

Likewise, here is the Proofing pane for the "ya" spelling error.

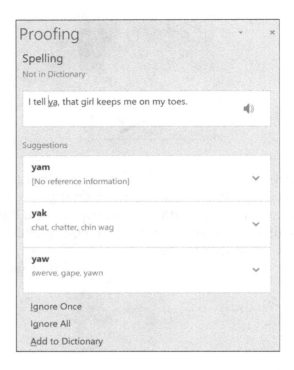

If you agree that there is an error, you can just click on the suggested fix you want and Word will make that edit to your document for you.

If you agree that there's an error but want to fix it some other way, you can click back into your document and make the edit yourself.

If you don't believe there's an error, then at the bottom of the screen you can click on Ignore Once and Word will move on to the next grammar or spelling error.

With spelling errors you can choose to Ignore All and it will not flag that word again in the document but spellcheck sometimes will still flag related uses of a word such as a possessive, singular, plural, or upper or lower case.

For example, it treated all of these as separate words that had to be ignored individually: Winswald Winswalds Winswald's winswald winswald's winswalds.

With grammar errors you can click on Don't Check for This Error. Just be sure that you really want that to happen. Just because it was wrong on this particular instance does not mean it will always be wrong and the listed grammar rules tend to be high-level.

You can see what the grammar error is by looking at the top of the pane. In the case above it says, "After an introductory word or phrase, a comma is best." Before choosing to skip that rule I'd have to believe that there are never any introductory phrases I use where a comma is warranted but I failed to include one. I'm not comfortable deciding that so I'd let it stand.

The final option for spelling in the Proofing page is to add the word to the dictionary, which we already discussed.

The final option for grammar is to see the grammar options. When you click on that choice Word will bring up the Grammar Settings dialogue box.

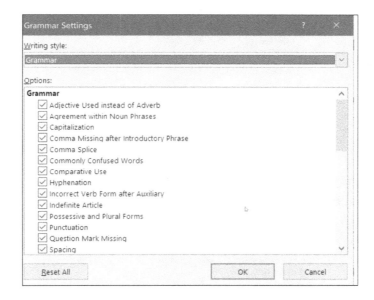

The first screen worth of options are pretty standard and they're all on by default. I don't think any of these give me enough problems that I'd need to turn one off, but you could. The capitalization one can be a little annoying when writing about Excel functions, but otherwise pretty standard stuff.

Where it gets interesting is if you scroll down to the categories for Clarity, Conciseness, Formality, Inclusiveness, Punctuation Conventions, and Vocabulary.

(Now, whether I really want developers who won't use Title Case for their text labels to be telling me about proper word usage is up for debate, but there are some interesting options in those sections.).

For example, in more formal settings, such as academic writing, contractions are frowned upon. The Formality section includes the ability to check your document for those.

So if you are writing an academic paper and want to be sure you didn't accidentally include a contraction, you can have Word check that for you.

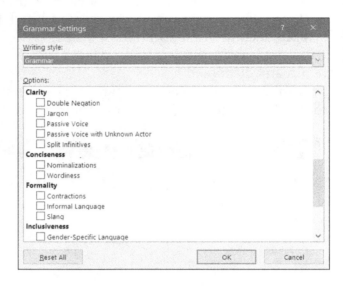

There's even a setting for the Oxford comma as well as one for checking for the number of spaces between sentences.

If any of that looks interesting to you, you can go into the Grammar Setup dialogue box and turn those options on by checking the relevant boxes.

Or if one of those rules keeps coming up and you don't want it to, this is the place to fix that.

One final note, once you've run spellcheck on a document and told Word to ignore spelling or grammar errors, it will continue to ignore those errors in that document. To run a clean spelling and grammar check of your document, go to the File tab, click on Options, click on Proofing, and finally click on the gray box labeled Recheck Document.

This will show you a notice that you're about to reset the spelling and grammar check. Click OK and all spelling and grammar errors will be flagged as they were originally.

Synonyms and Thesaurus

In the screenshot above where I showed you the Spelling & Grammar option you may have noticed that there was a Thesaurus option next to it.

A thesaurus, as you may know, is used to identify words with a similar or identical meaning, otherwise known as synonyms.

If I've used "happy" ten times and want to come up with a different word for it, I can use the thesaurus option in Word to find one.

The simplest way to do this is to right-click on the word and go to the synonyms choice in the dropdown menu and then look at the available options listed there:

If you like one of the choices simply click on it and your existing text will be replaced with the chosen word.

You can also select your word and then use the Thesaurus option from the Proofing section of the Review tab to open a Thesaurus task pane on the right-hand side of the workspace.

As you can see, at least in this instance, there are more choices provided in the Thesaurus task pane than there were in the synonyms dropdown menu.

The Thesaurus appears to work differently, however. If you click on one of the words listed it does not replace the word in your document but instead will provide synonyms for that word instead.

To insert the word into your document as a replacement you need to hold your mouse over the word so that it's highlighted, go to the end of the line where that word is, click on the dropdown arrow, and choose insert.

If you had a word or words highlighted in your document it or they will be replaced. If not, the new word will be inserted into the document where your cursor was.

Let me just step back for a moment and give a general caution about using a thesaurus. It's fantastic when what you're doing is triggering your memory of other similar words and you can go down the list and think about each one like a puzzle piece that you're trying to fit into place with what you're writing.

But it is a very bad idea to use a thesaurus to find words you don't already know.

For example, here with happy. One of the options is blissful. Another is exultant. But both of those convey a level of emotion that is not, in my mind, equivalent to being happy. And pleasant, which is another suggested word goes in the wrong direction. Someone is a pleasant person to be around but that is not the same thing as their being a happy person. One is what I feel around that person, another is what they feel.

(If that makes sense. I don't write dictionaries, so forgive me if my example there was bad.) The point is, you have to still know the words you choose when using a thesaurus or it's just not going to sound right.

But if you do need to use it, that's how.

Word Count

The other item in the Proofing section of the Review tab that I want to mention is Word Count. When I was in school we always had to hit a page limit, but for short stories and novels and online forms everyone wants to know the word count.

There are two main places you can find this. The first is actually just in the bottom left-hand corner of the Word screen. You can see there what page you're on and your total page count and then right next to that is the total word count for the document. If you highlight a selection of text the word count will change to show X of Y words so that you can see the number of words in your selection (X) as well as the total number of words in the document (Y).

You can also click on the Word Count option in the Proofing section of the Review tab. This will immediately bring up the Word Count dialogue box:

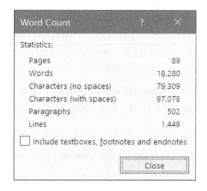

As you can see, it gives a little more information than just word count (which is the second line of information). You also have the number of pages, the number of characters with and without spaces, the number of paragraphs, and the number of lines.

I use the characters option sometimes when I complete online forms that have a character limit but don't tell me how many characters I've used. I type my entry up in Word, check the character count, and then copy it over to the website.

Read Aloud

Just to the right of those three options in the Speech section of the Review tab is the Read Aloud option.

With this option, you can highlight a selection of text in your document, click on Read Aloud, and a computerized voice will read the text to you.

I find this a nice way to review the final draft of my fiction, although it sometimes has very interesting ideas of how to pronounce certain words. For example, grimaced.

Overall, though, it's a good trick to catch those last few straggling errors that the eye tends to skip right over.

(Although not all of them. You never catch them all. I used to write business reports that were reviewed by six people, three of whom were detailed-oriented lawyers who'd gone to schools like Yale and Harvard ,and it never failed that we'd give the client the report and then I'd see a typo that we'd all missed. On page one.)

Show/Hide Paragraph Marks

By default I do not show paragraph and other marks in my document, but when I'm trouble-shooting issues in a document this can be invaluable. The option to show or hide these marks is found in the Paragraph section of the Home tab and is in the top left corner. It looks like a paragraph mark. Click on it to turn on marks, click on it again to turn them off.

Once you turn on paragraph marks you'll be able to see indents, tabs, paragraph breaks, line breaks, section breaks, etc. Like in this example here:

Alrighty·then.·Let's·start·with·some·basic·terminology.¶
→test¶·······································Section Break (Next Page)·······

If you look closely you should see a small dot between every single word. That indicates a space. Two dots in a row would indicate two spaces. At the end of every line that uses an Enter there is a paragraph mark. This example has two of those, one after "terminology." in the first line and one after "test" in the second line.

I've also included a tab which is indicated by the arrow on the second line before "test".

And there's a Section Break that will start the next line of text on the next page which is marked with a dashed line and text describing the type of break.

Showing paragraph marks is useful for finding those little annoyances like tabs or extra enters or a page or section break somewhere it wasn't supposed to be. You can often guess that they're there, but this is the only surefire way to know exactly what you're dealing with.

* * *

Alright, next we're going to cover some of the customized settings available under the Options section of the File tab.

File Options Customized Settings

Click on the File tab and then choose Options from the left-hand side and this will bring up the Word Options dialogue box which has a number of categories for options you can customize.

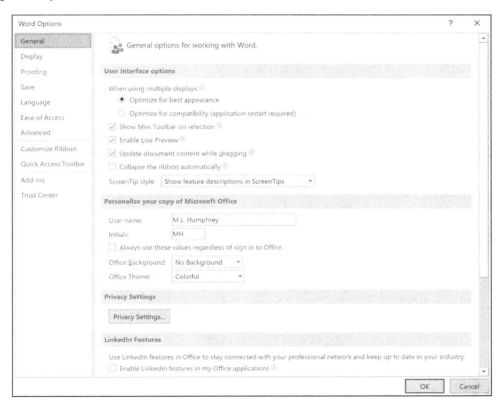

I'm not going to cover everything you can do here because there are easily over a hundred different settings, but I will point out some of the ones I've needed to use in the past.

General

The main change I've needed to make here is in the Personalize Your Copy of Microsoft Office section. As you can see in the screenshot above it defaults to showing my initials as MH, but I've in the past been on work teams where someone else had those same initials and that can be problematic for track changes. So this is where to adjust that to MLH for me, for example.

It also shows the ability to change the user name, but I want to say that I had to go into BIOS or somewhere to actually change my name to my initials for Office. So you can try it here, but it may not work or it may not hold for anything other than track changes. Be sure to check the box that says to always use those values regardless of sign in to Office, but then be careful if you have multiple users on the same computer.

(Basically, if this matters for you, double-check that it's working properly before you send the document off or take screenshots.)

Display

It looks like it's the default in Word 2019, but I always make sure that it says show white space between pages in print layout view. Without this box checked, you can't visually see page breaks in your document, one page of text rolls right into the next with just a thin gray line to indicate a page break.

That's especially annoying if you're working with a document that has very short sections that are supposed to fall on their own page because you can end up with three or four of them displayed on a single page.

I never customize the section that asks to show formatting marks on the screen because I only turn that on when I need that as discussed above, otherwise I want them hidden. But if find that you have marks showing in a document that won't turn off, check here to see if someone changed the settings so that some marks would be permanently visible.

Proofing

The Proofing section allows you to control when Word applies its AutoCorrect options and which ones it applies.

This one I always make changes to. (I haven't yet on this version of Word because I wanted to write this book first and it's driving me crazy to deal with the defaults.)

AutoCorrect Options

Most of the changes I make in this section are under the AutoCorrect Options. I click on that button and it brings up the AutoCorrect dialogue box which has five available tabs. I use the AutoCorrect, AutoFormat as You Type, and AutoFormat tabs to make adjustments.

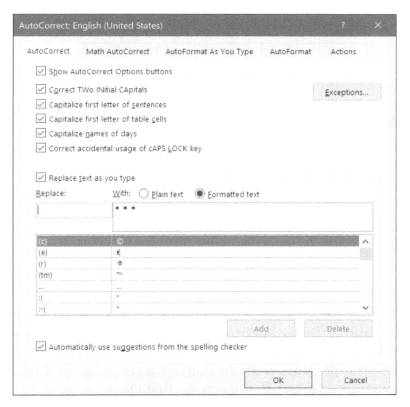

For example, at my old job on the AutoCorrect tab I would always delete that first option to change (c) into the copyright sign because my job involved a lot of rule citations, where you write things like Rule 3070(c) which made it really annoying each time Word automatically changed that over to a copyright sign.

Your other option is to use Ctrl + Z when Word makes a correction you don't want. (My problem is that I'm usually about three words past the change before

I realize what's happened. At that point it becomes more of a hassle than it's worth.)

The AutoFormat As You Type and AutoFormat tabs include the setting for smart quotes versus straight quotes, which is another one I often change.

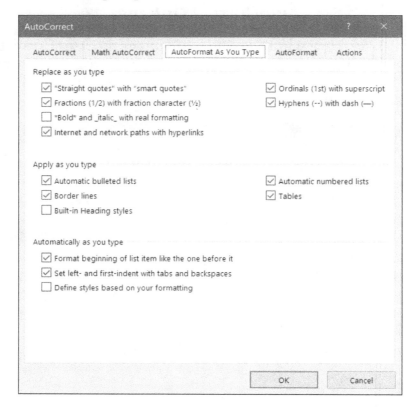

Smart quotes curve towards the text and are what you're supposed to use for dialogue, for example. But straight quotes are what you need to use in Excel formulas. So when I'm writing my Excel books I usually turn this one off.

It actually needs to be turned off in both of those tabs for it to work properly.

I will also sometimes turn off the setting that converts a fraction and the one that automatically creates hyperlinks, depending on what I'm working on.

Now, don't get me wrong. A lot of the autocorrect options are very handy—I often type too fast and mistype "the" as "teh" and Word always catches that for me—but do keep an eye out for "errors" you don't want fixed as you type like turning a single i into a capital I.

The AutoCorrect dialogue box is also where you can see that Word will automatically convert two dashes in a row into an em-dash.

(But only after you type a word, two dashes, another word, and a space.)

This is also where you can see that three periods in a row will turn into an ellipsis which treats them as one single character and keeps them together.

If you like to learn shortcuts or ways to make life easier that it's probably worth looking through these tabs to know what Word will do on your behalf so you can leverage it.

But if you're more like me then you'll probably wait to look at this section until you get annoyed with something that keeps happening that you want to turn off.

Check Spelling As You Type

In the third section of the Proofing screen you can uncheck the box that says to check spelling as you type so that you no longer have to see those red squiggly lines under words.

Mark Grammar Errors As You Type

Same for grammar errors. You can uncheck the box for that option to turn that off so that you aren't seeing the blue double underline in your document as you type.

This is also the section for turning off the grammar check altogether. Uncheck Check Grammar With Spelling and Word will no longer check for grammar when you select the Spelling and Grammar option on the Review tab.

Reset Spelling and Grammar Check

As mentioned previously, you can click on Recheck Document to reset the spelling and grammar check for the document. If you checked the document previously and told it to ignore errors but want to see those errors now, this is the way to do that.

Save

Prior to Word 2019 I would have recommended saving documents as a .doc instead of the default format which is .docx to ensure backward compatibility. Versions of Word from 2007 onward use .docx as their default but it's a format that users of Word versions prior to that can't open.

We're probably now in the safe range where most users have upgraded to new enough versions of Word that this isn't a concern. But if it ever is and you don't want to have to think about it you can change the default file format that Word uses to save your documents here.

This is also where you can specify how often Word saves an AutoRecovery version of your file. The default is set to 10 minutes. If you're ever working in Word and it crashes on you, then when you reopen that file in Word it will offer to let you open the recovery version instead which by default was saved at some point in the last ten minutes.

Word does not crash on me often, but when it does this has been a lifesaver for me. (More often it's that my entire computer crashed on me, not just Word.)

Normally the AutoRecovery process is so seamless you won't even notice it's happening, but I do have a set of formatted templates I work with that for some reason take long enough to save that they will freeze my computer for a minute or so as they save. Having that happen every ten minutes can be annoying, to say the least, so when working with them I will sometimes adjust this setting.

This section also lets you choose your default location for saving files, so if you always want to save to an X drive or something, this is where to change that setting.

Advanced

There are many options in this section. I can see a few that might be useful to change, like unchecking the allow text to be dragged and dropped option since I don't do that intentionally but have had it happen a few times unintentionally.

This is also the section where if you're going to work with documents that need high resolution images for print you'll want to change the default. Otherwise all of your images, no matter what their quality is when you bring them into Word will be 220 dpi which is generally considered too low for printing standards.

Customize Ribbon

The Customize Ribbon option lets you choose which tasks are available at the top of the screen in your Word workspace. So, for example, the options under the Home tab.

I would advise against this unless you work for yourself and have no expectation that you will ever use anyone else's computer or any public computer. Because what makes things faster for you in your version will significantly slow you down on anyone else's computer.

Also, you'll have to do this again with any new version of Word you buy which means another significant slowdown every couple of years as you upgrade to a new software version.

Not to mention, if you get stuck no one else will have the display you do so you'll be on your own trying to figure out where something is.

Quick Access Toolbar

Customizing the Quick Access Toolbar, on the other hand, makes a lot of sense if there are just one or two tasks that you use often that are located in a tab other than the one you usually need.

For me, for example, I usually put Breaks and Format Painter here so that I can access those from wherever I am.

File Info

We just discussed the File Options choices, but there's another section of the File tab that I want to explore and that's the Info section.

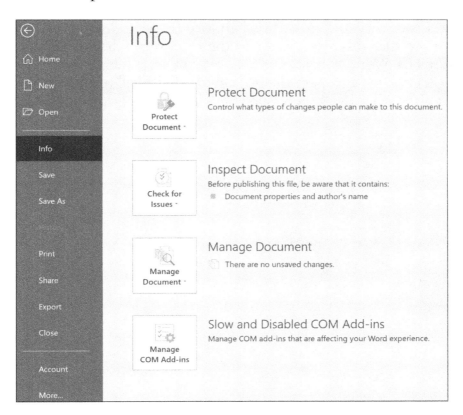

You reach it by clicking on the File tab and then the Info option on the left-hand side of the screen.

One of the things you can do here is strip the document of any personal information. So the author name, any track changes, any comments, etc. There are definitely times this is called for and you should always check a document for track changes before you hand it off to a client or professor or some other person who wasn't meant to see your comments and changes.

(I've been on the receiving end a few times of documents where that didn't happen and let's just say that you don't want to give you regulator the track changes version of your response to their inquiry...)

Which means it's a useful and necessary thing to be able to do. BUT. I hesitate to tell you about it because when used at the wrong time it can be a disaster. I have had people strip out the author information on a working document and then every single person's comments were listed as "Author" even if those comments were added after that point in time. So be careful with this, please.

Okay. The way you review a document for information you might want to remove is by clicking on the Check for Issues box next to where it says Inspect Document. From that dropdown then choose Inspect Document.

(You can see that this also gives you the option to Check Compatibility with older versions of Word, too, should that ever be an issue.)

When you choose to inspect the document Word will prompt you to save it if you haven't already and will then give you a list of categories it can scan for:

I usually scan for everything. When the scan is done it will display another dialogue box with any issues it found and let you choose which issues to fix:

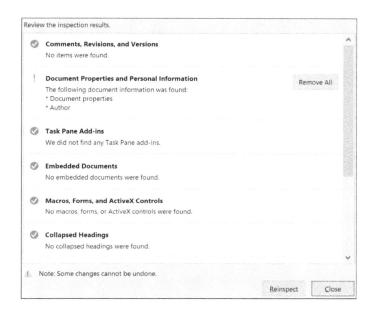

BE VERY CAREFUL at this point that you don't remove something you will need and can't get back. (Like author information in a working document.)

What I recommend is that you save a copy of the file before you inspect it and then save the inspected and stripped down version as a new file. That way if you did delete something you shouldn't, you can go back and fix it.

That's basically all I use this section for, but as I mentioned above you can check for compatibility with older versions of Word.

You can also protect the document so that people can't edit it and password protect the document so that no one can open unless they have the password. (Just be sure you remember your password or you won't be able to open the file either.)

Okay. Now we're up to printing a document. But before we can print we need to know how to format the page so that it has page numbers and headers and footers. So let's cover that next.

Page Formatting

If you're going to print a document that is more than one page long, chances are you'll want to add page numbering to the document as well as maybe a header or footer that includes the document title or your name or both. Let's talk about how to do that.

Page Numbering

First, do not ever manually number your pages. Word will do this for you. By letting Word do this, you ensure that the page numbering will still work even when you make edits to the document.

Nothing worse than putting a 1 at the bottom of what you think is page one and then deciding to add a title to the document and suddenly there's a random 1 in the middle of the second page.

So don't do that. Please.

(Says the person who has occasionally been stuck fixing a document where someone did in fact do this. That and the person who manually formatted the text to *look* like track changes...Took me ages to realize what that person had done. And even longer to fix it. But you're reading this book so you won't do that kind of thing, right? Right.)

To add page numbers to your document, go to the Header & Footer section of the Insert tab which is towards the right-hand side, and click on the arrow next to Page Number.

This will bring up a dropdown menu that lets you choose where on the page you want your page numbers to display. If you hold your mouse over those options, you can then choose how you want those page numbers to look.

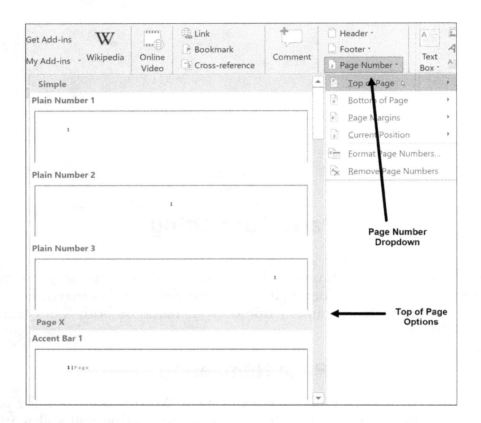

Above I've held my mouse over Top of Page and you can see the first four options I have to choose from, left, middle, right, and a left-hand accented option. If I scroll down in that list there are actually twenty-five total options to choose from some of which are quite distinctive.

Click on the choice you want and Word will insert it into the header (for top of page) or footer (for bottom of page). If you choose the page margins options, that is inserted into a standalone text box on the side of the page.

Current Position will insert the page number where your cursor currently is, so I'd only use that one if you already have a header or footer in your document (or a text box you want to use) and you're clicked into that space.

The Format Page Number option in that dropdown can be used to change the numbering format (to small case Roman numerals for example), the starting page number, or to specify that the numbering should or should not continue from a prior section. (This becomes much more relevant when you have sections in your document that require separate numbering. I cover how to create sections in *Word 2019 Intermediate*.)

For a basic simple page number using the dropdown menu and choosing one of the defaults should really be all you have to do.

Headers and Footers

Inserting a page number is basically a specialized version of inserting a header or footer. When you insert the page number at the top of the page or the bottom of the page Word creates a space that is separate from your main text and puts the page number there. But you can also put other text into the header or footer like your name or the title of the document.

Doing so will repeat that text at the top or bottom of the page for the entire document. (Or section if you're using sections. Also, you can set it up so that alternating pages have different text in them like a book does. But for basic headers and footers it repeats throughout the document.)

A header goes at the top of your page.

A footer goes at the bottom of your page.

To add one, go to the Header & Footer section of the Insert tab and click on the arrow below the one you need (header or footer), and then choose the option that works best for you, just like you did with page numbering.

Just like with page numbering you will have various pre-formatted options to choose from like these three for the footer:

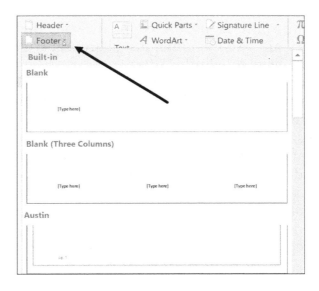

You're not stuck with the format you choose. For example, with short story submissions, they usually want the header to be in the top right corner. If you choose the Blank header option, that creates a header that's in the top left corner. But you can simply go to the Home tab and choose to right-align the text in your header and that will put it in the right corner instead.

After you choose your header or footer option, Word creates a header or footer and inserts [Type here] into the designated spots where you're supposed to put text.

To edit that text, just start typing because it will already be highlighted in gray. If it isn't highlighted in gray, select the text and then start typing.

Text in your header or footer works just like text in your document. You can use the same options from the Home tab to change your font, font size, color, etc.

As mentioned above, headers and footers are in a separate area from the main text of your document. If you're in a header or footer and want to go back to the main document, you can (1) double-click back onto the main body of your document, (2) click on Close Header and Footer in the menu bar which should be showing in the Design tab under Header & Footer Tools, or (3) hit the Esc key on your keyboard.

If you're in your main document and want to edit your header or footer, you can (1) double-click on the text in the header or footer, or (2) right-click on the header or footer and choose "Edit Header" or "Edit Footer" from the dropdown.

Margins

Margins are the white space along the edges of your document. The default margins in Word 2019 are one-inch margins all around which is pretty standard so you probably won't have to edit this often.

But if you need to edit your margins, you can go to the Layout tab and under the Page Setup section click on the dropdown under Margins. This will give you the choice of Normal, Narrow, Moderate, Wide, Mirrored, Office 2003 Default, and Custom Margins.

Mirrored margins are for printed texts where the inside margins are the same for facing pages and the outside margins are the same for facing pages. (As opposed to thinking about the left-hand margin and the right-hand margin which is what you think about with a report or other printed document that is seen one single page at a time.)

Each option, except Custom Margins, shows what the margins are for that option.

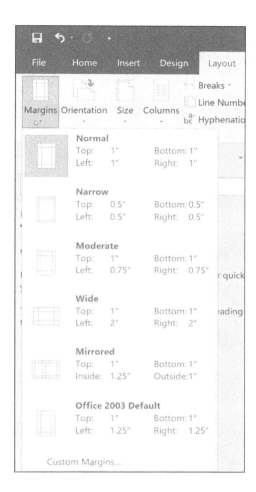

Clicking on Custom Margins, will open the Page Setup dialogue box directly onto the Margins tab. You can also open the Page Setup dialogue box to the Margins tab by clicking on the expansion arrow for the Page Setup section.

This lets you specify a custom value for each margin as well as for the document gutter. (Which matters if you're printing book-style.) In the Pages section dropdown you can also specify that the margins should be mirrored.

Page Orientation

A standard document has a page orientation of portrait. That's where the long edge of the document is along the sides and the short edge is across the bottom and top. This is how most books, business reports, and school papers are formatted, and it's the default in Word.

But sometimes you'll create a document where you need to turn the text ninety degrees so that the long edge is at the top and bottom and the short edge is on the sides.

A lot of tables in appendixes are done this way. Also presentation slides are often this way. That's called landscape orientation.

(Think paintings here. A drawing of a person—a portrait—is generally taller than it is wide. A drawing of a mountain range—a landscape—is generally wider than it is tall.)

To change the orientation of your document, go to the Page Setup section of the Layout tab, click on the arrow under Orientation, and choose the orientation you want.

If you use section breaks--which are covered in *Word 2019 Intermediate*—you can set the page orientation on a section-by-section basis. But if you're not using sections, changing the orientation on any page will change the orientation of the entire document so be careful with this one.

You can also change the orientation in the Page Setup dialogue box which can be opened via the expansion arrow for the Page Setup section. The orientation option is on the Margins tab directly below the Margins settings.

Printing

Printing in Word, at its most basic, is incredibly easy. You can simply type Ctrl + P or go to File and choose Print from the list of options on the left-hand side. Both options will bring you to the Print screen.

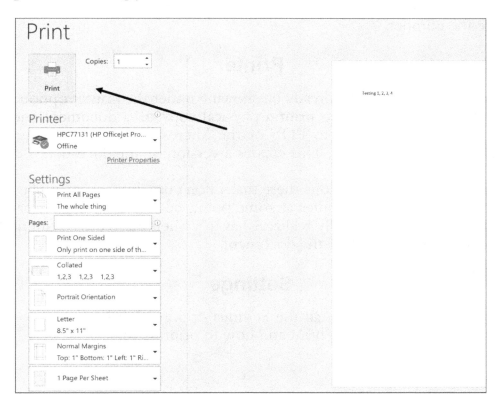

If all you want is to print the document with no adjustments, click on the printer image (see screenshot above) that's directly below where it says Print.

A lot of times this should be fine. It's not like Excel where you really need to check what it's going to look like because in Word as you were working you could see what it was going to look like.

But just in case, on the right-hand side Word will show you a preview of what the document will look like when it prints. For documents that are longer than a page, you can use the arrows at the bottom to navigate through the document preview.

There are a number of adjustments you can make before you print that will impact what prints and how.

Let's walk through those now from top to bottom.

Copies

Right next to the Print icon you can specify the number of copies you want to print. The default is one copy. To increase that amount, either click into the box and type a new number or use the arrows on the right-hand side to increase or decrease the number.

Printer

Your default printer should already be showing under the printer option.

Sometimes I don't want to print a physical copy of a document and so I'll choose the Microsoft Print to PDF or the Microsoft XPS Document Writer option instead of my printer. This creates a version of the document I can save to my computer.

There are a few other options there that I don't use, but you may, like fax.

If you do change your printer at some point, be sure to change it back next time you go to print. I usually realize I haven't when instead of printing Word asks me where I want to save the document.

Settings

Below the printer choice are all the Settings options that let you choose what portions of the document to print and how to print them.

Print All Pages Or Other Page Selections

The first choice you have is what portion of the document to print. The default is Print All Pages which will print the entire document.

If you click on that dropdown, however, there are a number of other choices. Print Selection will print any text that you have selected in the document.

Print Current Page will print the page you were clicked onto when you chose to print. You can verify that it's the right page in the print preview to the right.

Custom Print uses the pages box directly below the dropdown. You can type in the specific pages you want there. For page ranges, use a dash. For a list of individual pages, use commas.

So if you want to print pages 3, 5, and 7 you would enter "3,5,7" in the Pages box. If you wanted to print pages 3 through 7, you would enter "3-7" in the box.

If you go directly to the pages box and start typing in a page range it will automatically change the dropdown to "Custom Print."

You can also print in Word 2019 the Document Info, List of Markup which is your tracked changes, a list of the styles being used in the document, a list of items in your autotext gallery, and a list of any custom shortcut keys you have.

You can also choose to print only odd pages or only even pages.

And there's a choice to print the document with markup.

Print One-Sided or Two-Sided

The default is for Word to print on one side of the page, but you can change it to print two-sided documents.

To do so, click on the arrow next to the default choice of one-sided. You'll now see a dropdown with four options, one-sided, both sides with the long edge, both sides with the short edge, and manually print on both sides.

Choose the manual option if you have a printer that isn't set up to print two-sided documents automatically.

Choose to flip pages on the long edge for documents with a portrait orientation. Choose to flip pages on the short edge for documents with a landscape orientation.

Collation

This is only relevant if you're printing more than one copy of a document that's more than one page long.

The default when printing multiple copies of a document is to print one entire copy of the document and then print the next copy of the document. (That's the *collated* option that shows 1,2,3 1,23 1,2,3.)

The other option you can choose is to print all of your page ones and then all of your page twos and then all of your page threes. (That's the *uncollated* option that shows 1,1,1 2,2,2, 3,3,3)

The uncollated option is useful for situations where you might be giving out handouts one page at a time, but generally you'll want to stick with collated copies.

Orientation

We talked about this one before, but if you want the text on your page to go across the long edge instead of across the short edge, this is another place where you can make that choice.

The default is Portrait Orientation, but if you click on the arrow, you can instead choose Landscape Orientation.

Paper Size

The default in Word (at least in the U.S. version) is to print on 8.5"x11" paper. If you want to print your document on a different size of paper (say A4 or legal), then this is where you'd change that setting.

There are an insane number of choices both on the dropdown menu and if you click on More Paper Sizes, but for most documents you'll probably be using the default.

Make sure you have whatever paper you end up choosing if you're printing to an actual printer.

Margins

We already talked about how to change the margins on your document, but this is also another place where you can do that. You have the same pre-formatted margin choices here as in the Layout tab as well as the custom option.

Pages To Print Per Sheet

If you want to save paper because perhaps you're reviewing a document and it's not the final version, you can print more than one page of your document onto a single sheet.

The default is to print one page on one sheet, but if you click on the dropdown menu you can choose to print 2, 4, 6, 8, or 16 pages per sheet.

You can also choose to scale your text to a chosen paper size.

Be careful with this setting because Word will let you make a choice that results in an illegible document. Four pages on one page is still legible, but I suspect that sixteen pages on one page would be a challenge for most people to read. (But it may be useful if you're ever in a situation where your teacher said you could bring one page of notes and you're trying to cram an entire semester's worth of knowledge on that one page...)

Page Setup

As a beginner, I'd ignore the Page Setup link at the bottom of the page. Most of what it covers we've already addressed above. It's just the older way of specifying your print settings.

Conclusion

Alright. There you have it. Enough knowledge about Word to let you do most of what you need to do on a daily basis.

If you want to learn more, in *Word 2019 Intermediate* I dive into how to create complex numbered lists, insert tables, use section breaks, insert a table of contents, use styles, add watermarks and hyperlinks, deal with track changes, and more. Things that you may need to do at some point, but aren't essential to get started with Word.

You don't have to continue with that book, though. Word also has excellent help available.

The first option is to hold your mouse over any of the options in the menu at the top, like here for Format Painter. This will give you a basic description of what the option does as well as list any control shortcut that exists for it.

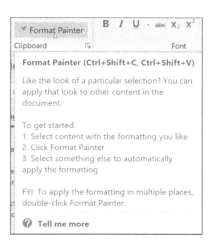

Many of the options will include Tell Me More at the bottom. You can click on that and it will open the Help task pane to a help pane specific to that topic.

You can also click on Help under the Help tab. This will open the Help task pane as well but to a generic starter screen where you can then browse the subject categories or search for what you're trying to do.

The Help tab also has a Show Training option which brings up a list of topics where you can then watch videos on each of the listed topics which can be helpful in learning something new.

If none of that works I will often do an internet search for what I'm looking for using "microsoft word" as part of my search string. So I might search for "how to add a hyperlink microsoft word." I then choose the support.microsoft. com option.

That's an excellent resource for how things work, but sometimes I need "is this possible" help, in which case I'll look to user forums to see if anyone else has asked my question before. (I find I need this less with Word than with Excel, though.)

You can also email me at mlhumphreywriter@gmail.com. I'm happy to point you in the right direction or figure out the answer myself and share it if I don't already know it. Sometimes it's just a matter of knowing the right buzz words to use to ask the question.

Okay. So that's it. Good luck with it! Don't let it scare you. If you're nervous then save drafts of what you're working on so you can go back to a prior version that was working for you. But generally just take it slow and easy and you should be fine. Especially if you stick to the basics we covered here.

Control Shortcuts

The following is a list of useful control shortcuts in Word. For each one, hold down the Ctrl key and use the listed letter to perform the command.

Command	Ctrl +
Bold	B
Center	E
Copy	C
Cut	X
Find	F
Italicize	I
New	N
Paste	V
Print	P
Redo	Y
Replace	H
Save	S
Select All	A
Underline	U
Undo	Z

Excel 2019 Beginner

EXCEL ESSENTIALS 2019 BOOK 1

M.L. HUMPHREY

CONTENTS

Copyright © 2021 M.L. Humphrey

All Rights Reserved.

ISBN: 978-1-63744-030-8

Introduction

Microsoft Excel is an amazing program and I am so grateful to have learned it because I use it all the time as a small business owner as well as personally.

It allows me to organize and track key information in a quick and easy manner and to automate a lot of the calculations I need.

For example, on a personal level I have a budget worksheet that lets me track whether my bills have been paid, how much I need to keep in my bank account, and where I am financially.

In my professional career I've used it in a number of ways, from analyzing a series of financial transactions to see if a customer was overcharged to performing a text-based comparison of regulatory requirements across multiple jurisdictions.

(While Excel works best for numerical purposes, it is often a good choice for text-based analysis as well, especially if you want to be able to sort your results or filter out and isolate certain results.)

The purpose of this specific guide is to teach you the basics of what you need to know to use Microsoft Excel on a daily basis. By the time you're done with this book you should be able to do over 95% of what you need to do in Microsoft Excel and should have a solid enough grounding in how Excel works and the additional help resources available that you can learn the rest.

The series does continue with *Excel 2019 Intermediate*, which covers more advanced topics such as pivot tables, charts, and conditional formatting, and *Excel 2019 Formulas & Functions*, which goes into more detail about how formulas and functions work in Excel and then discusses about a hundred of those functions, sixty in detail.

You are welcome to continue with those books but you shouldn't have to in order to work in Excel on a daily basis. This book should be enough for that.

It was written specifically for Excel 2019, so all of the screenshots in this book are from Excel 2019 which, as of the date I'm writing this, is the most recent version of Excel.

However, because this book is about the basics of Excel, even if you are working in a different version of Excel most of what we'll cover here should be the same. The basic functions of Excel (like copy, paste, save, etc.) haven't changed much in the twenty-five-plus years I've been using the program.

If you previously purchased *Excel for Beginners* which was written using Excel 2013, most of the content of this book is the same and you probably don't need to buy this book as well.

The visual appearance of Excel 2019 has been changed just enough from the 2013 version to be annoying, so it may help to have the updated screenshots, but don't feel that you need to buy this book to use Excel 2019 if you've already read *Excel for Beginners*.

This book is not a comprehensive guide to Excel. The goal here is to give you a solid grounding in Excel that will let you get started using it without bogging down in a lot of information you don't need when you're getting started.

In this book I will often cover multiple ways of doing the same thing to show you the various options available to you. I may not cover *all* of the possible ways of doing something (I think we're up to five or six ways of doing the same thing on some of this stuff), but I will usually cover at least two ways.

I highly recommend learning any of the control shortcuts that I give you. For example, to copy something you can use the Control key and the C key (which I will write as Ctrl + C). The reason to learn these shortcuts is because they have not changed in all the years I've been using Excel. Which means that even when Microsoft issues the next version of Excel and moves things around a bit (which they will because that's one major way they make money is through new product releases) you'll still know at least one easy way to perform the core tasks.

Also, when in doubt go with the right-click and open a dialogue version of doing something because that too seems to have remained relatively stable over the years and versions of Excel.

If what I just said didn't make sense to you, don't worry. The first thing we're going to do is cover basic terminology so that you know what I'm talking about when I say things.

Alright then. Let's get started with that.

Basic Terminology

First things first, we need to establish some basic terminology so that you know what I'm talking about when I refer to a cell or a row or a column, etc.

Column

Excel uses columns and rows to display information. Columns run across the top of the worksheet and, unless you've done something funky with your settings, are identified using letters of the alphabet. As you can see below, they start with A on the far left side and march right on through the alphabet (A, B, C, D, E, etc.).

If you scroll far enough to the right, you'll see that they continue on to a double alphabet (AA, AB, AC, etc.).

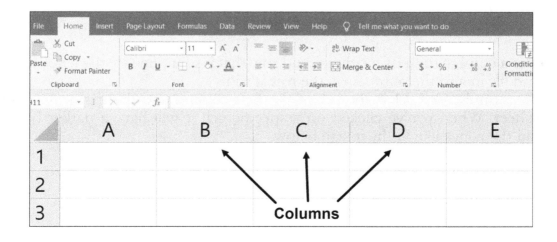

Row

Rows run down the side of the worksheet and are numbered starting at 1 and up to 1,048,576 in Excel 2019.

(Be aware that earlier versions of Excel have less rows in a worksheet so that if you have a lot of data that uses all of the available rows your file may not be compatible with earlier versions of Excel.)

You can click into any cell in a blank worksheet, hold down the ctrl key, and hit the down arrow to see just how many rows your version of Excel has. To return to the first row use the ctrl key and the up arrow.

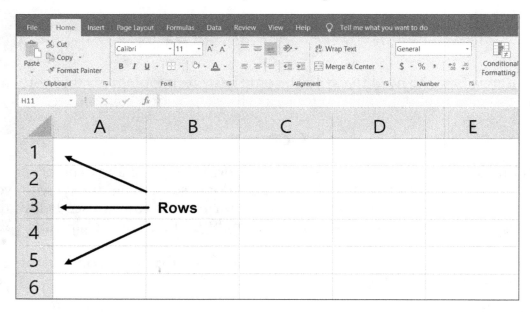

Cell

A cell is a combination of a column and row that is identified by the letter of the column it's in and the number of the row it's in.

For example, Cell A1 is the cell in the first column and the first row of the worksheet. When you've clicked on a specific cell it will have a darker border around the edges like in the image below.

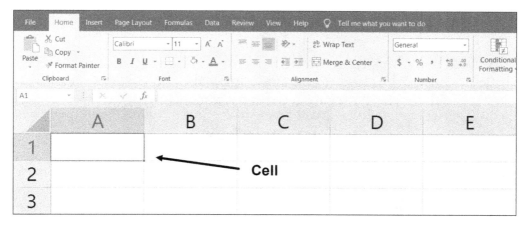

Cell

Click

If I tell you to click on something, that means to use your mouse (or trackpad) to move the arrow on the screen over to a specific location and left-click or right-click on the option. (See the next definition for the difference between left-click and right-click).

If you left-click, this selects the item. If you right-click, this generally creates a dropdown list of options to choose from.

If I don't tell you which to do, left- or right-click, then left-click.

Left-click/Right-click

If you look at your mouse or your trackpad, you generally have two flat buttons to press. One is on the left side, one is on the right. If I say left-click that means to press down on the button on the left. If I say right-click that means press down on the button on the right.

(If you're used to using Word you may already do this without even thinking about it. So, if that's the case then think of left-click as what you usually use to select text and right-click as what you use to see a menu of choices.)

Not all track pads have the left- and right-hand buttons. In that case, you'll basically want to press on either the bottom left-hand side of the track pad or the bottom right-hand side of the trackpad.

Spreadsheet

I'll try to avoid using this term, but if I do use it, I'll mean your entire Excel file. It's a little confusing because it can sometimes also be used to mean a specific worksheet, which is why I'll try to avoid it as much as possible.

Worksheet

A worksheet is basically a combination of rows and columns that you can enter data in. When you open an Excel file, it opens to worksheet one.

Excel 2019 has one worksheet available by default when a new file is opened and that worksheet is originally labeled Sheet1.

It is possible to add more worksheets to a workbook (that's the entire Excel file) and we will cover that later. When there are multiple worksheets, the name of the current worksheet is highlighted in white to show that it's in use.

Formula Bar

The formula bar is the long white bar at the top of the screen with the $f\chi$ symbol next to it.

If you click in a cell and start typing, you'll see that what you type appears not only in that cell, but in the formula bar as well. When you input a formula into a cell and then hit enter, the value returned by the formula will be what displays in the cell, but the formula will appear in the formula bar when you have that cell highlighted.

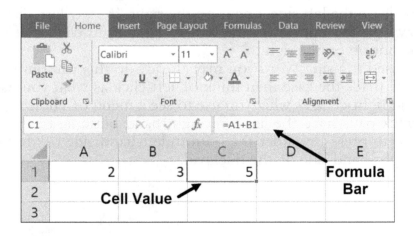

Tab

I refer to the menu choices at the top of the screen (File, Home, Insert, Page Layout, Formulas, Data, Review, View, and Help) as tabs. Note how they look like folder tabs from an old-time filing system when selected? That's why.

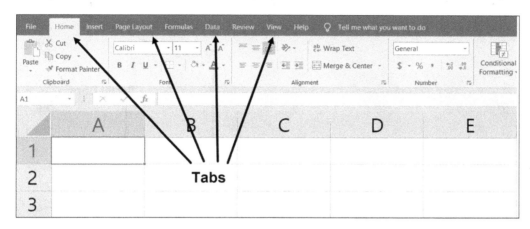

Each menu tab you select will show you different options. On my Home tab I can do things like copy/cut/paste, format cells, edit cells, and insert/delete cells, for example.

Scroll Bar

On the right side and along the bottom of the screen are two bars with arrows at the ends. If you left-click and hold on either bar you can move it back and forth between those arrows. This lets you see information that's off the page in your current view but part of the worksheet you're viewing.

You can also use the arrows at the ends of the scroll bar to do the same thing. Left-click on the arrow once to move it one line or column or left-click and hold to get it to move as far as it can go.

If you want to cover more rows/columns at a time you can click into the blank space on either side of the scroll bar to move an entire screen at a time, assuming you have enough data entered for that.

Using the scroll bars only lets you move to the end of the information you've already entered. You can use the arrows instead of clicking on the scroll bar to scroll all the way to the far end of the worksheet.

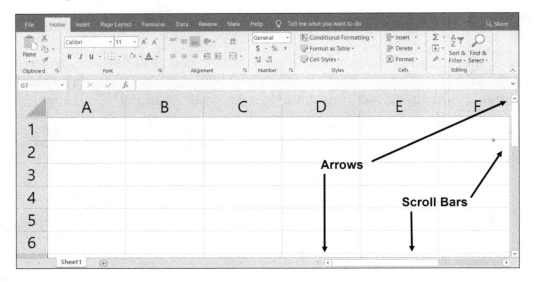

Data

I use data and information interchangeably. Whatever information you put into a worksheet is your data.

Table

I may also refer to a table of data or data table on occasion. This is just a combination of rows and columns that contain information.

This should not be confused with the Word version of a table which is a set aside combination of rows and columns. Even if you create a table in Excel with a border around the edges and nothing else in the document, you're still working in a worksheet that contains a set number of columns and rows that never changes no matter what you do.

Select

If I tell you to "select" cells, that means to highlight them. If the cells are next to each other, you can just left-click on the first one and drag the cursor (move your mouse or finger on the trackpad) until all of the cells are highlighted. When this happens, they'll all be surrounded by a dark box like below.

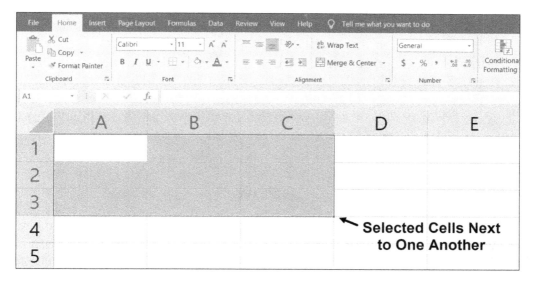

If the cells aren't next to each other, then what you do is left-click on the first cell, hold down the Ctrl key (bottom left on my keyboard), left-click on the next cell, hold down the Ctrl key, left-click on the next cell, etc. until you've selected all the cells you want.

The cells you've already selected will be shaded in gray. The last cell you selected will be surrounded by a dark border.

In the image below cells A1, C1, A3, and C3 are selected. Cell C3 was selected last.

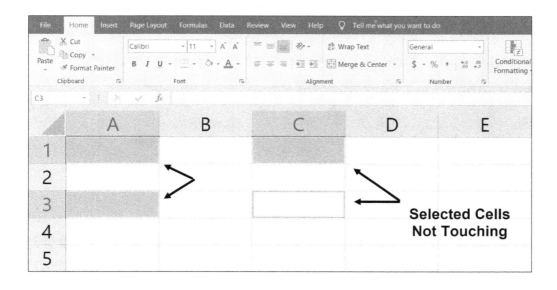

Cursor

If you didn't know this one already, it's what moves around when you move the mouse (or use the trackpad). In Excel it often looks like a three-dimensional squat cross or it will look like one of a couple of varieties of arrow. (You can open Excel and move the arrow to where the column and row labels are to see what I mean.) The different shapes the cursor takes represent different functions that are available.

Arrow

If I say that you can "arrow" to something that just means to use the arrow keys to navigate from one cell to another. For example, if you enter information in Cell A1 and hit Enter, that moves your cursor down to cell A2. If instead you wanted to move to the right to Cell B1, you could do so by using the right arrow.

Dropdown

I will occasionally refer to a dropdown or dropdown menu. This is generally a list of potential choices that you can select from. The existence of the list is indicated by an arrow next to the first available selection. You can see a number of examples in the image below.

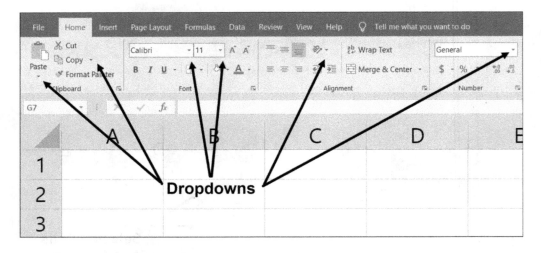

I will also sometimes refer to the list of options you see when you click on a dropdown arrow as the dropdown menu.

Dialogue Box

Dialogue boxes are pop-up boxes that contain a set of available options and appear when you need to provide additional information or make additional choices. For example, this is the Find and Replace dialogue box which appears when you select the Replace option from the Editing section of the Home tab:

Absolute Basics

It occurs to me that there are a few absolute basics to using Excel that we should cover before we get into things like formatting.

Opening an Excel File

To start a brand new Excel file, I simply click on Excel from my applications menu or the shortcut icon I have on my computer's taskbar, and it opens a new Excel file for me.

If you're opening an existing Excel file, you can either go to the folder where the file is saved and double-click on the file name, or you can (if Excel is already open) go to the File tab and choose Open from the left-hand menu.

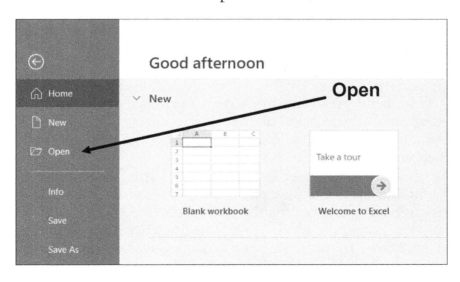

That will show you a list of Recent Workbooks. If it includes the one you're looking for, you can just click on it once and it will open.

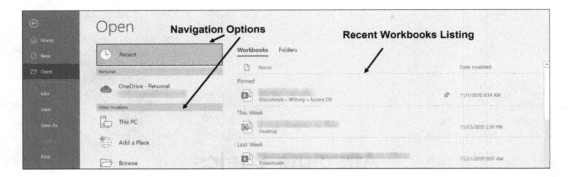

If you don't see the file you're looking for, you can click on the list of navigation options in between the left-hand menu and the list of Recent Workbooks and navigate to where the file is stored. When I click on This PC it gives me a list of recently used folders. If the document I want isn't in one of those folders, I can use the Browse option instead. If you use the cloud, OneDrive is also an option.

Excel may show an error message when you open some files in Excel. The one I usually see is about Excel opening a file in Protected View because it's a file I didn't create.

Don't panic, it's fine. You can see the contents without doing anything or if you need to edit just click on Enable Editing as long as you trust the source of the file.

Saving an Excel File

Excel has two options for saving a file, Save and Save As. If you have an existing file that's already been saved before and no changes to make to its name, location, or type, you can use Ctrl + S or click on the small computer disc image in the top left corner to save the file once more. Simply closing the file will also prompt Excel to ask if you'd like to save your changes to the document.

If the file you are saving is an .xlsx file type, you should really see nothing else at that point. The file is saved when you use Ctrl + S or the disc image or click on Save when you close the file..

If the file you're trying to save is an .xls file type (so an older file type) or another type of file like a .csv file or a .txt file, you may see an additional message when you try to Save about compatibility. The dialogue box that appears will tell you the issue that saving the file as-is will create and you need to decide whether that's okay or whether to go back into the file and fix the issue before saving.

(Usually I can just say continue when this happens because it opened from the old format and is saving to the old format so isn't going to be a huge concern as long as I didn't do some new fancy analysis in the meantime.)

All of the above options will also work for a brand new file, but they will bring up a dialogue box asking what you want to name the file and where you want to save it.

Clicking on More Options from that dialogue box will take you to the Save As screen that can also be reached by clicking on Save As on the left-hand side after clicking on the File tab.

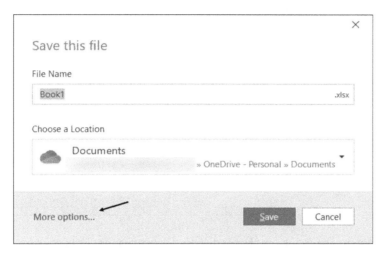

With the Save As option available under the File tab, Excel will ask you to choose which folder to save the file into. You can either choose from the list of recent folders on the right-hand side, or navigate to the folder you want using the locations listing on the left-hand side (OneDrive, This PC, and Browse).

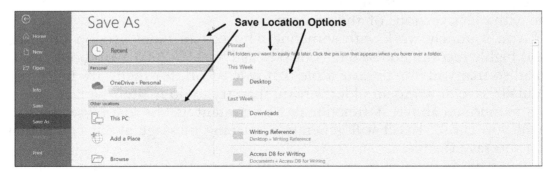

Once you choose Browse or select a folder, a dialogue box will appear where you can name the file and choose its format.

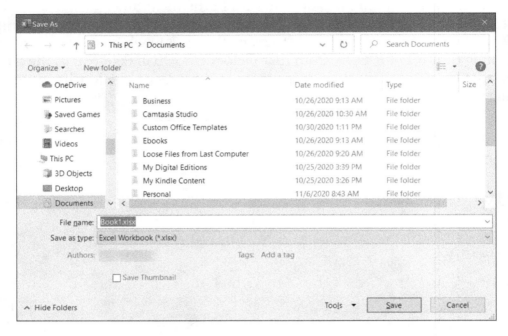

You can also navigate to a different file location at this point if you're more comfortable working in the Save As dialogue box.

To change the file type, click on the dropdown arrow for the option next to Save As Type under the File Name.

The default in Excel 2019 is to save to an .xlsx file type. Know that this file type is not compatible with versions of Excel prior to Excel 2007. At this point you're probably safe working with the default .xlsx file type, but this can be an issue with older versions of the program.

If you routinely work with someone who has an older version of Excel I would highly recommend saving your files as Excel 97-2003 Workbook .xls files instead so that you don't create a file that won't work for them. It's much easier to initially save down to an older version than try to do it after the fact.

As mentioned above, if functionality or content will be lost by saving to the format you chose, Excel will generate a warning message about compatibility when you save the file.

If you have an existing file that you want to rename, save to a new location, or save as a new file type, use the Save As option by going to the File tab and choosing Save As from there.

Deleting an Excel File

You can't delete an Excel file from within Excel. You'll need to navigate to the folder where the file is stored and delete the file there without opening it.

To do this, first, click on the file name. (Only enough to select it. Make sure you haven't double-clicked and highlighted the name which will then try to rename the file.) Then choose Delete from the menu at the top of the screen, or right-click and choose Delete from the dropdown menu.

Renaming an Excel File

You might want to rename an Excel file at some point. You can Save As and choose a new name for the file, but that will mean you now have two versions of the file, one with the old name and one with the new name.

A better option is to navigate to the folder where you have the file saved, click on it once to highlight the file, click on it a second time to highlight the name, and then type in the new name you want to use. If you do it that way, there will only be one version of the file, the one with the name you wanted.

However, if you do rename a file by changing the name in the source folder, know that you can't then access it from the Recent Workbooks listing under Open file. Even though it might be listed there, Excel won't be able to find it because it no longer has that name. (Same thing happens if you move a file from the location it was in when you were last working on it. I often run into this by moving a file into a new subfolder when I suddenly get inspired to organize my records.)

Closing an Excel File

When you're done with Excel you're going to want to close your file. The easiest way to do so is to click on the X in the top right corner of the screen. Or you can use Alt +F4. (If you use Alt+F4 this will only work if the F functions are set up to be the default keys on your keyboard.)

To just close a worksheet but keep Excel open you can use Ctrl + W.

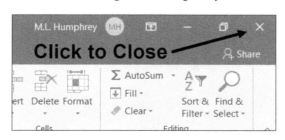

Navigating Excel

The next thing we're going to discuss is basic navigation within Excel. These are all things you can do that don't involve inputting, formatting, or manipulating your data.

Basic Navigation Within A Worksheet

Excel will automatically open into cell A1 of Sheet1 for a new Excel file. For an existing file it will open in the cell and worksheet where you were when you last saved the file. (This means it can also open with a set of cells already highlighted if that's what you were doing when you last saved the file.)

Within a worksheet, it's pretty basic to navigate.

You can click into any cell you can see in the worksheet using your mouse or trackpad. Just place your cursor over the cell and left-click.

From the cell where you currently are (which will be outlined with a dark border), you can use the up, down, left, and right arrow keys to move one cell at a time in any of those directions.

You can also use the tab key to move one cell at a time to the right and the shift and tab keys combined (shift + tab) to move one cell at a time to the left.

To see other cells in the worksheet that aren't currently visible, you can use the scroll bars on the right-hand side or the bottom of the worksheet. The right-hand scroll bar will let you move up and down. The bottom scroll bar will let you move right or left. Just remember that the bars themselves will only let you move as far as you've entered data or the default workspace. You need to use the arrows at the ends of the scroll bars to move farther than that.

For worksheets with lots of data in them, click on the scroll bar and drag it to move quickly to the beginning or end of the data. To move one view's worth at a time, click in the blank gray space around the actual scroll bar.

If you're using the scroll bars to navigate a large amount of data or records, know that until you click into a new cell with your mouse or trackpad you will still be in the last cell where you had clicked or made an edit. So be sure to click into one of the cells you see rather than try to immediately type or to use the tab or arrow keys to navigate. (I run into this frequently when I have Freeze Panes on and then try to use an arrow key to move from the first row of column labels into my data, forgetting that the data I'm actually seeing is hundreds of rows away from that top row. Don't worry, we'll discuss Freeze Panes later.)

F2

If you click in a cell and hit the F2 key, this will take you to the end of the contents of the cell. This can be very useful when you need to edit the contents of a cell or to work with a formula in that cell. I use it often enough that every time I get a new computer I make sure that the F keys are the default rather than the volume controls, etc.

Adding a New Worksheet

When you open a new Excel file in Excel 2019, you'll have one worksheet you can use named Sheet1.

If you need another worksheet, simply click on the + symbol in a circle next to that Sheet1 tab.

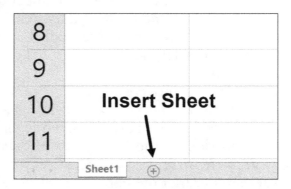

If you already have multiple worksheets in your workbook, the + sign will be located to the right of the last worksheet.

You can also go to the Home tab under the Cells section and left-click the arrow under Insert and then select Insert Sheet from the dropdown menu there.

Deleting a Worksheet

Sometimes you'll add a worksheet and then realize you don't want it anymore. It's easy enough to delete. Just right-click on the name of the worksheet you want to delete and choose the Delete option from the dropdown menu (which will actually drop upward.)

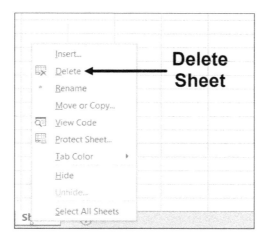

If there was any data in the worksheet you're trying to delete, Excel will give you a warning message to that effect in a dialogue box.

If you don't care, click Delete. If you do care and want to cancel the deletion, click Cancel.

Another way to delete a worksheet is to go to the Cells section in the Home tab, left-click on the arrow next to Delete, and choose Delete Sheet from the dropdown menu there.

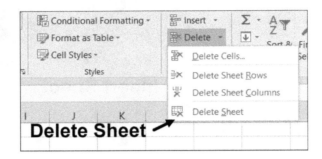

Be sure you want to delete any worksheet you choose to delete, because you can't get it back later. This is one place where undo (which we'll discuss later) will not work.

Basic Navigation Between Worksheets

Once you have multiple worksheets in your workbook, you can navigate between them by either clicking on the name of the worksheet you want at the bottom of the screen or by using Ctrl + Page Up to move one worksheet to the left or Ctrl + Page Dn to move one worksheet to the right.

The Ctrl shortcuts do not loop around, so if you're at the first worksheet and want to reach the last one you need to use Ctrl + Page Dn to move through all of the other worksheets to get there.

Or you could just click onto the last one like I do and skip the ctrl shortcut.

If you have too many worksheets to see their names on one screen, use the arrows at the left-hand side of the worksheet names or the … at the ends (when visible) to see the rest. The … will take you all the way to the beginning or the end.

Insert a Cell in a Worksheet

Sometimes you will just want to insert one cell or a small handful of cells into your worksheet. This will happen when you already have data entered into the worksheet and realize that you need to put additional data in the midst of what you already have entered.

(Because, remember, Excel worksheets have a fixed unchanging number of cells based upon the numbers of rows and columns they contain. So inserting a cell isn't really inserting a cell so much as telling Excel to move all of your information from that point over or down to make room for the new cell or cells.)

To insert a cell or cells, select the cell or cell range where you want to insert your new blank cells, right-click, and choose Insert from the dropdown menu.

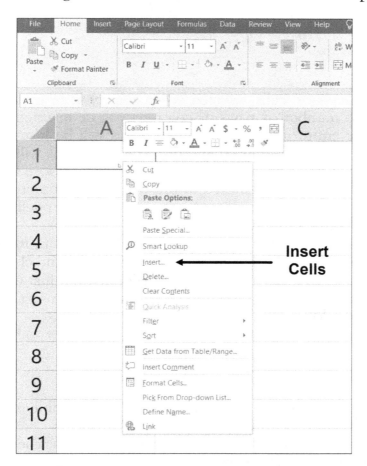

You'll be given four choices, Shift Cells Right, Shift Cells Down, Entire Row, and Entire Column. (See dialogue box screenshot on next page.)

Shift Cells Right will insert your cell or range of cells by moving every other cell in that row or rows to the right to make room for the new cell or cells.

Shift Cells Down will insert your cell or range of cells by moving every other cell in that column or columns down to make room.

Entire row will insert an entire new row at that point.
Entire column will insert an entire new column at that point.

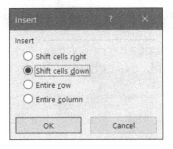

If you have a range of cells selected when you choose entire row or entire column then that number of rows or columns will be inserted. So, select three rows and choose entire row and three new rows will be inserted. Select three columns and choose entire column and three new columns will be inserted.

(Be sure that the cells you select and the option you choose make sense given the other data you've already entered in the worksheet. Sometimes I find that I need to actually highlight a larger range of cells and insert cells for all of them in order to keep the rest of my data aligned.)

You can also highlight the cell or cells where you want to insert and then go to the Cells section of the Home tab where it says Insert and choose Insert Cells from the dropdown to bring up the Insert dialogue box. Just clicking on Insert instead of using the dropdown menu will automatically insert a cell or cells by moving everything down.

There is also a control shortcut for this one (Ctrl+Shift+=) but I never use it.

Insert a Column or Row

From the above discussion you can see that it's also possible to insert an entire row or column into your existing data.

The easiest way to do so is to select the row or column where you want your new row or column to go, right-click, and choose Insert from the dropdown menu.

(To select a row or column you just click on either the letter of the column or the number of the row. You'll know it worked if all cells in that row or column are then shaded gray showing that they've been selected.)

For columns, when a new column is inserted all of your data will shift to the right one column. For rows all of your data will shift down one row. So data in Column C will move to Column D and data in Row 2 will move to Row 3.

As we saw above, you can also just right-click in a single cell, choose Insert, and then choose Entire Row or Entire Column from the Insert Dialogue Box.

Another option is to click in a cell or highlight the row or column where you want to insert and then go to the Cells section of the Home tab and use the Insert dropdown to choose Insert Sheet Rows or Insert Sheet Columns.

Delete a Cell in a Worksheet

Deleting a cell or range of cells in a worksheet is a lot like inserting one. Select the cell or cells you want to delete, right-click, and choose Delete from the dropdown menu.

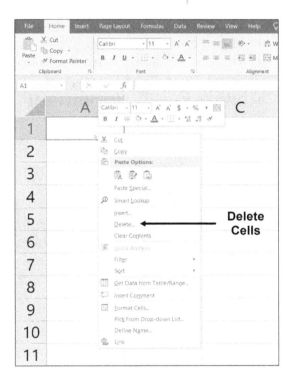

Next, choose whether to shift cells up or left, keeping in mind that when you remove a cell everything will have to move to fill in the empty space it leaves.

Double-check to make sure that deleting that cell or range of cells didn't change the layout of the rest of your data. (I sometimes find I need to delete more than one cell to keep things uniform.)

(Note that you can also delete an entire row or column this way as well just like you could with inserting.)

Another option is to highlight the cell(s) you want to delete, and then go to the Cells section of the Home tab where it says Delete and choose the delete option you want from there. Just clicking on Delete will shift the remaining data upward one row. Using the dropdown to choose Delete Cells will open the Delete dialogue box which gives you the option to shift the remaining data to the left.

Delete a Column or Row

Same as with inserting a column or row. The easiest option is to highlight the entire row or column you want to delete, right-click, and select Delete.

You can also highlight the row or column and then go to the Cells section of the Home tab where it says Delete and choose the delete option you want from the dropdown there. Or you can click into one cell, right-click, select Delete, and then choose Entire Row or Entire Column from the dialogue box.

Renaming A Worksheet

The default name for worksheets in Excel are Sheet1, Sheet2, Sheet3, etc. They're not useful for much of anything, and if you have information in more than one worksheet, you're going to want to rename them to something that lets you identify which worksheet is which.

If you double left-click on a worksheet name (on the tab at the bottom) it will highlight in gray and you can then delete the existing name and replace it with whatever you want by simply typing in the new worksheet name.

You can also right-click on the tab name and choose Rename from the dropdown menu and it will highlight the tab name in gray and let you type in your new name that way as well.

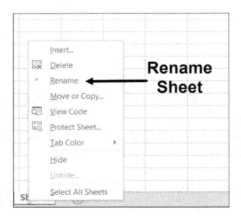

A worksheet name cannot be more than 31 characters long, be blank, contain the forward slash, the back slash, a question mark, a star, a colon, or brackets (/ \ ? * : [ ]), begin or end with an apostrophe, or be named History.

Don't worry about memorizing that. In Excel 2019 it won't let you type the prohibited characters or let you type more characters than the limit allows.

Moving or Copying Worksheet

There may be times that you want to move a worksheet around, so change the order of the worksheets in a workbook or even move that particular worksheet into a new Excel workbook. I've also on more than one occasion wanted to take a copy of a worksheet in one workbook and put that copy into a different workbook.

To move a worksheet within an Excel workbook, click on the name of the worksheet you want to move, hold down that click, and drag the worksheet to the new position you want for it. While you're dragging you should see what looks like a little piece of paper under your cursor arrow. This shows you where you're dragging the worksheet to. Once it's where you want it, just release the click and it should drop into the new position.

To move a worksheet to a new workbook or to copy one to a new workbook is basically the same. Right-click on the worksheet name and choose Move or Copy from the dropdown menu.

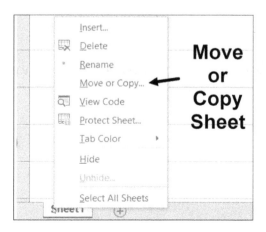

This will open the Move or Copy dialogue box. There are three options available in the dialogue box. The first is "To Book" which is where you select the file you'd like to move your worksheet to. If you're just copying the worksheet and keeping that copy within the current workbook, then leave this option alone. If you want to move or copy the worksheet to a new workbook, then use the dropdown menu to select that new workbook. Your options will consist of all of the workbooks you have open at the time as well as an option to create a new workbook.

The second choice you have is where to place the copied or moved worksheet. This is in a box labeled Before Sheet and it will list all of the current worksheets in the selected workbook. Choose the (move to end) option to place the worksheet at the end.

If you are copying the worksheet and not just moving it, so you want the original version to stay where it is but to use a copy in either that workbook or another, be sure to check the Create a Copy checkbox at the bottom.

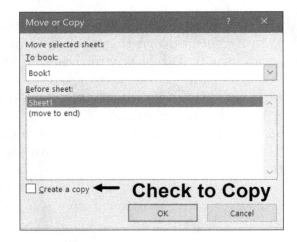

Click OK when you're done and the worksheet will be moved or copied.

Inputting Your Data

At its most basic, inputting your data is very simple. Click in the cell where you want to input information and type. But there are some tricks to it that you'll want to keep in mind.

First, let's take a step back and talk about one of the key strengths of using Excel and that's the ability to sort or filter your data. For example, I publish books, and every month I get reports from the places where my books are published listing all of the sales of my books at those locations. But what if I only care about the sales of book A? How can I see those if I have a couple hundred rows of information about various books in the report they've given me?

Well, if the site where I sold those books is nice and helpful and they understand data analysis, they've given me my sales listings in an Excel worksheet with one header row at the top and then one row for each sale or for each book. If they've done that, then I can very easily filter my data on the title column and see just the entries related to a specific title. If they haven't, then I'm stuck deleting rows of information I don't need to get to the data I want.

Which is all a roundabout way of saying that you can input your data any way you want, but if you follow some key data principles you'll have a lot more flexibility in what you can do with that data once it's entered.

Those principles are:

1. Use the first row of your worksheet to label your data.

2. List all of your data in continuous rows after that first row without including any subtotals or subheadings or anything that isn't your data.

3. To the extent possible, format your data in such a way that it can be analyzed. (So rather than put in a free-text field, try to use a standardized

list of values instead. See below. Column E, which uses a 1 to 5 point ranking scale, is better for analysis than Column D, which is a free text field where anyone can say anything.)

4. Standardize your values. Customer A should always be listed as Customer A. United States should always be United States not USA, U.S.A., or America.

5. Store your raw data in one location; analyze or correct it elsewhere.

I get into all of this much more in a book called *Data Principles for Beginners*, but that's the basic gist of how to best store data in an Excel worksheet if you're planning to do any analysis on it.

Here's an example of how it looks.

	A	B	C	D	E	F	G	H
1	Customer Name	Invoice	Date	Customer Feedack	Customer Satisfaction Score		Row 1 Identifies	
2	Customer Name A	$110	1-Jan	asbasbdasdas	1		Contents	
3	Customer Name B	$125	15-Feb	asdas	1			
4	Customer Name C	$150	7-Apr	kjjkhj	1		Other Rows	
5	Customer Name D	$225	21-Jan	adsas	4		Contain Data	
6	Customer Name E	$250	10-Sep	aiasdasd	5			

This is for data analysis, but there are many ways in which I use Excel that don't require that kind of analysis so don't follow those types of rules. My budgeting worksheet, for example, is not meant to be filtered or sorted. It's a snapshot of information that summarizes my current financial position. But my worksheet that lists all vendor payments for the year? You bet it's formatted using this approach.

So before you enter any data into your Excel file, put some time into thinking about how you want to use that data.

Is it just a visual snapshot? If so, don't worry about structuring it for sorting or filtering.

Will it be hundreds of rows of values that you want to summarize or analyze? If so, then arrange it in the way I showed above. You don't have to have Row 1 be your column headings (although it does make it easier), but wherever you do put those headings, keep everything below that point single rows of data that are all formatted and entered in the same way so that they can be compared to one another.

Okay?

Now that we've gotten that out of the way, let's discuss a few quick tricks that will make entering your data and analyzing it easier, starting with Undo and Redo.

Undo

If you enter the wrong information or perform the wrong action and want to easily undo it, hold down the Ctrl key and the Z key at the same time. (Ctrl + Z) You can do this multiple times if you want to undo multiple actions, although there are a few actions (such as deleting a worksheet) that cannot be undone.

You can also click on the left-pointing hooked arrow at the very top of the Excel workbook to undo an action. It's located in the Quick Access Toolbar right above the File and Home tabs next to where you can click on the disc image to save a file.

Clicking on the dropdown arrow next to the undo arrow will give you a list of all of the actions that you can undo at that point in time. You can then select the first action or a series of actions from there. If you want to undo something you did four actions ago, you have to undo the last three actions as well.

Undo is a life saver. If you only remember one control shortcut, make it this one. Ctrl + Z is your friend.

Redo

If you mistakenly undo something and want it back, you can hold down the Ctrl key and the Y key at the same time to redo it. (Ctrl + Y)

In the Quick Access Toolbar there is an arrow that points to the right that will be available if you just undid something which you can click on as well instead of using the control shortcut.

If you undo multiple actions at once, you can redo all of them at once as well using the Quick Access Toolbar. But again, if you want to redo actions 1, 2, and 4 you will also have to redo action 3. You can't pick and choose.

Auto-Suggested Text

If you've already typed text into a cell, Excel will suggest that text to you in subsequent cells in the same column.

For example, if you are creating a list of all the books you own (something I once tried to do and gave up after about a hundred entries), and in Cell A1 you type "science fiction", when you go to Cell A2 and type an "s", Excel will automatically suggest to you "science fiction". If you don't want to use that suggestion, then keep typing. If you do, then hit enter.

This is very convenient because instead of typing fifteen characters you only have to type one, but it only works when you have unique values for Excel to identify. If you have science fiction/fantasy and science fiction as entries in your list then it's not going to work because Excel waits until it can suggest one single option. So you'd have to type "science fiction/" before it made any suggestions in that scenario

Also, if there are empty cells between the entries you already completed and the one you're now completing and you have no other columns with completed data in them to bridge that gap and let Excel know the cells are related, Excel won't make a suggestion.

(Which means if you're going to use Auto-Suggested text it helps to have a column next to where you're inputting your data that is a numbered entries column that will let auto-complete work even if you're not entering your data row by row but are instead jumping around a bit.)

Another time this doesn't work is if you have a very long list that you've completed and the matching entry is hundreds of rows away from the one you're now completing.

Excel also doesn't make suggestions for numbers. If you have an entry that combines letters and numbers, it won't make a suggestion until you've typed at least one letter from the entry.

Despite all these apparent limitations, auto-suggested text can be very handy to use if you have to enter one of a limited number of choices over and over again and can't easily copy the information into your worksheet. It's also helpful to factor this in when deciding what your values will be. For example, I have a book *Excel for Beginners* and a book *Excel for Beginners Quiz Book*. Rather than list them that way in my advertising tracker where I have to make manual entries I list the quiz book as *Quiz Book: Excel for Beginners*. This lets me just type E or just type Q and have Excel complete the rest of both titles for me.

(We're not going to get into it in this book, but if you do have a limited list of values that you want available to enter and can't use auto-suggested text because maybe it's Widget1 and Widget2 so it won't help, then one alternate workaround would be to set up Data Validation with a list of values. Data Validation is covered in *Excel 2019 Intermediate*.)

Alright. Next.

Copying the Contents and Formatting of One Cell To Another

Copying the contents and formatting of a cell to another is something you will probably need to do often. And it is very easy to do.

First, highlight the information you want to copy, next, hold down the Ctrl and C keys at the same time (Ctrl + C), and then go to the cell where you want to put the information you copied and hit Enter.

If you want to copy the information to more than one location, instead of hitting Enter at the new cell, hold down the Ctrl and V keys at the same time (Ctrl + V) to paste.

If you use Ctrl + V, you'll see that the original cell you copied from is still surrounded by a dotted line which indicates that the information you copied is still available to be pasted into another cell. You can see this by clicking into another cell and using Ctrl + V again. It will paste the information you copied a second time.

Another way to copy is to select your information and then right-click and choose Copy from the dropdown menu. You can then use Enter, Ctrl + V, or right-click and choose Paste from the dropdown menu to paste the information.

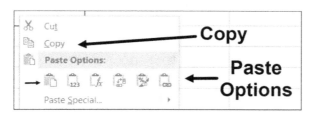

For a basic copy of the information choose the first option under Paste Options which is a clipboard with a blank piece of paper. Hold your cursor over it and you should see it described as Paste (P).

Once you're done pasting the values into new cells and want to do something else, just hit the Esc key. This will remove the dotted line from around the cell you were copying and ensure you don't accidentally paste it somewhere else. Typing text into a new cell also works to turn off the copy/paste that you've initiated.

(When in doubt in Excel using Esc is very helpful. It's kind of like an Undo function when you haven't yet done anything but have started something you don't want to finish.)

In the Clipboard section of the Home tab you can also find another set of Copy and Paste options (as well as Cut which we're about to discuss), but I almost never use them because these are tasks where learning your control shortcuts will save you a lot of time.

So, Ctrl + C to Copy, Ctrl + V to Paste, and, as we're about to learn, Ctrl + X to Cut. Memorize those and learn to use them. Trust me.

Moving the Contents of a Cell

To move selected information rather than just copy it, select the information, type Ctrl and X at the same time (Ctrl + X), click on the new location, and hit Enter or type Ctrl + V.

Unlike with copying, you can only move the contents of a cell to one new location. Once you hit Enter or use Ctrl + V that information will have moved and you cannot paste it anywhere else without first copying it from the new location.

Another option for moving your information is to highlight the information you want to move, right-click, and choose Cut from the dropdown menu and then paste your cell contents in the new location.

Copying the contents of a cell (Ctrl + C) is different from cutting and moving the contents of a cell (Ctrl + X), because when you copy the contents of a cell, (Ctrl + C), they remain in their original location. When you move the contents of a cell, (Ctrl + X), you are removing them from their original location to place them in their new location.

Note that I've been talking about Copying or Cutting information rather than cells, because you can actually click into a specific cell, highlight just a portion of the content of that cell and Copy or Cut that portion only. You do this by clicking into the cell and then going to the Formula Bar to highlight the text you want, or by clicking on a cell and then using F2 to access the contents of that cell and then the arrow keys and the Shift key to highlight the text you want.

Copying Versus Moving When It Comes to Formulas

If you're dealing with text, copying (Ctrl + C) or cutting the text (Ctrl + X) doesn't really change anything. What ends up in that new cell will be the same regardless of the method you use.

But with formulas, that's not what happens.

With formulas, moving the contents of a cell (Ctrl + X) will keep the formula the exact same as it was. So if your formula was =A2+B2 it will still be =A2+B2 in the new cell.

Copying the contents of a cell (Ctrl + C) will change the formula based upon the number of rows and columns you moved. The formula is copied relative to where it originated. If your original formula in Cell A3 is =A2+B2 and you copy it to Cell A4 (so move it one cell downward) the formula in Cell A4 will be =A3+B3. All cell references in the formula adjust one cell downward.

If you copy that same formula to Cell B3 (so one cell to the right) the formula in B3 will be =B2+C2. All cell references in the formula adjust one cell to the right.

If this doesn't make sense to you, just try it. Put some sample values in cells A2 and B2 and then experiment with Ctrl + C versus Ctrl + X.

Also, there is a way to prevent a formula from changing when you copy it using the $ sign to keep the cell references fixed. We'll talk about that next.

Copying Formulas To Other Cells While Keeping One Value Fixed

If you want to copy a formula while keeping the value of one or more of the cells fixed, you need to use the $ sign.

A $ sign in front of the letter portion of a cell location will keep the column the same but allow the row number to change. ($A1)

A $ sign in front of the number portion of a cell location will keep the row the same but allow the column to change. (A$1)

A $ sign in front of both the column and row portion will keep the referenced cell exactly the same. (A1)

This will be discussed in more detail in the manipulating data section because where it really comes up is in mathematical calculations and functions.

Paste Special

I often want to take values I've calculated in Excel and just keep the end result without keeping the formula. For example, with my advertising in the UK the values are reported to me in that currency (GBP) but I want to convert them to my currency (USD). Once I've done that, I don't need to keep the calculation because the only thing that matters for my purposes is the end value in my currency.

Other reasons to use Paste Special include wanting to copy the contents of a cell but not keep the formatting from that cell. Also, I use it to turn a series of values that are displayed across columns into a series of values that are displayed across rows, or vice versa.

The first thing to know about Paste Special is that you can only use it if you've copied (Ctrl + C) the contents of a cell or cells. It doesn't work with Cutting (Ctrl + X).

To Paste Special use the dropdown option for pasting or the dropdown option in the Clipboard section of the Home tab. You cannot use the Ctrl shortcut to paste.

So, right-click where you want to Paste and go to Paste Options or click on the dropdown arrow under Paste in the Clipboard section of the Home tab. You should see options that look like this:

In my opinion, not all of these choices are useful. So I'm just going to highlight two of them for you.

Paste Values, the second option above which has the 123 on its clipboard, is useful for when you want the results of a formula, but don't want the formula anymore. I use this often.

It's also useful when you want the contents of a cell, but would prefer to use the formatting from the destination cell(s). For example, if you're copying from one Excel file to another.

Another way I use it is when I've run a set of calculations on my data, found my values, and now want to sort or do something else with my data and don't want to risk having the values change on me. I highlight the entire data set, copy, and then paste special-values right over the top of my existing data. (Just be sure to type Esc after you do this so that the change is fixed in place.)

Paste Transpose, the fourth option with the little arrow arcing between two pairs of cells, is very useful if you have a row of data that you want to turn into columns of data or vice versa. Just highlight the data, copy, paste-transpose, and it will automatically paste a column of data as a row or a row of data as a column.

Just be sure before you paste that there isn't any data already there that will be overwritten, because Excel won't warn you before it overwrites it.

There are more paste options available than just the six you can see above. If you click on where it says Paste Special you'll see another dropdown menu to the side with eight more options, and if you go to the bottom of that breakout menu and click on Paste Special again, it will bring up the Paste Special dialogue box which allows you to pick and choose from the various paste options. The dropdown available from the Clipboard section of the Home tab is the same as the Paste Special dropdown list of options and you can also bring up the dialogue box from there by choosing Paste Special at the bottom.

Displaying The Contents Of A Cell As Text

Excel likes to change certain values to what it thinks you meant. So if you enter June 2015 into a cell, it will convert that entry to a date even if you intended it to be text. To see this, type June 2015 in a cell, hit enter, click back into the cell, and you'll see in the formula bar that it says 6/1/2015 and it displays as Jun-15 in the cell.

Excel also assumes that any entry that starts with a minus sign (-), an equals sign (=), or a plus sign (+) is a formula.

To keep Excel from messing with your entries, you can type a single quote mark (') before the contents of the cell. If you do that, Excel will treat whatever you enter after that as text and will keep the formatting type as General.

So if you want to have June 2015 display in a cell in your worksheet, you need to type 'June 2015.

If you want to have

- Item A

display in a cell, you need to type it as:

'- Item A

The single quote mark is not visible when you look at or print your worksheet. It is only visible in the formula bar when you've selected the impacted cell.

Entering a Formula Into a Cell

The discussion just above about displaying the contents of a cell as text brings up another good point. If you want Excel to treat an entry as a formula, then you need to enter the equals (=), plus (+), or negative sign (-) as your first character in the cell. So, if you type

1+1

in a cell, that will just display as text in the cell. You'll see

1+1

But if you type

+1+1

in a cell, Excel will treat that as a formula and calculate it. You'll see 2 in the cell and

=1+1

in the formula bar.

Same with if you type

$$=1+1$$

It will calculate that as a formula, display 2 in the cell, and show

$$=1+1$$

in the formula bar.
If you type

$$-1+1$$

in a cell it will treat that as a formula adding negative 1 to 1 and will show that as 0 in the cell and display

$$=-1+1$$

in the formula bar.

Best practice is to use the equals sign to start every formula since Excel converts it to using the equals sign anyway.

Including Line Breaks Within a Cell

I sometimes need to have multiple lines of text or numbers within a cell. So instead of a, b, c, I need

a
b
c

You can't just hit Enter, because if you do it'll take you to the next cell. Instead, hold down the Alt key at the same time you hit Enter. This will create a line break within the cell.

Deleting Data

If you enter information into a cell and later decide you want to delete it, you can click on that cell(s) and use the delete button on your computer's keyboard. This will remove whatever you entered in the cell without deleting the cell as well.

You can also double-click into the cell or use F2 to get to the end of the contents in the cell and then use your computer's backspace key to delete out the contents of the cell from the end. If you double-click and end up somewhere in the middle of the cell you can use the delete key to delete text to the right of your cursor.

Deleting the contents of a cell does not remove its formatting. To delete the contents of a cell as well as its formatting, go to the Editing section of the Home tab, click on the dropdown next to the Clear option, and choose Clear All.

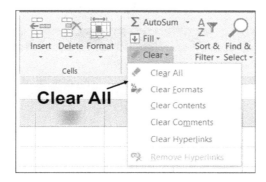

Find and Replace

Sometimes you have a big worksheet and you need to find a specific entry. An easy way to do this is to use the Find option. The easiest way to access it is to type Ctrl and F at the same time (Ctrl + F). This opens the Find dialogue box. Type what you're looking for into the "Find what" field and hit enter.

The other way to access Find is through the Editing section of the Home tab. The Find & Select option has a dropdown menu that includes Find.

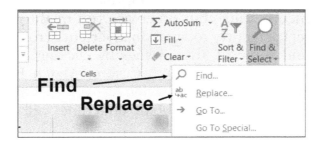

The default is for find to look in formulas as well, so if you search for "f" and have a formula that references cell F11, it will hit on that as much as it will hit on the cell that actually contains the letter f in a word.

You can change this setting under Options where it says Look In at the bottom left. Change the dropdown from Formulas to Values.

If you're looking for something in order to change it, you can use Replace instead. Type Ctrl and H (Ctrl + H) at the same time (or just Ctrl + F and then click over to the Replace tab), or you can access it through the Editing section of the Home tab.

When the Replace dialogue box opens, you'll see two lines, "Find what" and "Replace with." In the "Find what" line, type what you're looking for. In the "Replace with" line, type what to replace it with.

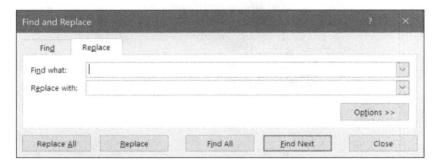

Be VERY careful using Replace.

Say you want to replace "hat" with "chapeau" because you've suddenly become pretentious. If you don't think this through, you will end up replacing every usage of hat, even when it's in words like "that" or "chat". So you'll end up with "tchapeau" in the middle of a sentence instead of "that" because the hat portion of "that" was replaced with "chapeau". (This probably happens in Word more than in Excel, but it's still something to be aware of.)

Replace is good for removing something like double spaces or converting formatting of a particular value, but otherwise you might want to use find and then manually correct each entry to avoid inadvertent errors.

You can get around some of these issues by clicking on Options and then using the checkboxes that let you Match Case or Match Entire Cell Contents Also, that brings up a Format dropdown that lets you search by pretty much any formatting you want such as italics, bold, underline, cell color, border, font, alignment, etc.

Searching by format can come in really handy when you need to, for example, replace italics with bold or change out a font that you used. But again, Find and Replace is used more with Microsoft Word than with Microsoft Excel in my experience.

Copying Patterns of Data

Sometimes you'll want to input data that repeats itself. Like, for example, the days of the week. Say you're putting together a worksheet that lists the date and what day of the week it is for an entire year. You could type out Monday, Tuesday, Wednesday, Thursday, Friday, Saturday, Sunday, and then copy and paste that 52 times. Or…

You could take advantage of the fact that Excel can recognize patterns. With this particular example, it looks like all it takes is typing in Monday. Do that and then go to the bottom right corner of the cell with Monday in it and position your cursor so that it looks like a small black cross. Left-click, hold that left-click down, and start to drag your cursor away from the cell. Excel should auto-complete the cells below or to the right of the Monday cell, depending on the direction you move, with the days of the week in order and repeating themselves in order for as long as you need it to.

If you're dealing with a pattern that isn't as standard as days of the week sometimes it takes a few entries before Excel can identify the pattern.

For example, if I type 1 into a cell and try to drag it, Excel just repeats the 1 over and over again. If I do 1 and then 2 and highlight both cells and start to drag from the bottom of the cell with the 2 in it, then it starts to number the next cells 3, 4, 5 etc.

You'll see the values Excel suggests for each cell as you drag the cursor through that cell, but those values won't actually appear in those cells until you're done highlighting all the cells you want to copy the pattern to and you let up on the left-click. (If that doesn't make sense, just try it a few times and you'll see what I mean.)

	E	F	G	H
1	Customer Satisfaction Score			
2		1	1	
3		1	2	
4		1		
5		4		
6		5		
7		3		

Excel Copying a Pattern Into Three Cells

(You can combine Excel's ability to copy patterns with the AutoFill option by double-clicking in the bottom right-hand corner instead. This only works for columns and when your current column is next to a column that already has values in it for all the rows where you want to copy your pattern. (See the Manipulating Your Data section for more detail on AutoFill.)

Freeze Panes

If you have enough information in a worksheet for it to not be visible in one page, there's a chance you'll want to use freeze panes. What it does is freezes a row or rows and/or a column or columns at the top and side of your page so that even when you scroll down or to the right those rows or columns stay visible. So if you have 100 rows of information but always want to be able to see your header row, freeze panes will let you do that.

To freeze panes, go to the Window section of the View tab and click on the arrow under Freeze Panes.

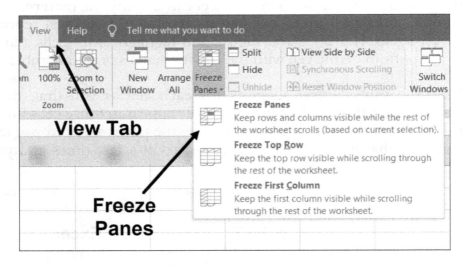

It gives you three options: Freeze Panes, Freeze Top Row, and Freeze First Column.

Those second two are pretty obvious. Choose "Freeze Top Row" and you'll always see Row 1 of your worksheet no matter how far down you scroll. Choose "Freeze First Column" and you'll always see Column A of your worksheet no matter how far to the right you scroll. When you use either of those options you are limited to just that one option, top row or first column.

However, the first option, Freeze Panes gives you the ability to freeze any number of rows AND columns at the same time. You just have to choose your cell first before choosing your freeze panes option.

So if I click on cell C4, which has three rows above it and two to the left, and then choose Freeze Panes, Excel will keep the top three rows AND the left two columns of my worksheet visible no matter where I scroll in the document.

For example, if you had customer name, city, and state in your first three columns and wanted to be able to see that information as you scrolled over to see other customer data, you could.

Or say your worksheet has a couple of rows of descriptive text and then the real row labels begin in row 5, you can click in Cell A6, choose to freeze panes, and those top five rows will always stay visible.

Freeze panes is very handy when dealing with large amounts of data. Just be careful that you don't accidentally lose where you are. If you click into a frozen row or column and then arrow down or over from there, it will take you to the next row, not the data you're seeing on the screen. So if you were looking at row 10,522 and you had the top row frozen and clicked into Row 1 for some reason and then arrowed down from there it would take you to Row 2 not Row 10,522 which is what you see on the screen. (It happens to be something I do often, so figured it was worth mentioning.)

Another thing to be cautious about with freeze panes is that you don't freeze so many rows and columns that you can't see any new data. But that would probably take quite a lot to make happen. But if you are arrowing down or to the right and can't see any new data, you just keep seeing what's already on the screen, that could be the cause.

To remove freeze panes, you can go back to the View tab and the Freeze Panes dropdown and you'll now see that that first option has become Unfreeze Panes. Just click on it and your document will go back to normal. Use that option regardless of whether you initially choose freeze panes, freeze top row, or freeze first column.

Formatting

If you're going to spend any amount of time working in Excel then you need to learn how to format cells, because inevitably your column won't be as wide as you want it to be or you'll want to have a cell with red-colored text or to use bolding or italics or something that isn't Excel's default.

That's what this section is for. It's an alphabetical listing of different things you might want to do. You can either format one cell at a time by highlighting that specific cell, format multiple cells at once by highlighting all of them and then choosing your formatting option, or format just a portion of the contents of a cell by selecting the specific text you want to format and then choosing your formatting option.

There are four main ways to format cells in Excel 2019.

The first is to use the Home tab and click the option you want from there.

The second is to right-click and select the Format Cells option from the dropdown menu which will bring up the Format Cells dialogue box.

The third is to right-click and select an option from what I refer to as the mini formatting menu (pictured below) which is located either just above or just below the dropdown menu and looks like a condensed version of the Home tab options.

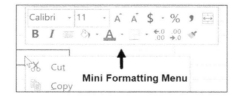

The fourth option is to use control shortcuts. These are available for some of the key formatting options such as bolding (Ctrl + B), italicizing (Ctrl + I), and underlining (Ctrl + U).

For basic formatting, I use the control shortcuts or the Home tab. If you're new to Excel you may want to use the mini formatting menu instead of the Home tab. (I don't use it because it didn't exist when I was learning Excel and it doesn't save so much time that I found it worth learning.)

For less common formatting choices, you will likely need to use the Format Cells dialogue box instead.

Aligning Your Text Within a Cell

By default, text within a cell is left-aligned and bottom-aligned. But at times you may want to adjust this. I often will center text or prefer for it to be top-aligned because it looks better to me that way when I have some column headers that are one line and others that are multiple lines.

To change the alignment in a cell or range of cells, highlight the cell(s) you want to change, and go to the Alignment section on the Home tab. There are a total of six choices which make nine possible combinations as shown below.

The six choices are on the left-hand side of the Alignment section and represented visually.

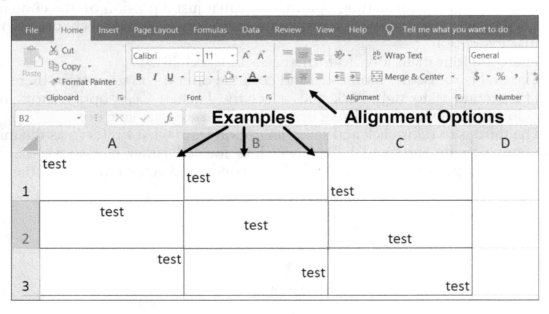

The first row has the top aligned, middle aligned, and bottom aligned options. You can choose one of these three options for your cell.

The second row has the left-aligned, centered, and right-aligned options. You can also choose one of these three options for your cell.

So you can have a cell with top-aligned and centered text or top-aligned and right-aligned text or bottom-aligned and centered text, etc. The image on the opposite page includes an example of the nine possible combinations.

You can also change the direction of your text so that it's angled or vertical.

To do so from the Home tab, click on the arrow next to the angled "ab" in the top row of the Alignment section and select one of the pre-defined options listed there.

You can choose Angle Counterclockwise, Angle Clockwise, Vertical Text, Rotate Text Up, and Rotate Text Down. (The last option, Format Cell Alignment, will bring up the Format Cells dialogue box.)

Another way to change the text alignment within a cell(s) is to highlight your cell(s) and then right-click and choose Format Cells from the dropdown menu. This will also bring up the Format Cells dialogue box. You can then go to the Alignment tab to see your available choices.

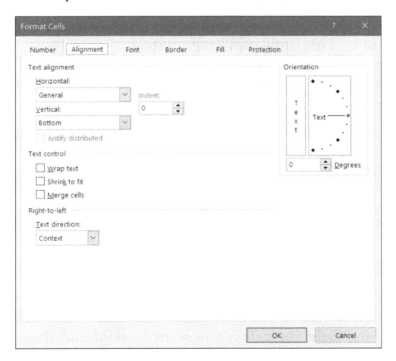

Choose from the Horizontal and Vertical dropdown menus to change the basic alignment of your text (Top, Center, Bottom, Left, Right, etc.).

The dropdown menus do have a few additional choices (like Justify and Distributed), but you generally shouldn't need them. And be wary of Fill which it seems will repeat whatever you have in that cell over and over again horizontally until it fills the cell. (Remember, if you do something you don't like, Ctrl + Z is your friend.)

On the right-hand side of the dialogue box you can also change the orientation of your text to any angle you want by entering a specified number of degrees (90 to make it vertical) or by moving the line within the Orientation box to where you want it. This is generally how I choose to angle text since I usually want an angle of about 30 degrees instead of the default choice in the Home tab which is 45 degrees.

If all you want to do is center your text, you can also use the third option in the bottom row of the mini formatting menu.

Bolding Text

You can bold text in a number of ways.

First, highlight the content you want bolded and then type Ctrl and B (Ctrl + B) at the same time. This is my preferred method.

Second, highlight your content and click on the large capital B in the Font section of the Home tab or in the bottom left row of the mini formatting menu.

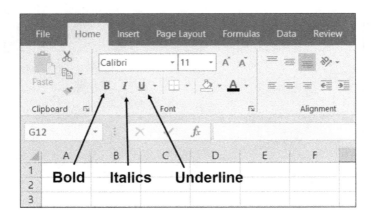

Third, you can highlight the cell(s) you want to bold and then right-click and choose Format Cells from the dropdown menu. Once you're in the Format Cells dialogue box, go to the Font tab and choose Bold from the Font Style options.

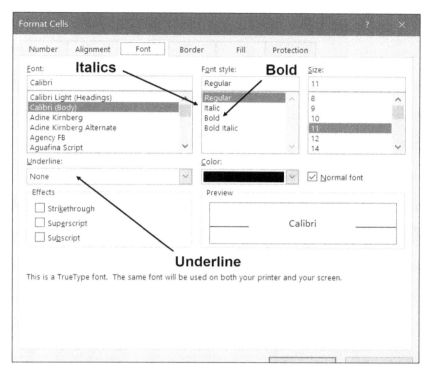

If you want text that is both bolded and italicized, choose Bold Italic.

To remove bolding from text or cells that already have it, highlight the bolded portion and then type Ctrl + B or click on the large capital B in the Font section of the Home tab or the mini formatting menu.(If you happen to highlight text that is only partially bolded you may have to do it twice to remove the bold formatting since the first time it will apply it to the rest of the text.)

Borders Around Cells

It's nice to have borders around your data to keep the information in each cell distinct, especially if you're going to print your document.

There are two main ways to add borders around a cell or set of cells. First, you can highlight the cells you want to place a border around and then go to the Font section on the Home tab and choose from the Borders dropdown option. It's a four-square grid with an arrow next to it that's located between the U used for underlining and the color bucket used for filling a cell with color.

Click on the arrow next to the grid to see your available options, and then choose the type of border you want.

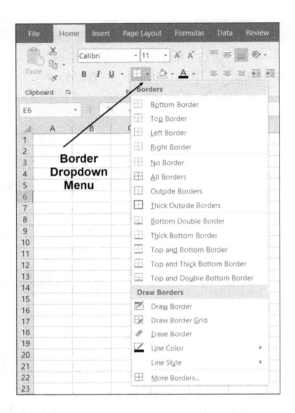

If you just want a simple border all around the cells and between multiple cells click on the All Borders option.

To adjust line thickness or line colors use the options in the Draw Borders section at the bottom, but be sure to choose your colors and line style *before* you choose your border type because the color and line type you choose will only apply to borders you draw after that.

You can also combine border types to get the appearance you want. For example, you could choose All Borders for the entire set of cells and then Thick Box Border to put a darker outline around the perimeter.

Your second choice for adding a border to your cells is to highlight the cells where you want to place a border and then right-click and select Format Cells from the dropdown menu.

When the Format Cells dialogue box appears, go to the Border tab and choose your border style, type, and color from there. (See image on next page.)

There are three Preset options at the top. If you want a basic outline or inside lines, just click on that option. To clear what you've done and start over you can select None from the Presets section.

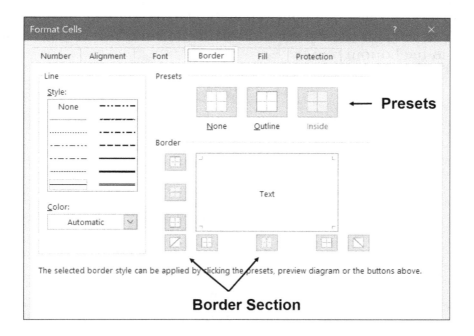

The Border section of the dialogue box allows you to pick and choose which lines you want to have in your cells, including diagonal lines. Simply click on the choice(s) you want.

You will see a preview of how it will appear in that Text box in the center section of the dialogue box.

You can click on more than one of the lines in the Border section. So you could have, for example, a top and bottom border, but nothing else.

If you want to change the style of a line or its color from the default, you can do so in the Line section on the left-hand side, but be sure to do so before you select where you want your lines to appear.

If you forget to change the style or color first, change it then just select the line placement again and it will apply the new style and/or color.

The fact that it works this way allows you to have multiple line styles or colors on a single cell which can come in handy at times.

Coloring a Cell (Fill Color)

You can color (or fill) an entire cell with almost any color you want. To do this, highlight the cell(s) you want to color, go to the Font section of the Home tab, and click on the dropdown arrow for the paint bucket that has a colored line under it. (The color will be bright yellow by default but will change as you use the tool.) You can also use the mini formatting menu where the fill color icon is the fourth in the bottom row.

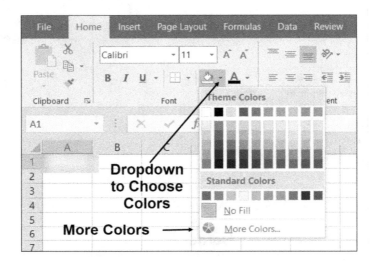

Either option will bring up a dropdown menu with 70 different colors to choose from, including the theme colors which consist of ten columns of color with six shades per color.

If you want to use any of the seventy colors you can see in the dropdown, just click on it.

If none of those colors work for you, or you need to use a specific corporate color, click on More Colors at the bottom of the dropdown menu.

This will bring up a Colors dialogue box. The first tab of that box looks like a honeycomb and has a number of colors you can choose from by clicking into the honeycomb.

The second tab is the Custom tab. It has a rainbow of colors that you can click on and also allows you to enter specific RGB or HSL values to get the exact color you need. (If you have a corporate color palette, they should give you the values for each of the corporate colors.)

On the Custom tab, you can also click and drag the arrow on the right-hand side to darken or lighten your color.

With both tabs, you can see the color you've chosen in the bottom right corner. If you like your choice, click on OK. If you don't want to add color to a cell after all, choose Cancel.

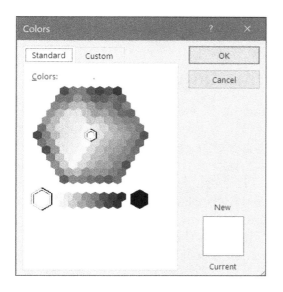 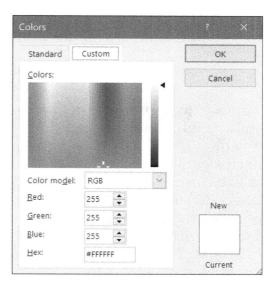

Column Width (Adjusting)

If your columns aren't the width you want, you have three options for adjusting them.

First, you can right-click on the column and choose Column Width from the dropdown menu. When the box showing you the current column width appears, enter a new column width.

Second, you can place your cursor to the right side of the column name—it should look like a line with arrows on either side—and then left-click and hold while you move the cursor to the right or the left until the column is as wide as you want it to be.

Or, third, you can place your cursor on the right side of the column name and double left-click. This will make the column as wide or as narrow as the widest text currently in that column. (Usually. Sometimes this one has a mind of its own.)

To adjust all column widths in your document at once, you can highlight the entire worksheet and then double-left click on any column border and it will adjust each column to the contents in that column. (Usually. See comment above.)

To have uniform column widths throughout your worksheet, highlight the whole worksheet, right-click on a column, choose Column Width, and set your column width. Highlighting the whole worksheet and then left-clicking and dragging one column to the desired width will also work.

(We cover it later, but to select the entire worksheet you can click in the top left corner at the intersection of the columns and rows. Or you can use Ctrl + A.)

Currency Formatting

In addition to applying basic formatting like bold, italics, and underline, Excel can also apply more complex formatting such as currency formatting or date formatting. The first of these we're going to cover is currency formatting. There are actually two default options for formatting numbers in Excel so that they look like currency notation such as $25.00. They are Accounting and Currency.

Excel defaults to the Accounting option which places the $ sign to the left-hand side of the cell even when the numbers don't fill the cell.

I tend to prefer the Currency option which keeps the $ sign with the numbers but that's because I'm usually only using this for a small range of values that are about the same size.

To apply the default Accounting format to your cells, highlight them, and then go to the Number section of the Home tab or the mini formatting menu, and click on the $ sign.

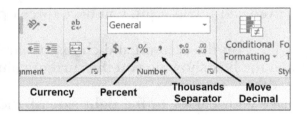

You can also use the dropdown menu in the Number section of the Home tab (which by default shows General) to choose either the Currency or Accounting format.

The final formatting option is to highlight the cell(s), right-click, choose the Format Cells option from the dropdown menu, go to the Number tab of the Format Cells dialogue box, and choose either Currency or Accounting from there.

Date Formatting

Excel can also format your entries as dates. Doing so will allow Excel to use those dates in calculations. But sometimes Excel has a mind of its own about how to format dates.

For example, if I type in 1/1 for January 1st, Excel will show it as 1-Jan and immediately turn it into a date in the current year. It may means the same thing as what I wanted, but if I'm going to display a current year date I would rather it display as 1/1/2020. That means I need to change the formatting.

One option is to click on the cell(s) with your date in it, go to the Number section on the Home tab, click on the dropdown menu, and choose either Short Date or Long Date.

If you select a cell or range of cells where the first cell already has a number in it, you will see examples of what the format will look like when you choose it. In the example above it's showing what the number 25 will look like in each format.

I prefer Short Date because I don't really need to see the day of the week named as well, which is what Long Date does.

Another option, and the one I probably use more for this, is to highlight your cell(s), right click, choose Format Cells from the dropdown menu, go to the

Number tab of the Format Cells dialogue box, and choose your date format from there by clicking on Date and then selecting one of the numerous choices it provides.

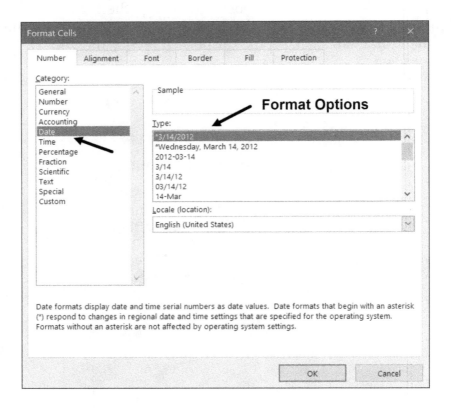

Keep in mind when selecting date formats that different countries write dates in different ways. So in the United States if I write 3/1/20 that means March 1, 2020 but in other countries that can mean January 3, 2020. You can see that the first couple of date options listed in the dialogue box will adjust for regional differences on different computers, but sometimes it's better to choose a spelled-out date to avoid any confusion.

And, just to reiterate because it's been an issue for me in the past, as mentioned above, Excel will always assign a year to a date no matter what you have it display or what information you provide. Always. So if that matters to you, be sure to control that information yourself.

Font Choice and Size

In Excel 2019 the default font choice is Calibri and the default font size is 11 point. You may have strong preferences about what font you use or work for a company that uses specific fonts for its brand or just want some variety in terms of font size or type within a specific document. In that case, you will need to change your font.

There are multiple ways to do this.

First, you can highlight your selection, go to the Font section on the Home tab, and select a different font or font size from the dropdown menus there.

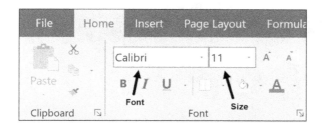

You also have the option there to increase or decrease the font one size at a time by clicking on the A's with little arrows off to the right-hand side of the dropdowns.

The same choices are also available on the left side of the first row of the mini formatting menu.

You can also highlight the cells or text you want to change, right-click, and choose Format Cells from the dropdown menu, and then go to the Font tab and choose your Font and Size from the listed values there. (I almost never find myself needing to use this option since the Home tab is so convenient.)

With any of the above options you can also choose a font size that isn't listed by clicking into the font size box and typing the value you want. So if you want a font size of 13 or 15, etc. you can just type it in.

Font Color

The default color for all text in Excel is black, but you can change that if you want or need to. (For example, if you've colored a cell with a darker color you may want to consider changing the font color to white to make the text in that cell more visible.)

You have multiple options here as well.

First, you can highlight the cells or the specific text you want to change, go to the Font section on the Home tab, and click on the arrow next to the A with a line under it. (The line is red by default but changes as you use this option.)

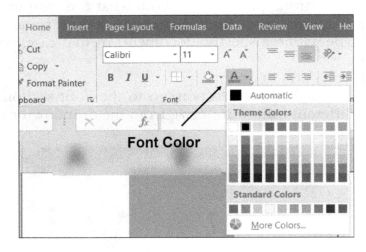

You can then choose from one of the 70 colors that are listed, and if those aren't enough of a choice you can click on More Colors and select your color from the Colors dialogue box. (See Coloring a Cell for more detail about that option.)

Second, you can use the fifth option in the bottom row of the mini formatting menu.

Third, you can highlight your selected text, right-click and choose Format Cells from the drop-down menu, go to the Font tab of the Format Cells dialogue box, and then click on the dropdown menu under Color which will bring up the same seventy color options and the ability to choose More Colors and add a custom color instead. Again, not an option I use often since the Home tab option is so convenient.

Italicizing Text

To add italics to a selection, highlight your selection and hold down the Ctrl key and the I key at the same time. (Ctrl + I)

Or you can highlight what you want italicized, and click on the slanted I in the Font section on the Home tab (see image under the Bolding description) or the bottom row of the mini formatting menu.

Another option is to highlight your selection, right-click, choose Format Cells from the dropdown menu, go to the Font tab of the Format Cells dialogue box, and choose Italic from the Font Style options.

As mentioned before, you can italicize just part of the text in a cell by only selecting that portion and then using one of the methods above.

To remove italics from text or cells that already have it, you follow the exact same steps. (Highlight your selection and then type Ctrl + I or click on the slanted I in the Font section on the Home tab or the mini formatting menu.) You may need to do it twice if your selection was not fully italicized already.

Merge & Center

Merge & Center is a specialized command that can come in handy when you're working with a table where you want a header that spans multiple columns of data.

If you're going to merge and center text, make sure that the text you want to keep is in the top-most and left-most of the cells you plan to merge and center. Data in the other cells that are being merged will be deleted. (You'll get a warning message to this effect if you have values in any of the other cells.)

You can merge cells across columns and/or down rows. So you could, for example, merge cells that span two columns and two rows into one big cell while keeping all of the other cells in those columns and rows separate.

To merge and center, highlight all of the cells you want to merge. Next, go to the Alignment section of the Home tab and choose Merge & Center. You can also find the Merge & Center option in the top right corner of the mini formatting menu.

Choosing Merge & Center will combine your selected cells into one large cell and center the contents from the topmost, left-most cell that was merged across the selection and then bottom-align the remaining text.

The Home tab also has a dropdown menu that includes additional options.

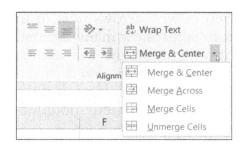

Merge Across will merge the cells across each individual row of the selected range rather than create one giant merged cell.

Merge Cells merges the cells into one cell but places the resulting text in the bottom right corner instead of the center.

Also, if you ever need to unmerge merged cells (like I do with one of my sales reports I receive) you can do so by selecting the Unmerge Cells option from the Merge & Center dropdown in the Home tab.

You can also Merge Cells by highlighting the cells, right-clicking, selecting the Format Cells option, going to the Alignment tab in the Format Cells dialogue box, and then choosing to Merge Cells from there. If you choose that option, you have to center the text separately.

A quick warning: Don't merge and center your cells if you plan to do a lot of data analysis with what you've input because it will mess with your ability to filter, sort, or use pivot tables. It's really for creating a finalized, pretty-looking report.

Number Formatting

Sometimes when you copy data into Excel it doesn't format it the way you want. For example, I have a report I receive that includes ISBN numbers which are 10- or 13- digit numbers. When I copy those into Excel, it sometimes displays them in Scientific number format (9.78E+12) as opposed to as a normal number.

To change the formatting of your data to a number format, you have a few options.

First, you can highlight the cell(s) and go to the Number section of the Home tab. From the drop-down menu choose Number. (Sometimes General will work as well.)

That will then convert your entries to numbers with two decimal places but no commas. So 100.00 instead of 100.

You can also click on the comma right below the dropdown to create a number with two decimal places and commas separating the thousands, hundred thousands, millions, etc.

You can then use the zeroes with arrows next to them that are located right below the drop-down box to adjust how many decimal places to display.

The one with the right-pointing arrow will reduce the number of decimal places. The one with the left-pointing arrow will increase them.

Second, the mini formatting menu has an option to format a cell as a number with commas for the thousands, hundred thousands, millions, etc. and will display with two decimal places.

To use it, select your cell(s), right-click, and from the mini formatting menu click on the comma in the top row on the right.

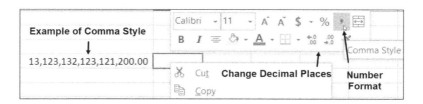

To adjust your decimal places then click on the zeroes with arrows under them in the bottom row. You can see an example of what the default looks like on the left-hand side of the image above.

Finally, you can highlight the cell(s), right-click, select Format Cells from the dropdown, go to the Number tab in the Format Cells dialogue box, choose Number on the left-hand side listing, and then in the middle choose your number of decimal places and how you want your negative numbers to display.

If I'm working with negative numbers a lot I'll use this option so that I can display my negative numbers either as red text or with ( ) around them.

You can also choose whether to use a comma separator or not here by checking the box that says "Use 1000 Separator".

Percent Formatting

To format numbers as a percentage, highlight the cell(s), and click on the percent sign in the Number section of the Home tab or in the top row of the mini formatting menu.

This one will take the number 5 and turn it into 500% or the number 0.1 and turn it into 10%, for example, so be sure your numbers are formatted to work as percentages.

You can also highlight the cell(s), right-click, select Format Cells from the dropdown, go to the Number tab, of the Format Cells dialogue box choose Percentage on the left-hand side, and then in the middle, choose your number of decimal places.

Row Height (Adjusting)

If your rows aren't the correct height, you have three options for adjusting them.

First, you can right-click on the row you want to adjust, choose Row Height from the dropdown menu, and when the box showing you the current row height appears, enter a new row height.

Second, you can place your cursor along the lower border of the row number until it looks like a line with arrows above and below. Left-click and hold while you move the cursor up or down until the row is as tall as you want it to be.

Third, you can place your cursor along the lower border of the row, and double left-click. This will fit the row height to the text in the cell. (Usually.)

To adjust all row heights in your document at once you can highlight the entire worksheet and then double-left click on any row border and it will adjust each row to the contents in each individual row. (Again, usually. It doesn't work particularly well for cells with lots and lots of text in them.)

To have uniform row heights throughout your worksheet, you can highlight the whole sheet, right-click on a row, choose Row Height and set your row height that way or select the entire worksheet, left-click on the border below a row, and adjust that row to the height you want for all rows.

As mentioned above, to select all rows at once you can use Ctrl + A or you can click in the corner at the intersection of the rows and columns.

Underlining Text

You have three options for underlining text.

First, you can highlight your selection and type Ctrl and U at the same time. (Ctrl + U). This is the easiest method and the one I use most often.

Second, you can highlight your selection and click on the underlined U in the Font section on the Home tab. (See the Bolding section for a screen shot.)

Third, you can highlight the selection, right-click, choose Format Cells from the dropdown menu, go to the Font tab of the Format Cells dialogue box, and choose the type of underlining you want (single, double, single accounting, double accounting) from the Underline drop down menu.

As noted above, you can apply formatting to just part of the text in a cell by clicking into the cell, highlighting the portion of the text that you want to underline, and then applying your chosen format.

To remove underlining from text or cells that already have it, highlight the text or cells and then use one of the above options.

Wrapping Text

Sometimes you want to read all of the text in a cell, but you don't want that column to be wide enough to display all of the text in a single row. This is where the Wrap Text option becomes useful, because it will keep your text within the width of the column and display it on multiple lines by "wrapping" the text.

To Wrap Text in a cell, select the cell(s), go to the Alignment section of the Home Tab, and click on the Wrap Text option on the right-hand side in the Alignment section.

Or you can highlight the cell(s), right-click, choose Format Cells from the dropdown menu, go to the Alignment tab in the Format Cells dialogue box, and choose Wrap Text under the second section, Text Control.

You will likely have to adjust the row height after you do this to see all of the text. The double-click method to auto-adjust your row height will generally work here, but if you have lots of text Excel has a limit to how much it will auto-adjust the height of a row and you may have to click and drag to get the row height you need.

* * *

One final trick that I use often, probably more in Word than in Excel, but that's still handy to know:

Format Painter
(Or How To Copy Formatting From One Cell To Another)

In addition to the specific formatting options discussed above, if you already have a cell formatted the way you want it to, you can take the formatting from that cell to other cells you want formatted the same way.

You do this by using the Format Painter

First, highlight the cell(s) that have the formatting you want to copy. (If the formatting is identical across all cells then just highlight one cell.)

Next, click on the Format Painter which is either located in the bottom right corner of the mini formatting menu or in the Clipboard section of the Home tab. It looks like a little paint brush. (I call it format sweeping because it always looked like a little broom to me, but given the name it's obviously a paint brush.)

Finally, select the range of cells where you want to copy the formatting.

The contents of the destination cells will remain the same, but the font, font color, font size, cell borders, italics/bolding/underlining, text alignment and text orientation will all change to match that of the cell that you took the formatting from.

As I alluded to above, you can select a range of cells and take their formatting and apply it to another range of cells. So I can have the first cell be bold, the second be italic, the third be red, etc. and I can select that cell range and then use Format Painter to apply that same different formatting across as many cells as I swept the formatting from.

If you do that, you can just click into the first cell of the range where you're applying the formatting. Excel will change the formatting of X number of cells where X is the original range of cells you chose your formatting from.

You need to be careful using the Format Painter because it will change *all* formatting in your destination cells.

So, if the cell you're copying the formatting from is bolded and has red text, both of those attributes will copy over even if all you were trying to do was copy the bold formatting. This is more of a problem when using the tool in Word than in Excel, but it's still something to watch out for especially if you have borders around cells. If you, for example, copy formatting from a cell that's in the center of a formatted table to a cell that's on the edge of that table you could end up removing the edge border.

(If that sounds confusing, just play around with it a bit and you'll see what I'm talking about.)

Also, the tool copies formatting to whatever cell you select next, which can be a problem if the cell you're copying from isn't near the one you're copying to. I sometimes have the temptation to use the arrow keys to move to the cell where I want to place the formatting, but that obviously does not work because the minute I arrow over one cell the formatting transfers to that cell.

To avoid this issue, click directly into the cell where you want to transfer the formatting.

(And remember, that Ctrl + Z is your friend if you make a mistake.)

Also, if you have more than one isolated cell that you need to apply formatting to, you can double-click the Format Painter instead of single clicking and it will continue to copy the formatting of the original cell to every cell you click in until you click on the Format Painter again or hit Esc. (You'll know the tool is still in operation because there will be a little brush next to your cursor as you move it around.)

If you format sweep, realize you made a mistake, and then use Ctrl + Z to undo, you'll see that the cell(s) you were trying to take formatting from will be surrounded by a dotted border as if you had copied it. Hit the Esc key before you continue. Otherwise you risk copying the contents of that cell or cells to a new one if you click in another cell and hit Enter.

(Not a common problem, but one to be aware of.)

Manipulating Your Data

Once you've entered your data into a worksheet, you are then ready to work with that data by filtering it, sorting it, and performing calculations on it.

This section will walk you through the basics of selecting, sorting, filtering, and analyzing your data. I'm just going to touch on formulas and the most essential functions, but this series does have an entire book (*Excel 2019 Formulas and Functions*) that is devoted to the topic if you find that you need or want to know more. Also, PivotTables and charts can be very useful for data analysis, but those are covered in *Excel 2019 Intermediate* because the goal in this book is to firmly ground you in the basics.

So, let's start with a few quick tricks for selecting your data that you want to analyze.

Select All

I mentioned this already in the formatting chapter when we discussed changing row height and column width, but I want to cover it again. If you want to select every single active cell in a worksheet, you can use Ctrl + A. (To select all of the rows and columns in a worksheet you may need to apply it more than once because it may just select your cells with data in them the first time.)

As mentioned above, it can be helpful when trying to adjust the row height or the column width in an entire worksheet quickly.

I also use it to copy the entire contents of a worksheet at once.

I will often combine Select All with Paste Special – Values onto the same worksheet. This is a simple way to remove any formulas from the worksheet as well as any PivotTables.

Another way to select all of the cells in your worksheet is to click in the small box at the intersection of the rows and columns labels. It does the exact same thing as Ctrl + A.

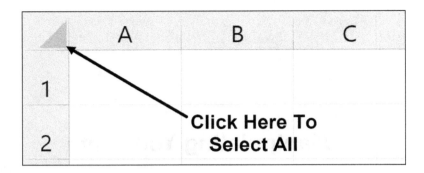

One caution when selecting all is that you don't then do something like apply borders to the entire worksheet. This can mess with your file size as well as printing because Excel stores that information for all of those cells even if you don't have any information in them. So don't do that. If you do so accidentally, you can Undo or select all and then go to the Clear dropdown in the Editing section of the Home tab and choose Clear Formats.

Select A Row

I often will want to select a row of data in my worksheet To do so, click on the row number on the left-hand side. (You may have to do it twice to select the row)

All of the cells in that row except the first one should turn gray to show that they've been selected.

Be careful about applying formatting if you do this, because you will rarely need to format an entire row and doing so can mess with printing.

To select more than one row, you can select left-click on the first row you want and then hold that down as you drag the mouse up or down to select more rows.

If the rows you need are not touching, use the Ctrl key as you click on each row number. You can also click on one row, hold down the shift key and click at the end of the range you select to select all of the rows in between.

Select A Column

Selecting a column works just like selecting a row. Click on the letter of the column you want to select. (You may have to do so twice to actually select the cells)

When the column is selected all cells in that column will be shaded gray except for the first one. You can select multiple columns by clicking and dragging, using the control key as you click on each one you want, or using the shift key to select a range of columns.

Again, selecting columns is useful for copying the data in a column or when writing a formula that references the values in a column, but don't apply formatting to the entire column.

Select A Range of Cells

It's very easy to select an entire table of data as long as it has a header row that labels all of the columns and an identifier column that has a value in it for every row of the table. (This helps define the range of columns and rows in the table.)

To do so, click in the top left corner of your data and then while holding down the Shift and Ctrl keys use the down arrow key followed by the right arrow key to highlight all of your cells in the table. (You can also arrow right and then down.)

Once the cells are selected, you can then apply all the formatting you want to that range of cells or copy it, etc.

What is happening when you do this is that you are telling Excel to start where you are and go in the direction of the arrow you used and select all of the cells it finds that have content in them until it reaches one that doesn't and then stop.

Because we were talking about a table that had column labels and row labels that selects the entire range of the table, even the blank cells within the table.

Sometimes your data won't be that neatly arranged and there will be gaps. If that happens, just keep arrowing in the direction you wanted until you reach the end of your data.

Also, I tell you to start in the top left corner of your data because that's the easiest way to make sure you select it all, but you can do this from any point. The only problem is you can go left OR right but not left AND right. Same with up and down. You can go up OR down but not up AND down. So start in a corner.

Being able to select a data range is very helpful when it comes to sorting and filtering. I can usually get away with just selecting all, but there are times when it is better to select a specific range of cells.

Also, selecting a range of cells comes in very useful when you don't want to bring over header information from another worksheet but just want the data.

Reach The End Of A Data Range

What if you want to reach the end of your data but you don't want to select it?

You can do so with just the Ctrl key and the arrows. Using Ctrl and an arrow will take you to the cell in that direction that is the last cell with something in it before an empty cell.

Depending on how your data is set up, that may not be the absolute end. But if your data is set up cleanly where it's all labeled and kept together Ctrl + an arrow key should take you to the edge of your existing data. You can then use the arrow key one more time from there to get to an empty cell.

Sorting

Now that we know how to select a range of data, let's talk about sorting.

Sorting allows you to take a data set and display it in a specific order. For example, chronologically by date, in increasing or decreasing value, or alphabetically.

Excel also allows you to sort at more than one level at a time. So you can sort by date and then by customer name and then by transaction value, for example. This would put all April 12th orders together and then all orders by each customer together, making them easy to locate.

Okay, so how do you do this?

First, select all cells that contain your information, including your header row if there is one.

(If you set your data up with the first row as the header and all of the rest as data, you can use Ctrl + A or click in the top left corner to select all.)

If you have a table of data that starts lower down on the page or that has a summary row or that is followed by other data that you don't want to use, then you need to be careful to only select the cells you want to work with.

Be very careful also to keep your data together. What I mean by that is, say you want to sort by date and customer name, but you have ten other columns of data related to each transaction by each customer on each day. You need to select all twelve columns of data even though you're only sorting on two of those columns.

If you don't do that then Excel will sort the two columns you selected but leave the other ten columns in their original position. That will mean that Customer Jones's July 3rd transaction information is now listed as Customer Smith's August 5th transaction.

So always, always before you sort make sure that all of your related data has been selected.

Once you've selected your data, go to the Editing section of the Home tab. Click on the arrow for Sort & Filter and then choose Custom Sort.

Your other option is to go to the Data tab and click on the Sort option there.

You can also right-click and choose Sort and then Custom Sort from the dropdown menu. All three options will open the Sort dialogue box.

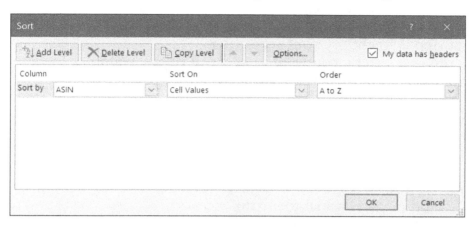

The first choice you need to make is to indicate whether or not your data has headers. In other words, does the first row of your data contain column labels?

If so, click on that box in the top corner that says, "My data has headers." If you indicate that there is a header row, it will not be included in your sort and will remain the first row of your data.

When you do this, you'll see that your Sort By dropdown now displays your column labels.

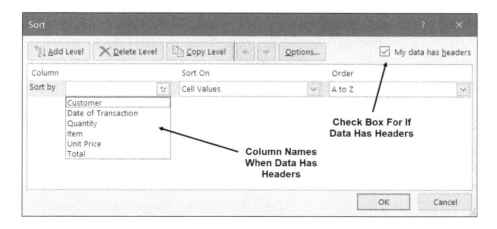

If you don't check this box, the dropdown will show generic column names (Column A, Column B, etc.) and *all* of your data will be sorted, *including* the first row.

Sometimes Excel tries to decide on its own whether there are headers or not and is wrong, so always make sure that your Sort By choices make sense given the data you selected, and that you check or uncheck the "My data has headers" box to get the result you want.

The next step is to choose your sort order.

What is the first criteria you want to sort by? In the examples I've mentioned above it would be date because I want all of my data grouped by date first and then I'll sort by customer name. But if you cared more about looking up information by customer name first and then by date of transaction you'd want to choose customer name for your first Sort By option.

Whatever that primary criteria is, choose that column from the Sort By dropdown menu.

Next, choose how to sort that column of data. You can sort on cell values, cell color, font color, or conditional formatting icon.

I almost always use values but if you were working with a data set where you'd used conditional formatting (which is discussed in detail in *Excel 2019 Intermediate*) you could, for example, sort by font color and have all of your overdue payments listed first.

After you choose what to sort on, then you can choose what order to use for your sort.

For text it's usually going to be A to Z to sort alphabetically but you can also choose Z to A to sort in reverse alphabetical order.

The third option, Custom List, is very useful for when you have text entries that should be in a specific order but that order is not alphabetical. I use this for when I have data broken down by month. I can choose Custom List and then in the Custom Lists dialogue box there are two month-based sort options. (As well as two day-of-the-week-based sort options.)

The Custom Lists dialogue box also allows you to create a brand new sort order with the NEW LIST option.

For date fields, your sort choices are Oldest to Newest, Newest to Oldest, and Custom List.

For numbers your short choices are Smallest to Largest, Largest to Smallest, and Custom List.

That's the first sort order and often it will be all you need. For example, if you just want your data sorted by month. If that's the case, click OK in the bottom right corner of the Sort dialogue box.

If, however, you want to use a second sort criteria, so sort first by date and then by customer, you need to add another level to your sort. You do this by clicking on Add Level and then repeating the same process for the next row of choosing your Column, Sort On criteria, and Order.

If you ever add a level you don't need, highlight it by clicking on the words "sort by" or "then by" on the left-hand side of the row, and then choose Delete Level from the list of options at the top of the dialogue box.

If you have listed out multiple levels to sort by but then decide that they should be sorted in a different order, you can select one of the levels and use the arrows at the top of the dialogue box to move that level up or down.

The default is to sort your data from top to bottom, so in rows.

Row 2 (assuming you have a header in Row 1) will be the first entry based on your sort criteria, Row 3 will be the second, etc.

You can click on Options in the Sort dialogue box, however, if you want to sort across columns instead.

(I think I've only ever needed to do that once. But just spitballing here, if I had, for example, a table of information and had listed student names across my columns and wanted those sorted alphabetically so that Column B was Anna and Column C was Bob, etc. I could use this option to make that happen.)

Options is also where you can do a case-sensitive sort, but I've never found myself needing to do that.

When you're done with all of your sort options, click OK.

(If you change your mind about performing a sort, click Cancel.)

Immediately check your results. Look across an entire row of data and ask if that still makes sense. Did you properly select and sort the data so that all of Customer Smith's transaction information stayed together?

If not, use Ctrl + Z to undo and try again because if you save the file with a bad sort order it's done for. You'll have to go back to your original raw data and start over. (Assuming you were smart enough to save your raw data in one location and do any analysis work in another. Which you should always, always do. As discussed previously and in *Data Principles for Beginners*.)

One final note about sorting, Excel also offers quick-sort options (the ones that say Sort A to Z or Sort Z to A) which are basically options to sort in ascending or descending order based upon the cell you're in at the time you make the selection.

Theoretically these options identify your data range, figure out if you have a header or not, and then sort based on the column you chose. But be wary when using them. Sometimes they work great, most times they sort in the wrong order for me or on the wrong column or miss that I have a header row.

Filtering

Okay. Now on to filtering which is also incredibly useful. I often won't need to permanently change the order of my data, I just want to see a subset of my data that meets a certain criteria. For example, I only want to see sales for Title A or Author B.

Filtering allows me to do that without having to sort.

This works best with a data table that has continuous and labeled columns and continuous rows.

If you have non-continuous columns, you need to manually select all of your columns when you choose to filter in order for the filter option to show for all of them. Otherwise, Excel will only show the filter option for the column in which you were clicked at the time you turned on filtering as well as for any columns that are connected to that column.

This sounds confusing, so let me show you what I mean.

	A	B	C	D	E	F	G
1	Customer	Date of Transaction		Quantity	Item	Unit Price	Total
2	Richard Martinez	4/7/2016		20	Whasit	$ 1.50	$ 30.00
3	Richard Martinez	3/7/2016		10	Who knows what	$ 3.50	$ 35.00
4	Albert Jones	9/1/2015		3	Whatchamacallit	$ 15.00	$ 45.00
5	Albert Jones	8/30/2015		10	Widget	$ 25.00	$250.00
6	Albert Jones	8/1/2015		1	Widget	$ 20.00	$ 20.00
7	Albert Jones	8/1/2015		1	Other	$ 5.00	$ 5.00
8							

Here I have six columns of data, but I have a blank column in Column C so that the data is not continuous. When I click into Cell A1 and turn on filtering, it only turns on filtering for Columns A and B. (You can tell filtering is on by looking at those little arrows in the corners in Cells A1 and B1.)

Because Column C was blank, Excel didn't know to also turn on filtering for Columns D, E, F, and G. I can work around this by turning off filtering, selecting Cells A1 through G1 and turning filtering back on. That will apply filtering to all of the columns.

Or I can make my life simpler and simply not have the blank column in the middle of my data in which case when I click into Cell A1 (or any of the cells in Row 1) filtering will be available for all of the columns of data.

If for some reason you don't want to filter starting at the top row of your data, you can highlight a row of data that is not at the top of the range and Excel will apply the filtering options starting at the highlighted row. (Usually for me what happens is I do that accidentally and notice that the filtering is in Row 3 where my data is instead of Row 1 where my header row is and I have to go turn off filtering and reapply it at Row 1.)

To apply filtering, click into the appropriate spot in your data, and then in the Editing section of the Home tab, click on the arrow next to Sort & Filter and choose Filter.

Once you turn on filtering you should see small gray arrows in the bottom right corner of each cell in your header row. (Like on the previous page with Customer and Date of Transaction in Cells A1 and B1.)

Filtering in Excel has evolved over the years, which means the complex type of filtering we're about to discuss was not always available in prior versions of Excel. So if you filter a file and try to share that with someone using an older version of Excel it may do weird things. Namely, they won't be able to remove or adjust your filtering easily. (Easy way to deal with that is never save your data in a filtered form.)

Okay, so let's talk filtering options. Once you have filtering turned on, you can click on that little arrow in the corner at the top of a column and it will bring up a dropdown menu that has a variety of options for you to use to filter the contents of your data table. (See the next page for an example.)

The very top options in that dropdown are sort options.

The first filter option, Filter by Color, will generally be grayed out unless you have different font colors or fill colors in your data.

If you have used different font or fill colors, you can hold your cursor over where it says Filter by Color and it will then give you additional options to Filter by Cell Color or Filter by Font Color.

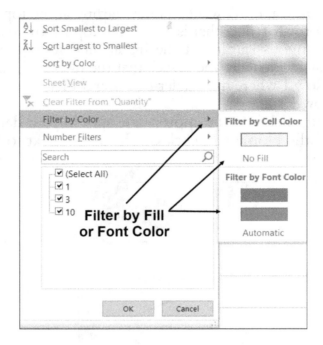

These options will only show the font or fill colors you've used in your data. If you want cells that are the standard color or the standard fill you can choose the No Fill or the Automatic filtering choices.

After the filter by color choices, there is another set of filter options that will be named based upon the type of data in that column. Above you can see that the next option is Number Filters, but you may also see Date Filters or Text Filters.

Holding your cursor over this option will show filter criteria for that type of data. For numbers you'll see choices such as Equals, Greater Than, Between, etc. For dates you'll see Before, After, Tomorrow, Today, etc. For text you'll see Begins With, Contains, etc.

I find these options to be useful when there are a large number of individual entries that all differ slightly from one another but that I want to include in my display. So if I want all of my Excel books, for example, I can use a Contains filter and look for entries with "Excel" in them. That's much easier than going through and checking boxes to select each title individually.

The filter approach I probably use the most, though, is the final option which is the checkbox option. You can see above and on the next page that the dropdown will list the possible values for that column with checkboxes next to each value. You can select one or more of the values in that list by checking or unchecking the box next to each value.

If you just want one value and there are a number of choices, click in that Select All box at the top to unselect everything and then go back and click on the entries you want. It's much faster than unchecking everything one box at a time.

You also have the option to use the Search field that's directly above the checkboxes. Excel will filter your data down to just those entries that contain the search term and then you can refine from there if you need to.

When cells in your worksheet are filtered, the row numbers in your worksheet will be colored blue, and you'll see that the row numbers skip since some rows won't be displayed. (In the screenshot below, Row 2 is not displayed because it had a date in April 2016 and I unchecked that box.)

Columns where filtering is in place will show a funnel instead of an arrow on the gray dropdown next to the column name.

To remove filtering from a specific column, click on the gray arrow, and select Clear Filter from [Column Name] in the dropdown menu.

To remove all filtering you've applied to a worksheet, go to the Editing section of the Home tab, click on Sort & Filter, and then choose Clear. This will leave the filtering option in place but remove all filters.

To remove filtering altogether, go to the Editing section of the Home tab, click on Sort & Filter, and click on Filter.

Some of this can also be done through right-click and using the dropdown available on the worksheet. If you're clicked into a cell and want to filter by that value or fill color or font color, you can right-click, move your cursor to the Filter option, and then choose Filter by Selected Cell's Value, Color, Font Color, or Icon. That will perform the filter task you wanted as well as turning on filtering for that range of cells.

Once filtering is on, you can also right-click, go to Filter, and choose to clear the filter from a specific column.

Because the right-click option is somewhat limited, I tend to just use the Editing section of the Home tab.

* * *

Basic Math Calculations

Alright, that was sorting and filtering. Now let's talk basic math calculations in Excel. I'm going to cover addition, subtraction, multiplication, and division.

Let's start with doing each of those tasks using standard math notation.

In Excel these are referred to as calculation operators, but you'll probably recognize them as the way you used to write an equation in math class.

For addition, you use a plus sign (+). For subtraction, you use a minus sign (-). For multiplication you use an asterisk (*). For division, you use a forward slash (/).

To perform one of these basic calculations in a cell in Excel, click into the cell where you want to perform the calculation, type an equals sign, type the first value you want to use, type the calculation operator for the calculation you want to perform (+ - * /), and then type the second value you want to use. Hit Enter. You will see the result of that calculation in the cell and if you go back to the cell you'll see your equation in the formula bar.

So, for example:

$$=23+23$$

would add 23 and 23 and when you hit enter you would see a value of 46 in that cell.

$$=23/23$$

would divide 23 by 23 and you would see a value of 1 in that cell after you hit enter.

$$=4*5$$

would return a value of 20.

And

$$=10\text{-}2$$

would return a value of 8.

If that's all that Excel could do it wouldn't be very useful. About as useful as a calculator. The power that Excel has is that it can perform those same calculations by using cell references. So rather than type in 23, you can have the value 23 in a cell and point Excel at that cell to retrieve the value for you.

That still doesn't sound too exciting until you realize that you can combine that task with copying formulas which means you can write a simple formula that says add this cell in Column A to that cell in Column B and then copy that one formula you wrote a hundred thousand times with a single click, and have Excel add those two cells in those two columns for all hundred thousand rows of your data in less than a minute.

But to make that happen requires using cell notation instead of numbers.

The easy way to use cell notation is to let Excel do it for you by simply clicking on the cells you want as you build your formula.

So you click in the cell where you want your calculation, type an equals sign, click on the cell that contains the first value you want to use in your calculation, type your calculation operator (+ - * /), and then click on the cell that contains the second value you want to use in your calculation, and then hit enter.

Excel will build your formula for you and write the name of the cell you click on each time into your formula.

You can even see if the correct cells were used by going back to the cell where you did the calculation and double-clicking on it. Excel will show you the formula it wrote and highlight all of the cells it used in the formula as well as color code each cell and cell reference in the formula. Cell A2 will be blue and the text A2 in the formula will also be blue, for example, so you can see exactly where each value was used.

Which is great, but I like to understand how to do it myself so I can better troubleshoot issues. So let's cover how that works real quick.

First, a quick refresher about how you reference a cell. A cell is the intersection of a row and a column and is always written with the column identifier first. So if I write A1 that means the cell that's at the intersection of Column A and Row 1. (You don't have to include Cell when you write this in a formula because that's implied.) Likewise, B2 is the cell that is at the intersection of Column B and Row 2.

To reference more than one cell at a time, you need to use either a colon (:) or a comma (,).

A comma (,) written between two cell references means "and.". So

A1,B3

means Cells A1 and B3.

A colon (:) written between two cell references means "through". So

A1:B3

means all cells in Columns A and B and all cells in those columns that are in Rows 1, 2, and 3.

Likewise,

D24:M65

means all cells in Columns D through M and in Rows 24 through 65.

To reference an entire column, you just leave out the row numbers. So

B:B

means all of the cells in Column B. And

B:C

means all of the cells in Columns B and C.

To reference an entire row you leave out the column letters. So

2:2

means all of the cells in Row 2. And

2:10

means all of the cells in Rows 2 through 10.

Putting that together with what we discussed earlier about using calculation operators, the following are how you would write addition, subtraction, multiplication, and division of values in Cells A1 and B1:

=A1+B1

$$=A1-B1$$

$$=A1*B1$$

$$=A1/B1$$

Remember from math class that with addition and multiplication order isn't going to matter, A1+B1 and B1+A1 give you the same result. But with subtraction and division, which value is listed first will impact the result you get. A1-B1 and B1-A1 are different equations.

Which is why there is no shortcut, quickie way to subtract or divide multiple values in Excel. But for addition and multiplication there are. You can use what are called functions to sum or multiply any number of cells that you want.

The function you use for addition is SUM. The function you use for multiplication is PRODUCT. (I often use SUM, I rarely use PRODUCT although I do use one we won't cover here that is SUMPRODUCT that combines the two.)

If you're going to use a function for a calculation, you click into the cell, type your equals sign, then type the function you want and an opening paren, then you type your cell references or highlight the cells you want, then type a closing paren and hit enter.

This table shows how to use the operators when just using two values and how to use the functions or operators when dealing with multiple values:

	With Two Values In Cells A1 and B1	With Six Values In Cells A1, B1, A2, B2, A3, and B3
Addition	=A1+B1	=SUM(A1:B3)
Subtraction	=A1-B1	=A1-B1-A2-B2-A3-B3
Multiplication	=A1*B1	=PRODUCT(A1:B3)
Division	=A1/B1	=A1/B1/A2/B2/A3/B3

A few more comments:

With addition, there are two other tricks to know.

First, if you don't care about recording the value you calculate, you can simply highlight the cells you want to add together and then look in the bottom right corner of the worksheet. It should show you the average, the count, and the sum of the cells you have highlighted.

Second you can use the AutoSum option in the Editing section of the Home Tab to add either a row or column of values without having to type in the formula. This is basically just another way to have Excel create your formula for you.

To use it, click into the empty cell at the end of your range of values and then click on the AutoSum icon which looks like the mathematical sum function (a big pointy E-like shape). Excel will then create and display a SUM function for you and highlight the cells it thinks you wanted to add.

The AutoSum option stops at blank cells, so if you need to sum across a blank space, you'll need to edit the formula for it to work properly, but it can be a nice way to get a quick start on writing your formula.

(You'll note that there's a dropdown there as well, so you can also use it for Average, Count Numbers, Max, and Min.)

Complex Formulas

Excel can handle incredibly complex formulas. You just have to make sure you write them properly so that Excel knows which functions to perform first.

Put something in parens and Excel will do that before anything else. Otherwise it will follow standard mathematical principles about which actions to perform in which order.

According to the Excel help documentation (under Operator Precedence), Excel will first combine cells (B1:B3 or B1,B2), then create any negative numbers (-B1). Next it will create percents, then calculate any exponentials (B2^2), then do any multiplication and division, then do any addition and subtraction, then concatenate any values, and then do any comparisons last.

All of this, of course, at least in the U.S., is done from left to right in a formula.

So, basically, Excel calculates starting on the left side of the equation and moves to the right, doing each of those steps above in that order throughout the entire formula before circling back to the start and doing the next step. Which means that multiplication and division are done first and then addition or subtraction.

Of course, anything in parens is treated as a standalone equation first. So if you have =3*(4+2), Excel will add the 4 and the 2 before it does the multiplication.

Basically, if you're going to write complex formulas they're definitely doable but you should be very comfortable with math and how it works. Also, be sure to test your equation to make sure you did it right. I do this by breaking a formula into its component steps and then making sure that my combined equation generates the same result.

Other Functions

We briefly discussed SUM and PRODUCT, but Excel has hundreds of available functions that can do all sorts of interesting things and not just with numbers.

To see what I'm talking about, go to the Formulas tab. There are seven different subject areas listed there (Financial, Logical, Text, Date & Time, Lookup & Reference, Math & Trig, and More Functions which shows an additional six categories). Click on each of those dropdowns and you'll see twenty-plus functions for each one.

But how do you know if there's a function that does what you want to do? For example, is there a function for trimming excess space from a string of values? (Yes. It's called TRIM.) Or for calculating the cumulative principal paid on a loan between two periods? (Yes.)

So how do you find the function you want without hovering over each function to see what it does because the names by themselves are certainly no help?

The simple way is to go to the Formulas tab and click on Insert Function. This will bring up the Insert Function dialogue box which includes a search function. Type a few words for what you're looking for.

For example, if I want to calculate how many days until some event occurs and I want to have this formula work no matter what day it is when I open my worksheet, then I need some way to set a value equal to today's date whatever day today is. So I search for "today" and get a function called TODAY that it says "Returns the current date formatted as a date." Perfect.

Once you've found a function you like, select it and click on OK. Excel will take you back to the worksheet and show you a Function Arguments dialogue box that tells you what inputs are needed to create that particular function.

If the function doesn't require any arguments, like TODAY doesn't, it will just let you know that and insert the function into your selected cell.

Sometimes selecting a function this way, even if you know what it does, is helpful because it shows you what order you need to put the information in and what form it needs to take. But you can also see this to a lesser degree when you start to type the function into your cell. Once you type the opening paren it will show you the components you need and their order. (Very helpful for things like SUMIF and SUMIFS that have different orders even though they do similar things.)

As mentioned before, *Excel 2019 Formulas and Functions*, which is 200 pages long, is going to be the best resource if you really want to dig in on how formulas and functions work.

Copying Cells With Formulas in Them

One of the nice things about working with formulas in Excel is that you don't have to type them over and over and over again. You can type a formula once and if you need to use it again, simply copy it to a new cell.

There are some tricks to copying formulas. So let's walk through those.

By default, formulas are relative. Meaning that if you have a formula that says

=B1+C1

and you copy it (Ctrl + C) over to the right one cell it will become

=C1+D1

See how the column value for each referenced cell changed by one column? If you copy that same formula down one cell from the original location it will become

=B2+C2

See how the row number for each referenced cell changed by one?

This is great when you have rows and rows of data with everything located in the same position and want to perform the exact same calculation on each of those rows. You can simply copy the formula and paste it down the entire column and it will perform that calculation on each and every row.

But sometimes you just want to move the calculation. Say it's in Cell B2 now and you want to put it in Cell A10. That's when you need to cut the formula (Ctrl + X) instead of copy it. By cutting and moving the formula, it stays the exact same. If it said =B1+C1 before it still will after you paste it into the new location..

Another way to do this is to click into the cell, highlight all of the text in the cell, copy it, and tab (or Esc) out of the cell, and then click on the new location and paste it that way.

(If you click into the cell, highlight all of the text, and try to click on where you want to paste it, you'll end up replacing your existing text in the source cell with a reference to the cell you clicked into.)

What if you want to copy the formula, but you want to keep some portion of it fixed? Say either the row reference, the column reference, or the reference to an entire cell. (Useful when calculating different scenarios where you build a table with different values for variable x in one row and different values for variable y in one column and then calculate what value you get for each combination of x and y. So, hourly pay and hours worked, for example.)

You can fix a portion of a cell reference by using the $ sign. (We discussed it earlier with respect to inputting data, but I'll run through it again here.)

To fix the reference to a cell, put a $ sign before both the letter and the number in the cell name. So cell B2 becomes B2 in your formula.

If you reference a cell that way (B2), no matter where you copy that formula to it will continue to reference that specific cell.

This is useful if you have a constant value in your formula. So say you're selling widgets and they're all priced at $100. You might list Widget Price at the top of your worksheet and put 100 in a cell at the top and then calculate how much each customer owes by multiplying their units purchased by that fixed value in that cell.

If you want to keep just the column the same, but change the row reference, then put the dollar sign in front of the letter only. So $B2 when copied would become $B3, $B4, etc. no matter where you copy that formula to it's always B.

If you want to keep the row the same, but change the column reference, you'd put the dollar sign in front of the number only. So B$2. When copied, that portion of the formula would change to C$2, D$2, etc. but the 2 would never change.

One more thought about copying formulas. I usually just highlight all of the cells where I want to copy the formula to and then paste, but there's a shortcut that you can sometimes use that's faster when you have many many rows of data.

If you have a formula in a cell and want to copy it downward and the column where that cell is located is touching another column of data that has already been completed (so you have a full column of data next to the column where you want to put your formula), you can place your cursor on the bottom right corner of the cell with the formula and double-left click. This should copy the formula down all of your rows of data.

It doesn't work if the other column of data hasn't been filled in yet. Excel only knows how far to copy the formula based on the information in the other column. But it can be a handy shortcut in a table with lots of completed information where you're just adding a calculation.

Okay. So that was manipulating data, let's now talk about how to print when you have a finished product that's ready to go.

Printing

You might not think that printing needs its own section, but it definitely does. Not because clicking on Print is so hard to do, but because you need to format your data well to get it to print well. If you just hit print without thinking about how that information in your worksheet will appear on a printed page, you'll likely end up with pages and pages worth of poorly-formatted garbage.

Now, it's possible you have no intent of printing anything (I never print my budget spreadsheet) in which case, skip this section. But if you are going to print, let's try and waste as little paper as possible.

First things first. To print, go to the File tab and select Print.

Typing Ctrl and P at the same time (Ctrl + P) will also take you to the print screen.

You should see a number of print options in the center of the screen and a preview section on the right-hand side.

If everything looks good, you can just click on the big Print button right there at the top and be done with it.

Sometimes that's the case if you're printing a small amount of data, but usually I find I need to make adjustments, especially if I have enough information that it carries over to additional pages.

Let's walk through all of the options you have with respect to printing, but first let me just show you what the print screen will look like:

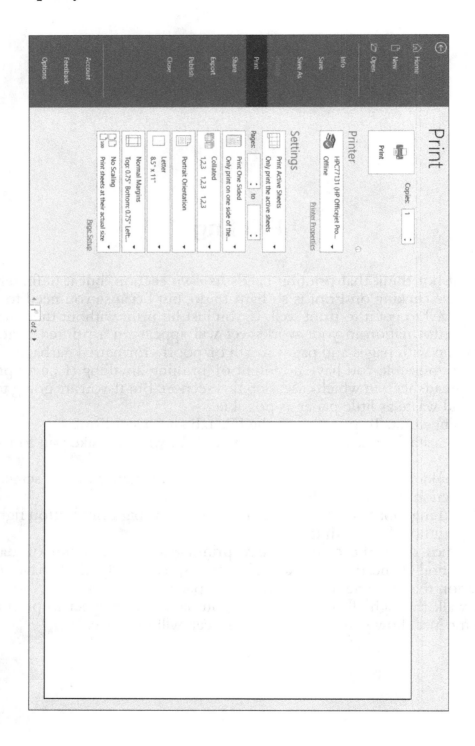

You can see in the image that you have a number of print options listed underneath the text Print and then on the right-hand side you have a print preview of what your document will look like on a page-by-page basis.

(In this case, mine is blank but you can see at the bottom where it says 1 of 2 and you can arrow to a second page.)

Let's walk through each of those options starting with the image of a printer right under the text Print.

Print

Once you're ready to print your page, you can click on the button on the top left with the image of a printer that says Print and your document will print.

Copies

To the right of that image where it says Copies is where you specify how many copies to print. If you want to print more than one copy, change that number by either using the up and down arrows or by clicking into the box and typing in a new value.

Printer

It should display your computer's default printer here, but if you want to use a different printer than that one, click on the arrow next to the printer name and choose from the listed options. If the printer you want isn't listed, choose Add Printer.

Print Active Sheets / Print Entire Workbook / Print Selection

The default is Print Active Sheets. This will generally be the worksheet you were working in when you chose to print.

However, you can select more than one worksheet by holding down the Control key and clicking on multiple worksheet names. (When you do this, you'll see that the names of all of your selected worksheets are highlighted, not just one of them.) If you do this before you choose to print, then when you do Print Active Sheets it will print all of the worksheets you've selected.

I would only print multiple worksheets if you're satisfied that each one is formatted exactly the way you want it formatted.

Also, choosing to print more than one sheet at a time either with Print Active Sheets or Print Entire Workbook, results in strange things happening to your headers and footers. For example, your pages will be numbered across worksheets. If you mean each worksheet to be a standalone report with numbered pages specific to that report, then you need to print each worksheet separately.

As I just alluded to, the Print Entire Workbook option prints all of the worksheets in your workbook. Print Selection allows you to just print a highlighted section of a worksheet or worksheets.

(I happened to have three worksheets selected at once and then highlighted the first twenty cells in one of those worksheets and when I went to Print Selection Excel printed those twenty cells in *each* of those three worksheets.)

Pages

Just below the Print Active Sheets option is a row that says Pages and has two boxes with arrows at the side. You can choose to just print a specific page rather than the entire worksheet by using the options here. To figure out which page to print, look at your preview. To specify the pages numbers either use the up and down arrows or click into the boxes and type in your value(s) using commas between page numbers.

Print One Sided / Print on Both Sides (long edge) / Print on Both Sides (short edge)

The default is to just print on one side of your paper. If you have a printer that can print on both sides of the page you can change your settings to do so. You want the long-edge option if your layout is going to be portrait-style and the short-edge option if your layout is going to be landscape-style. (See below.)

Whether or not you have the option to choose to print on both sides will depend on the printer you have selected. I have occasionally printed to PDF and then come back to print in Excel and found that I couldn't print on both sides because my printer had been changed to the PDF option and I had forgotten to change it back.

Collated / Uncollated

This only matters if what you're printing has more than one page and if you're printing more than one copy.

In that case, you need to decide if you want to print one full copy at a time x number of times or if you want to print x copies of page 1 and then x copies of page 2 and then x copies of page 3 and so on until you've printed all pages of your document. In general, I would choose collated (one copy at a time), which is also the default. The uncollated option (one page at a time) could be good for handouts.

Portrait Orientation / Landscape Orientation

You can choose to print in either portrait orientation (with the short edge of the page on top) or landscape orientation (with the long edge of the page on top). You can see what difference it will make by changing the option in Excel and looking at your print preview.

Which option you choose will likely depend on how many columns of data you have.

Assuming I'm dealing with a normal worksheet with rows of data listed across various columns, my goal is to fit all of my columns on one page if possible. Sometimes changing the layout to landscape allows me to do that because it allows me to have more columns per page than I'd be able to fit in portrait mode.

If I have just a few columns of data, but lots of rows I'll generally stick with portrait orientation instead.

You'll have to decide what works best for you and your specific situation.

Letter / Legal / Statement / Etc.

This is where you select your paper type. Unless you're in an office, chances are you'll leave this exactly like it is. I'm sure my printer could print on legal paper, but I don't have any for it to use so it's a moot point for me. In the U.S. the default is. 8.5"x11" but I assume that overseas it is A4 or some other regional standard.

Normal Margins / Wide Margins / Narrow Margins / Custom Margins

I would expect you won't use this often, but if you need to then this would be where you can change the margins on your document. The normal margins allow for .7" on each side and .75" on top and bottom. If you have a lot of text and need just a little more room to fit it all on one page, you could use the narrow margin option to make that happen. I generally adjust my scaling instead although that does change the text size which changing the margins will not do.

No Scaling / Fit Sheet on One Page / Fit All Columns on One Page / Fit All Rows on One Page/ Custom Scaling Options

I use this option often when I have a situation where my columns are just a little bit too much to fit on the page or my rows go just a little bit beyond the page. If you choose "Fit All Columns on One Page" that will make sure that all of your columns fit across the top of one page. You might still have multiple pages because of the number of rows, but at least everything will fit across the top.

Of course, depending on how many columns you have, this might not be a good choice. Excel will make it fit, but it does so by decreasing your font size. If you have too many columns you're trying to fit on one page your font size may become so small you can't read it.

So be sure to look at your preview before you print. (And use Landscape Orientation first if you need to.)

Fit All Rows on One Page is good for if you have maybe one or two rows too many to naturally fit on the page.

Fit Sheet on One Page is a combination of fitting all columns and all rows onto one page. Again, Excel will do it if you ask it to, but with a large set of data you won't be able to read it.

Custom Scaling brings up the Page Setup dialogue box. This is often where I will go to adjust my scaling for a document because it has the most flexibility. You can specify exactly how many pages to scale by in each direction. (We'll talk about that more below.)

Page Setup

The Page Setup link at the very bottom of the Print Screen Options gives you access to even more print options by opening the Page Setup dialogue box.

A few things to point out to you that I find useful:

Scaling

On the Page tab you can see the scaling option once more in the second section of the box where it says Scaling.

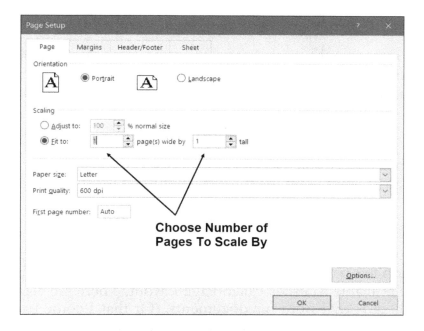

The nice thing here is that you can fit your information to however many pages across by however many pages long. You're not limited to 1 page wide or 1 page tall.

So say you have a document that's currently one page wide and four pages long but the last page is just one row. You can scale that document in the Page Setup dialogue box so that the document that prints is one page wide by three pages long and that last row is brought up onto the prior page.

Center Horizontally or Vertically

On the Margins tab there are two check boxes that let you center what you're printing either horizontally or vertically on the page, or both.

I will often choose to center an item horizontally if there aren't many columns.

Header/Footer

We're going to talk about another way to do this in a moment, but if you want to set up a header and/or a footer for your printed document you can do so on the Header/Footer tab.

The dropdown boxes that say (none) include a number of pre-formatted headers and footers for you to use. So if you just want the page number included, there should be a pre-formatted one that you can select via the dropdown options.

Same with including the worksheet name or file name in the header or footer. As you look at each one it will show you examples of the actual text that will be included. You also have the option of customizing either the header or footer.

Sheet

The sheet tab has a couple of useful options, but I'm going to show you a different way to set these options through the Page Layout Tab.

Page Layout Tab

If you exit out of the File tab go back to your worksheet by clicking the little arrow in the top left corner of the screen or using Esc, you'll see that one of the tabs you have available to use is called Page Layout. There are certain attributes that I set up here *before* I print my documents. (Or that I come back here to set up if I forget before I try to print, which is more often the case.)

Let's walk through them.

(Also, note that you can change margins, orientation, and size here just as easily as in the print preview screen.)

Print Area

If you only want to print a portion of a worksheet, you can set that portion as your print area by highlighting it and then clicking on the arrow next to Print Area and choosing Set Print Area in the Page Setup section of the Page Layout tab.

Only do it this way (as opposed to highlighting the section and choosing Print-Selection) if it's a permanent setting. Because once you set your print area it will remain set until you clear it. You can add more data to your worksheet but it will never print until you change your print area or clear that setting and it's easy to forget you've done that and then not be able to figure out why the whole document won't print for you.

I use this setting when I have a worksheet that either has extra information I don't want to print or where the formatting extends beyond my data and Excel keeps trying to print all those empty but formatted cells. (Sometimes removing that extra formatting is more of a hassle than it's worth and using print area is a quick workaround.)

Breaks

You can set where a page break occurs in your worksheet. So say you have a worksheet that takes up four pages and you want to make sure that rows 1 through 10 are on a page together and then rows 11 through 20 are on a page together even though that's not how things would naturally fall.

You can set a page break to force that to happen by clicking in a cell in your worksheet and then going to Breaks and choosing Insert Page Break from the dropdown menu. This will insert a page break above the cell where you clicked and to the left of the cell.

You can see where the breaks are located because Excel will insert a solid line through your worksheet above your selected cell and, if it wasn't the first column, to the left of your selected cell. It's not terribly easy to see in the worksheet itself, but if you go to print and look at the preview you'll see that your information is now broken into new pages at the place or places where you inserted the break(s).

To remove a page break, click into the cell below it or to the right of it and go to Breaks in the Page Setup section of the Page Layout tab and choose Remove Page Break. You can also choose Reset All Page Breaks.

Personally, I find page breaks a challenge to work with, so I usually try to get what I need some other way.

Print Titles

This is the one we came here to discuss. I find Print Titles incredibly valuable. When you click on this option you'll see that it brings up the Page Setup dialogue box and takes you to the Sheet tab. The top section of the Sheet tab lets you choose rows to repeat at the top of every page or columns to repeat at the left. This is invaluable. If you learn nothing else about printing, learn this.

Why? Say you have a worksheet with a thousand rows of data in it that will print on a hundred pages. How do you know what's in each column on each page? You need a header row. And you need that header row to repeat at the top of each and every page.

"Rows to repeat at top" is where you specify what row(s) is your header row. Click in that box and then click on the row number in your worksheet that you want to have repeat at the top of each page. Excel will do its thing and put $1:$1 or whatever row reference it needs to for you. (You can also just type this same information in from the Print screen if you remember cell notation. Just use $ signs and your row or row numbers that you want. So $1:$3 would repeat Rows 1 through 3 on every page.)

To set a column(s) you want to repeat on the left-hand side of each page, such as a customer name or student name or record number, click in the box that says "Columns to repeat at left", and then click on the letter for the column(s) you want to repeat on each page. Again, Excel will do its magic and convert that to cell notation for you. But, again, you can write it yourself I you want, too by using $ and the letter for the column. So, $C:$C would repeat the values in Column C on every page.

Do be careful if you're going to choose more than one row or column to repeat that you don't end up selecting so many rows or columns to repeat that you basically just print the same thing over and over and over again. You need to leave room for the rest of the data in your worksheet.

Conclusion

Alright, so there you have it. A beginner's guide to Excel. This wasn't meant to be a comprehensive guide to Excel, but to instead give you the basics you need to do 95% of what you'll ever want to do in Excel. I hope it did that.

If something wasn't clear or you have any questions, please feel free to reach out to me at mlhumphreywriter@gmail.com.

As I mentioned previously, the next book in this series is *Excel 2019 Intermediate* which covers more advanced topics such as charts, pivot tables, conditional formatting, subtotaling and grouping data, and limiting the set of values that can be entered into a cell.

There is also *Excel 2019 Formulas and Functions* which gets much more in depth about how formulas and functions work in Excel and then goes one-by-one through about sixty functions in detail while covering approximately one hundred functions total.

But you can also just research specific topics on your own. The Microsoft website has a number of tutorials and examples that I think are very well-written and easy to follow at www.support.office.com. I usually find what I need there with a quick internet search for something like "bold text Excel 2019" and then choose the Microsoft support link to take me directly to the page I need.

The help available directly in Excel 2019 is excellent as well. Click on the Help tab and then click on the blue circle with a question mark that says Help. This will bring up a search box on the right-hand side of the screen where you can type in the topic that you need to know more about.

Another source of more information is to simply hold your mouse over the tasks listed on the various tabs. This will usually show a brief description of what that item does. A lot of the descriptions also have a "tell me more" link at the bottom of the description that will take you directly to the help screen related to that item. (The Format Painter on the Home tab is a good example of this. Just hold your cursor over it to see what I'm talking about.)

Your final option is to wade into the mess that is online help forums. I generally recommend against asking your own question in those forums because I find they're full of people who are rude if you don't ask your question in just the right way and provide every little piece of detailed information when you originally ask your question. How can a new user know what they don't know or what they need to provide to get their answer, right, so it always annoys me to see that.

But sometimes finding where someone else asked your question already and seeing what the answer was can be very helpful. Forums are best for the "is this possible" type of question rather than the "how does this work" type of question. Microsoft is very good at providing enough help on how things work that you can find that on their website or in the Excel help tab. But they are less helpful at telling you whether you can do something.

Again, if there's something specific you want to know, just ask. Happy to help if I can.

And thanks for reading this guide. Excel is an incredibly powerful tool and now that you have the foundation you need to use it effectively, I hope you see that.

Control Shortcuts

The following is a list of useful control shortcuts in Excel. For each one, hold down the Ctrl key and use the listed letter to perform the command.

Command	Ctrl +
Bold	B
Copy	C
Cut	X
Find	F
Italicize	I
Next Worksheet	Page Down
Paste	V
Print	P
Prior Worksheet	Page Up
Redo	Y
Replace	H
Save	S
Select All	A
Underline	U
Undo	Z

PowerPoint 2019 Beginner

POWERPOINT ESSENTIALS 2019 BOOK 1

M.L. HUMPHREY

Copyright © 2021 M.L. Humphrey

All Rights Reserved.

ISBN: 978-1-63744-035-3

CONTENTS

CONTENTS (CONT.)

Introduction

This guide focuses specifically on how to use Microsoft PowerPoint 2019. If you have an older version of PowerPoint, *PowerPoint for Beginners*, the predecessor to this book, is likely a better choice because it was written to be more generic and accessible to users of any version of PowerPoint from 2007 onward.

This guide, *PowerPoint 2019 Beginner*, just focuses on how to use Microsoft PowerPoint 2019. What that means, practically speaking, is that all screenshots in this book will be from PowerPoint 2019 and all instructions in this book will be written for users of PowerPoint 2019.

At the beginner level there really isn't a significant difference between the two books and you will likely be able to use either one to learn PowerPoint. You definitely do not need both of them.

Alright, then. Now that we have that out of the way.

The purpose of this guide is to introduce you to the basics of using Microsoft PowerPoint 2019, which is one of the go-to software programs for creating presentation slides. I've used it throughout my professional career and I know of a number of students who have also needed to use it for class presentations.

It is a fantastic tool, but if you've ever been on the receiving end of a consulting presentation, you likely also know how it can be misused by people who cram far too much information into a single slide for it to actually work as a presentation.

Same goes for if you've ever been subjected to someone who got a little too excited about the bells and whistles available through PowerPoint and created a presentation where every single page or bullet point whizzed and spun and danced onto the screen.

(As you can tell, I have opinions about proper presentations. To me a presentation should give enough information to prompt the speaker to remember what they need to say, but not be such a distraction that no one listens to the speaker. You want to write a report? Write a report. You want to have dancing, spinning, spiraling text? You better be in third grade.)

Anyway. PowerPoint is a useful and important program to learn. The goal for this book is to teach you enough of it that you can comfortably use one of the PowerPoint templates to create your own presentation which includes text, pictures, and/or tables of information.

You will also learn how to format any text you enter, how to add notes to your slides, how to animate your slides so that each bullet point appears separately, and how to launch your presentation as a slide show. We will also cover how to print a copy of your presentation as well as how to print handouts.

As you can see, I will also be sprinkling in my opinion throughout this guide so it isn't just going to be how to do things in PowerPoint but why you might want to do it in a certain way.

There are other aspects to PowerPoint that I'm not going to cover in this guide. For example, we're not going to discuss how to use SmartArt. Nor will we discuss how to insert charts or create a presentation from scratch. If you want to continue with your knowledge of PowerPoint, many of those topics are covered in *PowerPoint 2019 Intermediate*.

The goal of this guide is to give you enough information on how to create a basic presentation without overwhelming you with information you may not need. I will, however, end with a discussion of how to find help for any additional topics you need to learn. PowerPoint, just like Word and Excel, has a certain underlying logic to it and if you pay attention to that structure it's generally easy to find what you need when you need it.

There is definitely overlap between how things work in Word and Excel, so if you've already mastered one of those programs PowerPoint will be much easier for you to learn. But if you haven't, we'll cover what you need to know, don't worry.

Alright then. First things first, let's get started with some basic terminology.

Basic Terminology

Before we do anything else, I want to make sure that we're on the same page in terms of terminology. Some of this will be standard to anyone talking about these programs and some of it is my personal quirky way of saying things, so best to skim through if nothing else.

Tab

I refer to the menu choices at the top of the screen (File, Home, Insert, Design, Transitions, Animations, Slide Show, Review, View, etc.) as tabs. If you click on one you'll see that the way it's highlighted sort of looks like an old-time filing system.

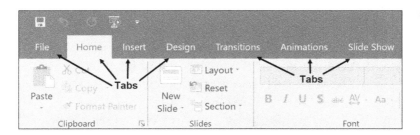

Each tab you select will show you different options. For example, in the image above, I have the Home tab selected and you can do various tasks such as cut/copy/paste, add new slides, change the slide layout, change fonts or font size or font color, change text formatting, add shapes, find/replace, etc. Other tabs will give other options.

Click

If I tell you to click on something, that means to use your mouse (or trackpad) to move the arrow on the screen over to a specific location and left-click or right-click on the option. (See the next definition for the difference between left-click and right-click).

If you left-click, this selects the item. If you right-click, this generally creates a dropdown list of options to choose from. If I don't tell you which to do, left- or right-click, then left-click.

Left-Click/Right-Click

If you look at your mouse or your trackpad, you generally have two flat buttons to press. One is on the left side, one is on the right. If I say left-click that means to press down on the button on the left. If I say right-click that means press down on the button on the right.

Now, as I sadly learned when I had to upgrade computers, not all trackpads have the left- and right-hand buttons. In that case, you'll basically want to press on either the bottom left-hand side of the trackpad or the bottom right-hand side of the trackpad. Since you're working blind it may take a little trial and error to get the option you want working. (Or is that just me?)

Select or Highlight

If I tell you to select text, that means to left-click at the end of the text you want to select, hold that left-click, and move your cursor to the other end of the text you want to select.

Another option is to use the Shift key. Go to one end of the text you want to select. Hold down the shift key and use the arrow keys to move to the other end of the text you want to select. If you arrow up or down, that will select an entire row at a time.

With both methods, which side of the text you start on doesn't matter. You can start at the end and go to the beginning or start at the beginning and go to the end. Just start at one end or the other of the text you want to select.

The text you've selected will then be highlighted in gray.

If you need to select text that isn't touching you can do this by selecting your first section of text and then holding down the Ctrl key and selecting your second section of text using your mouse.

(You can't arrow to the second section of text or you'll lose your already selected text.)

To select an object, you can generally just left-click on it. To select multiple objects, hold down the Ctrl key as you click on each object.

To select everything in your workspace, you can use Ctrl + A. (This is a control shortcut, which we'll define in a moment.)

Dropdown Menu

If you right-click on a PowerPoint slide, you will see what I'm going to refer to as a dropdown menu. (Sometimes it will actually drop upward if you're towards the bottom of the document.)

A dropdown menu provides you a list of choices to select from like this one that appears when I right-click on a presentation slide:

There are also dropdown menus available for some of the options listed under the tabs at the top of the screen. For example, if you go to the Home tab, you'll see small arrows below or next to some of the options, like the Layout option and the Section option in the Slides section. Clicking on those little arrows will give you a dropdown menu with a list of choices to choose from like this one for Section:

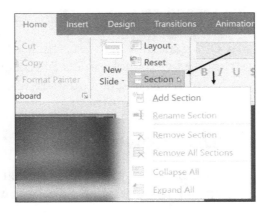

Expansion Arrows

I don't know the official word for these, but you'll also notice at the bottom right corner of most of the sections in each tab that there are little arrows pointing down and to the right.

If you click on one of those arrows PowerPoint will bring up a more detailed set of options, usually through a dialogue box (which we'll discuss next) or a task pane (which we'll discuss after that).

In the Home tab, for example, there are expansion arrows for Clipboard, Font, Paragraph, and Drawing. Holding your mouse over the arrow will give a brief description of what clicking on the expansion arrow will do like here for the Clipboard section on the Home tab where it tells you that clicking on the expansion arrow will allow you to see all items that have been copied to the clipboard.

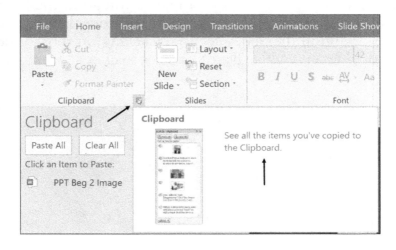

In this instance, clicking on the expansion arrow opens a task pane on the left-hand side of the screen, which is visible in the background of the image above.

Dialogue Box

Dialogue boxes are pop-up boxes that cover specialized settings. As just mentioned, if you click on an expansion arrow, it will often open a dialogue box that contains more choices than are visible in that section.

Also, if you right-click on the text in a PowerPoint content slide and choose Font, Paragraph, or Hyperlink from the dropdown menu that will open a dialogue box.

Dialogue boxes often allow the most granular level of control over an option. For example, this is the Font dialogue box which you can see has more options available than in the Font section of the Home tab.

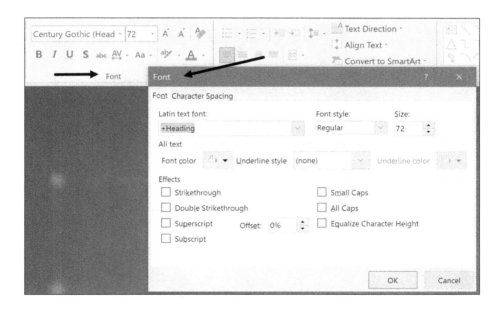

Task Pane

What I refer to as task panes are separate work spaces that are visible to the left- and right-hand sides of your main workspace. They may also occasionally appear below your main workspace.

For example, When you first open PowerPoint, there will generally be a task pane on the left-hand side that shows thumbnail images of the slides in your presentation. This is an area you can navigate in separate from your main workspace.

Here is an example of a business presentation template I opened with the slides in a task pane to the left and the title slide in the main workspace:

You can have multiple task panes open at once. To close a task pane that is not permanently visible, such as the Clipboard task pane, click on the X in the top right corner.

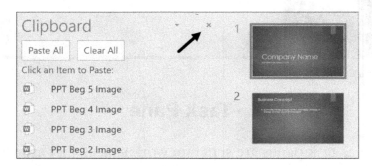

You can also click on the arrow next to the X and choose Close.

You can sometimes also move a task pane. To do so, click on the arrow in the top right corner and choose Move from the dropdown menu. That will detach the task pane from its current position. You can then left-click and drag the task pane to where you'd like.

To attach a task pane to the left-hand or right-hand side of the workspace, drag it off of the edge of the screen until it "docks" into place.

If you do move a task pane and then close it, when you reopen the task pane it will appear in the location you moved it to.

Scroll Bar

Scroll bars allow you to see content that isn't currently visible on the screen. PowerPoint usually has multiple scroll bars visible.

One scroll bar will appear on the right-hand side of the task pane that contains thumbnails of your presentation slides. This scroll bar lets you see the thumbnails of all available slides in the presentation by scrolling up and down.

Here is the top portion of that scroll bar:

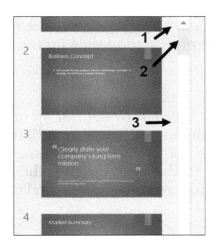

You can click on the up arrow (labeled 1) at the top or the down arrow (not visible here) at the bottom to move a small amount up or down.

If you click on the gray space above or below the scroll bar (labeled 2) that will move you one whole screen at a time. So if Slides 1 through 6 are currently visible, clicking below the scroll bar will make Slides 7 through 12 visible.

Or you can left-click on the scroll bar itself (labeled 3) and drag up or down to move through the available space at your own speed.

I personally tend to left-click and drag the scroll bar because that gives me the most control while still moving through my available slides at a relatively fast pace.

Another scroll bar will generally appear on the right-hand side of the main workspace. This scrollbar will by default let you navigate through each of the slides in your presentation one-by-one.

In the main workspace, there are a few more options. At the bottom of the scroll bar, you have a double up arrow and a double down arrow which can be clicked on to move to the previous slide or the next slide.

When you're at a normal zoom level, you will get that same result by clicking on the gray space above or below the scroll bar or on the arrows at the top or bottom of the scroll bar.

(If you increase the zoom level on your main workspace the scroll bar will instead move through portions of your slides.)

Generally, I don't use the scroll bar for the main workspace because I click onto the thumbnails in the left-hand task pane to move to the slide I want. Or to see an entire presentation one slide at a time I go into Slide Show mode, which we'll discuss later.

You won't normally see a scroll bar at the bottom of the screen, but it is possible. This would happen if you ever change the zoom level to the point that you're not seeing the entire presentation slide on the screen.

Arrow

If I ever tell you to arrow to the left or right or up or down, that just means use your arrow keys. This will move your cursor to the left one space, to the right one space, up one line, or down one line. If you're at the end of a line and arrow to the right, it will take you to the beginning of the next line. If you're at the beginning of a line and arrow to the left, it will take you to the end of the last line.

Cursor

There are two possible meanings for cursor. One is the one I just used. When you're clicked into a PowerPoint slide, you will see that there is a blinking line. This indicates where you are in the document. If you type text, each letter will appear where the cursor was at the time you typed it. The cursor will move (at least in the U.S. and I'd assume most European versions) to the right as you type. This version of the cursor should be visible at all times when you're clicked onto text.

The other type of cursor is the one that's tied to the movement of your mouse or trackpad. If you've clicked onto your text, the cursor will look somewhat like a tall skinny capital I when positioned over text. Move it up to the menu options or off to the sides, and it will generally become a white arrow or four-sided black arrow.

Usually I won't refer to your cursor, I'll just say, "click" or "select" or whatever action you need to take with it, and moving the cursor to that location will be implied.

Quick Access Toolbar

In the very top left corner of your screen above the Home tab, you should see a series of symbols. These are part of the Quick Access Toolbar. By default it appears to have options for Save, Undo, Redo, and Start from Beginning.

To see what each symbol stands for, hold your mouse over it and help text will appear.

You can customize what options appear there by clicking on the downward pointing arrow with a line above it located at the end of the line of symbols.

Click on any command you want that isn't currently visible to select it or click on one you no longer want to unselect it. The checkmarks next to each item indicate which are visible. For example, here the Save command is checked but none of the others are.

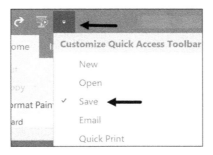

The Quick Access Toolbar can be useful if there's something you're doing repeatedly that's located on a different tab than something else you're doing repeatedly.

Control Shortcut

Throughout this document, I'm going to mention various control shortcuts that you can use to perform tasks like save, copy, cut, and paste like I did above with Select All, Ctrl +A.

Each of these will be written as Ctrl + a capital letter.

When you use the shortcut you do not need to use the capitalized version of the letter. For example, holding down the Ctrl key and the s key at the same time will save your document. I'll write this as Ctrl + S, but that just means hold down the key that says ctrl and the s key at the same time.

Undo

One of the most powerful control shortcuts in PowerPoint is the Undo option. If you do something you didn't mean or that you want to take back, use Ctrl + Z. This will reverse whatever you just did.

If you need to reverse more than one item, you can keep using Ctrl + Z until you've undone everything you wanted to undo, or you can use the Undo option in the Quick Access Toolbar.

If you use the Quick Access Toolbar there is a dropdown menu option that lets you choose to undo multiple steps at once.

Either way, though, you have to undo things in order. So if I bold, underline, and italicize text and want to undo the bolding on the text, I would also have to undo the italics and underline since those happened after I bolded the text. I can't choose to just undo the bolding. Undo walks you backwards one thing at a time.

(Which is why in that example, it might be easier to just unbold the text rather than try to use undo.)

Absolute Basics

Now let's discuss some absolute basics, like opening, closing, saving, and deleting presentations.

Start a New PowerPoint Presentation

To start a brand new PowerPoint presentation, I choose PowerPoint from my applications menu or click on the shortcut I have on my computer's taskbar. If you're already in PowerPoint and want to start a new PowerPoint presentation you can go to the File tab and choose New from the left-hand menu.

You can also use Ctrl + N to start a new presentation. That will bring up a Title Slide that has no theme and is just plain white.

Using the File→New option will give you a choice of a number of different presentations that are pre-formatted. The blank presentation option is also available, but I recommend using one of the pre-formatted options when you can since they've already thought through complementary colors and imagery and font choices.

Clicking on any of the themes will bring up a secondary display. You can actually use the arrows on the left- and right-hand sides of that display to navigate through the template choices and see a little description related to each template.

For some of the templates there will be variant versions shown. For example, for me if I click on the Circuit presentation template it shows that there are four color palettes available. I can click on any of the four variants to use that color palette. Here I've clicked on the gray option instead of the blue:

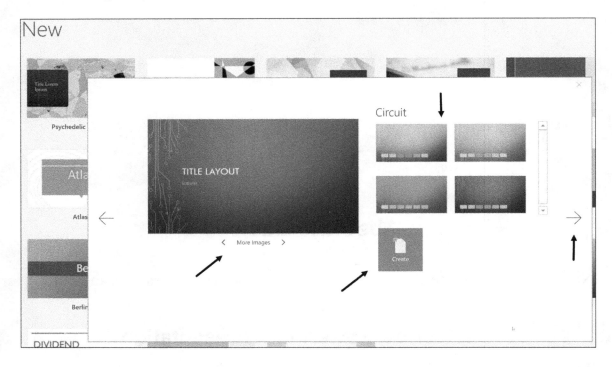

Also, some of the templates may have a More Images option underneath the title slide image. You can click on the arrows there to see what the interior slide layouts for that template will look like.

This can be important because, for example, if you're going to print a presentation chances are you don't want the main presentation slides to use a colored background. You'll want to instead use a template like Ion Boardroom that has a white background on the main presentation slides.

And don't worry if you choose a "bad" template initially. You can change the template and the variant on that template later if you realize the template you chose isn't going to work for you.

Okay, then.

Once you've found a template you like, click on it and then on Create to have PowerPoint start a draft presentation for you to work from.

The presentation should appear with a Title page that has draft text showing on it, usually "Click to Add Title" and often "Click to Add Subtitle."

As I mentioned above, you can always choose a template after you've started working on your presentation using the Design tab which we'll cover later. But if you chose a blank presentation using Ctrl + N you will also have a Design Ideas task pane appear.

I wouldn't recommend using one of the options from the Design Ideas task pane, though, because as far as I can tell it only provides you with a style for the title slide and not the rest of the presentation.

I don't see a way to then have the rest of the slides in your presentation match that title slide style. So the rest of your presentation would still be plain white with black text if you chose one of those options, which isn't very helpful.

Okay, then. That's how to start a brand new presentation. If you have a corporate template you're working from, chances are you'll need to use that instead, so let's talk about how to open an existing presentation next.

Open an Existing PowerPoint File

To open an existing PowerPoint file you can go to the folder where the file is saved and double-click on the file name. Or you can open PowerPoint without selecting a file and it will provide a list of recent documents to choose from under the Recent heading in the middle of the screen.

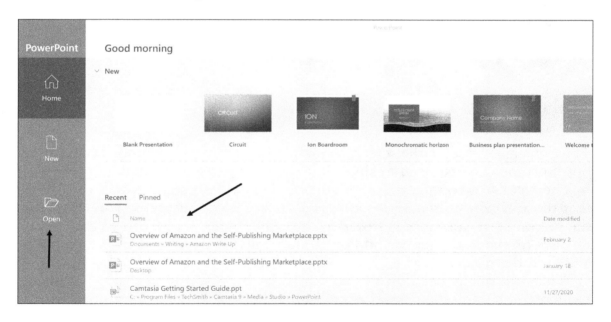

Double-click on one of those file names and the presentation will open.

Next to the Recent heading is a Pinned heading. If you have any presentations that you always want to be able to access easily you can pin them and no matter how long it's been since you opened that presentation last you'll be able to find it under the Pinned heading.

To pin a file, single-click on its name under Recent and look to the right-hand side of the listing. There should be a small thumbtack image. Click on that and the file will be added to the Pinned section.

To unpin a file, just click on the thumbtack again.

If you're in PowerPoint and don't see the file you want under either Recent or Pinned, you can either click on More Presentations at the bottom of the recent files listing or click on the Open option on the left-hand sidebar. Both will bring you to the Open screen.

You can also reach the screen by using Ctrl + O.

The right-hand side of the screen contains your recent presentations once more, but this time you just need to single left-click to open a presentation.

There is also an option there for Folders. This will generally display the folders that those recent presentations are saved in so it's only useful if you know that the presentation you want is stored in the same folder as one you recently used.

Click on the folder name and PowerPoint will display for you all presentations stored in that folder.

What I normally need on this screen is the Browse option that's available to the left of the presentations/folders listing. Left-clicking on that brings up the Open dialogue box which allows you to navigate to any location on your computer. Mine by default opens to the Documents folder.

Once you find the file you want, either click on it and then choose Open, or double-click on it.

Save a PowerPoint File

To quickly save your presentation, you can use Ctrl + S or click on the small image of a floppy disk in the Quick Access Toolbar.

For a document you've already saved that will overwrite the prior version of the document with the current version and will keep the file name, file type, and file location the same.

If you need to change the file name, type, or location you'll need to use the Save As option instead. This can be accessed via the File tab.

(With respect to file type, I sometimes need to, for example, save a presentation as a .pdf or a .jpg file instead.)

When you use Save As you wil need to navigate to where you want to save your file by either clicking on one of the listed file names or by clicking on one of the locations on the left-hand side.

Here I've clicked on Browse which opens a Save As dialogue box that shows the default name PowerPoint assigned, the default file type, and which shows my Documents folder so that I can navigate to where I want to save the file.

There are still defaults for name and format, but you'll want to change the name of the document to something better than the template name.

If you try to save a file that has never been saved before, it will automatically default to the Save As option and open a dialogue box which requires that you specify where to save the file and what to name it.

Clicking on More Options will let you also change the file type before you save. It does so by taking you to the Save As screen.

If you had already saved the file and you choose to Save As but keep the same location, name, and format as before, PowerPoint will overwrite the previous version of the file just like it would have if you'd used Save.

Rename a PowerPoint File

If you just want to rename a file, it's best to close the file and then go to where the file is saved and rename it that way rather than use Save As. Using Save As will keep the original of the file as well as creating the newer version. That's great when you want version control (which is rarely needed for PowerPoint), but not when you just wanted to rename your file from Great Presentation v22 to Great Presentation FINAL.

To do so, navigate to where you've saved the file, click on the file name once to select it, click on it a second time to highlight the name, and then type in the new name you want to use, replacing the old one. If you rename the file this way outside of PowerPoint, there will only be one version of the file left, the one with the new name you wanted.

Just be aware that if you rename a file by navigating to where it's located and changing the name you won't be able to access the file from the Recent Presentations list under Open since that will still list the old name which no longer exists. The next time you want to open that file you'll need to navigate to where it's stored and open it that way.

Delete a PowerPoint File

You can't delete a PowerPoint file from within PowerPoint. You need to close the file you want to delete and then navigate to where the file is stored and delete the file from there without opening it.

To do so, locate the file and click on the file name. (Only enough to select it. Make sure you haven't double-clicked and highlighted the name which will delete the file name but not the file.) Next, choose Delete from the menu at the top of the screen, or right-click and choose Delete from the dropdown menu.

Close a PowerPoint File

To close a PowerPoint file click on the X in the top right corner or go to File and then choose Close. (You can also use Ctrl + W, but I never have.)

If no changes have been made to the document since you saved it last, it will just close.

If changes have been made, PowerPoint should ask you if you want to save those changes. You can either choose to save them, not save them, or cancel closing the document and leave it open. I almost always default to saving any changes. If I'm in doubt about whether I'd be overwriting something important, I cancel and choose to Save As and save the current file as a later version of the document just in case (e.g., Great Presentation v2).

If you had copied an image or a large block of text before trying to close your presentation, you may also have a dialogue box pop up asking if you want to keep that image or text available for use when you close the document. Usually the answer to this is no, but if you had planned on pasting that image or text somewhere else and hadn't yet done so, you can say to keep it on the clipboard.

* * *

Okay. Now let's talk about your workspace. We touched on it a bit when we defined task panes, but I want to go over it in more detail now.

Your Workspace

Whether you choose to start a brand new file or open an existing file, you'll end up in the main workspace for PowerPoint. It looks something like this:

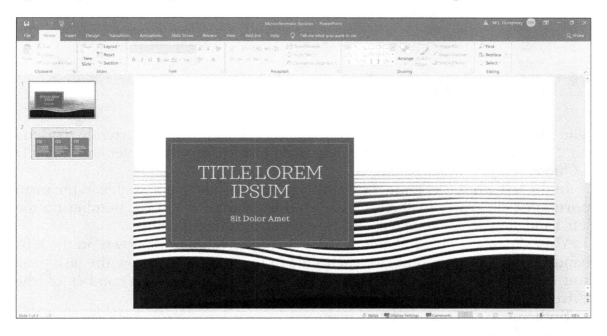

We'll walk through this in more detail in the Working with Your Presentation Slides section but I just wanted you to see right now that there's a left-hand task pane that shows all of the slides in the presentation and then a main section of the screen that shows the slide you're currently working on.

For a new presentation there's usually just the one title slide. This one happens to have two slides that it opens with.

The business presentation template opens with fourteen slides. Let's look through that one now:

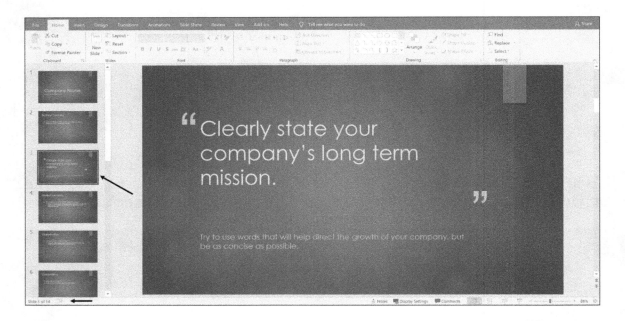

The main portion of the screen will contain the slide you're currently working on. So in this case I've selected a slide from farther into the presentation that is a Quote Name Card slide.

In the left-hand task pane the thumbnail of the slide that is visible in the main portion of the screen will have a dark border around it and the number on the left-hand side of the slide will also be colored a different color.

Your slides will be numbered starting at 1. The number is shown on the left-hand side of the thumbnail for each slide in the task pane. Below the task pane you can see how many slides are in the presentation and the number of the current slide. So here that says 3 of 14.

Both the task pane and the main workspace have scroll bars that let you navigate through the presentation. To move to a different slide you can also double-click on its thumbnail in the task pane and it will appear in the main workspace.

In the bottom right corner you can also change the zoom level for the main workspace. (I usually leave that alone, though.)

Across the top of the workspace are your menu tabs which you may need to use when formatting the text or appearance of your presentation.

There are also dropdown menus available in both the task pane and the main workspace. In the task pane dropdown you have the options to cut, copy, paste, add a new slide, duplicate a slide, delete a slide, add a section (which is an intermediate-level topic), change the slide layout, and more. These relate to the slides themselves.

In the main workspace you also have a dropdown with cut, copy, and paste options, but these generally relate to the text on a slide. There are also options for font, paragraph, bullets, numbering, and more.

We'll revisit some of this later, but for now let's focus on that left-hand task pane and what you can do there with respect to your slides.

Edit Presentation Slides

Before we continue I want to edit your presentation slides, most of which is done by working in the left-hand slide task pane.

Add a Slide

If you right-click into the blank space below your slide(s) in the left-hand task pane, you'll see a dropdown menu that includes the New Slide option.

Click on that and PowerPoint will add a new slide to your presentation. The layout of the slide will either match the layout of the slide directly above it or will be a Title and Content slide if the slide directly above it was a Title slide.

You can also right-click on an existing slide and choose New Slide from that dropdown menu as well. If you do that, the slide that is added to your presentation will have the same layout as the one you right-clicked on.

Another option is to go to the Slides section of the Home tab and click on New Slide there. If you add a slide via the Home tab and click on the New Slide dropdown arrow you can choose the layout you want. (See the chapter on slide layouts for a discussion of the various layout options.)

Select a Slide or Slides

To select a single slide, you simply left-click on the slide where it's visible in the left-hand slide task pane. When a slide is selected it should have a darker border around it. In my version that border appears to be a dark red.

If you want to select more than one slide, left-click on the first slide and then hold down the Ctrl key as you left-click on the other slides you want.

Each selected slide will have that dark border around it.

Slides do not need to be next to one another for you to select them this way.

If you have a range of slides that you want to select, you can use the Shift key instead. Click on the slide at the top or the bottom of the range of slides you want, hold down the Shift key, and then click on the slide at the other end of the range of slides you want. All slides within that range, including both of the slides you clicked, will be selected.

(You can also combine methods of selecting slides to, for example, select a range of slides using Shift and then select an additional slide using the Ctrl key.)

No matter how many slides you select, the main workspace will only show one of them.

To remove your selection of multiple slides, click in the gray area around any of the slides or into your main workspace.

Move a Slide or Slides

The easiest way to move a slide or slides to a different position within your presentation is to select the slide(s) (as noted above) and then left-click and drag the slide(s) to the new location using the left-hand slide task pane.

As you move your chosen slide(s) you'll see the slides moving upward or downward to leave a space for your slide(s) to be inserted.

If you're moving more than one slide, you can left-click on any of the slides you've selected and drag.

All of the selected slides will move to the new location even if they weren't next to one another before.

As you move multiple slides at once you'll see a number in the top right corner telling you how many slides you're moving.

Cut a Slide or Slides

Cutting a slide removes it from its current location but lets you paste that slide elsewhere.

In the task pane, you can right-click on your chosen slide(s) and choose Cut from the dropdown menu. Or you can select your slide(s) and then use Ctrl + X. Or you can select your slide(s) and then go to the Clipboard section of the Home tab and choose Cut from there.

Any of these options will remove the slide(s) from their current position but let you paste them either into another location in that presentation or into another presentation altogether. (Usually within the same presentation I'd just move the slides, but if it was a very long presentation it might be easier to cut and paste instead.)

Copy a Slide or Slides

Copying a slide keeps that slide in its current position but takes a copy of the slide that you can then paste elsewhere.

In the left-hand task pane, you can right-click on your chosen slide(s) and choose Copy from the dropdown menu. Or you can select your slide(s) and then use Ctrl + C. Or you can select your slide(s) in the task pane and then go to the Clipboard section of the Home tab and choose Copy from there.

You also have a Duplicate option in PowerPoint which will take a copy of your selected slide(s) and immediately paste that copy below the selected slide(s). It's available if you right-click or if you click on the dropdown arrow next to Copy in the Clipboard section of the Home tab.

This means you only need to use Copy if you want to paste your copied slide(s) elsewhere in your document or into another presentation.

Paste a Slide or Slides

If you copy or cut a slide or slides and want to use them elsewhere, you need to paste them into that new location.

You can do a basic paste by clicking into the space where you want to put those slides (so between two existing slides or in the gray space at the end of the presentation, for example) and using Ctrl + V.

If you are clicked onto a slide when you use Ctrl + V, your copied or cut slides will be pasted in below that slide you were clicked onto.

You can also right-click where you want to paste a slide and choose from the paste options in the dropdown menu.

The first option, which has a small a in the bottom right corner, is Use Destination Theme. If you're cutting or copying and pasting within an existing presentation this won't mean much. I have used this one, however, when working with a corporate PowerPoint template where someone had drafted their presentation slides without using the template and I had to bring their content into the corporate template.

In a situation like that you can copy all of the slides from the initial version of the presentation and paste them into the corporate template using the destination theme option which will convert the slides from whatever theme was initially used to the corporate theme. You'll still have to walk through your document and make sure nothing was impacted by the change of theme, but at least you won't have to change each slide's theme individually.

The second paste option you have, the one with the paintbrush in the bottom right corner, is Keep Source Formatting. This does exactly what it says, it keeps the formatting that the slide(s) already had.

Sometimes it's important to do this especially if you've done a lot of custom work on a slide and don't want your images, charts, etc. resized when you move them into a new presentation.

The third paste option, the one with a photo icon in the bottom right corner, is to paste a slide in as a Picture. That means the slide can no longer be edited. It's like someone took a snapshot of that slide and now you just have that snapshot. If you try to use this option with multiple slides only the first slide will paste in.

You can also paste slides by going to the Clipboard section of the Home tab and choosing Paste from there. The more advanced paste options are available by clicking on the arrow under Paste.

Delete a Slide

To delete a slide, you can click on that slide in the left-hand task pane and then hit the Delete or Backspace key. Either one will work. Or you can right-click on that slide and choose Delete Slide from the dropdown menu.

Reset a Slide

If you make changes to the layout of a slide, by for example changing the size of the text boxes or their location, and want to go back to the original layout for that slide type for that theme, you can right-click on the slide and choose Reset Slide from the dropdown menu. According to PowerPoint, this will "reset the position, size, and formatting of the slide placeholders to their default settings."

You can also do so by clicking on the slide you want to reset and clicking on the Reset option in the Slides section of the Home tab.

Presentation Themes

As a beginner, I highly recommend that you work with the presentation themes that PowerPoint provides you rather than trying to create a presentation from scratch. Presentation themes are pre-built to use colors, fonts, and imagery that all work together to provide a polished appearance.

As a matter of fact, the rest of this guide will assume that that's what you're doing. I do not cover here how to create a presentation from scratch.

We already covered above under how to create a new presentation how to start your presentation using one of the PowerPoint themes or a variation on that theme. This chapter will cover how to change your presentation theme once you've started to create your presentation.

There are a number of reasons why you might want to do so. For example, the audiences I've presented to in the past expect the title field on each slide to appear at the top of the slide. There are a handful of PowerPoint themes that place the title portion of the slide elsewhere. So if I were to inadvertently select one of those as I started to prepare, I'd need to change it once I realized that.

Also, some of the themes include a wider variety of slide layouts than others. If I knew I'd be using a certain slide layout that wasn't available in my chosen theme it might be easier to switch to a theme that did have that slide layout rather than try to create it myself.

So. How do you do this? How do you change your theme once you've started working on a presentation?

First, go to the Design tab.

You should see that the Themes section takes up most of the tab starting on the left-hand side of the screen. The first thumbnail in that section is your current theme followed by your other choices.

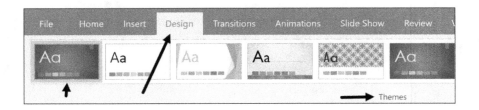

To see how each theme will look, you can hold your mouse over the thumbnail for that theme and PowerPoint will temporarily apply it to the slide in your main workspace.

To see more themes, click on the down arrow at the end. To see all themes at once, click on the down arrow with a line above it. That will give you something that looks like this:

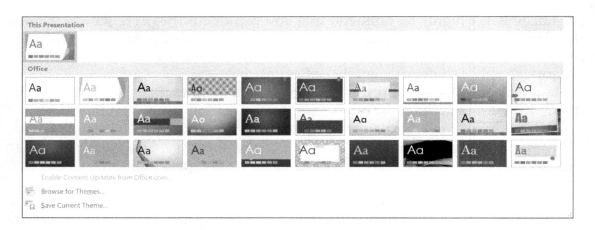

I recommend when choosing a theme that you look at how that theme will appear when applied to both a Title slide as well as a Title and Content slide before making your choice, because they can be very different.

For example, the slide on the next page is from the Integral theme and is very simple. But the title slide for that theme is dominated by a decorative pattern that is not.

Also, theoretically, the text color that will be used in the headers on your presentation is the same one used for the Aa on the thumbnail image but it's good to confirm that by seeing the theme on a slide.

And the colored boxes that run along the bottom of each thumbnail do show the main color palette for the theme, but most themes will only use the first color or two for bullets or effects.

For example, here is a slide using the Integral theme and it only uses one accent color:

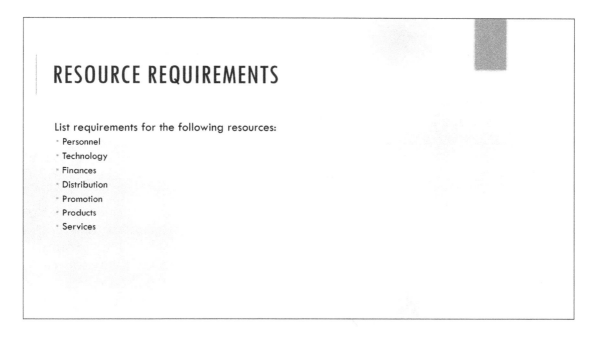

If you add charts, etc. you will see more of the theme colors used and they are all available for any text, element, etc. color choice that you make.

So always a good idea to preview your themes. And to do so on both a title slide and a content slide. (If you don't already have a content slide, right-click in the left-hand task pane and choose New Slide.)

Once you've found a theme you like, to permanently apply it to your slides, simply click on it.

That should apply the theme to every slide in your entire presentation. But it won't do so if you'd selected a subset of your slides before choosing the theme. It also may not do so if your presentation has sections in it.

(Which is why it's always good to start with the right theme so that you don't have to worry about these issues later.)

In addition to the choices you can see in the Themes section of the Design tab, some themes also have what are called variants. Variants use the same structure and design elements but have different color palettes or use different background colors or patterns.

Not every theme has a variant, but when a theme does have variants you will see them in the Variants section of the Design tab.

They only appear after you have selected that specific theme. Here, for example, is the variant section for the Integral theme.

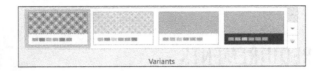

The first thumbnail is the default option for that theme. The remaining thumbnails show the variants.

Just like with the Themes section if there are more than three variants available you can use the arrows on the right-hand side to see the rest of the choices.

Also, as with the theme thumbnails, you can hold your mouse over each variant to see what it will look like when applied to your presentation.

In this example, at least two of the variants use a non-white background for the main slides in the presentation. A couple also use more than one of the theme colors, so there can definitely be some variety within a theme.

But they all do keep the general design elements the same. Here is an example of one of the variants for the Integral theme:

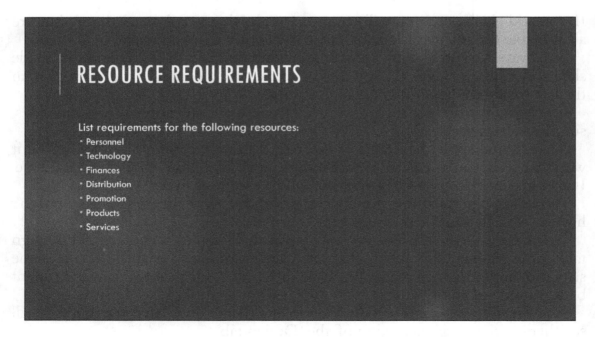

Be careful when applying a new theme that all of your existing slides work with that new theme. It is possible for the main slides to work but the title slide to no longer have an acceptable appearance. Or vice versa.

If you find a presentation theme that you like but still can't find colors that work for you amongst the variant thumbnails, you can instead change the colors using the Colors dropdown menu under Variants in the Design tab.

To access it, click on the downward arrow with a line on the right-hand side of the Variants thumbnail display. That will bring up a dropdown menu that includes the Colors option. Hold your mouse over that Colors option and a secondary dropdown menu will appear that shows various color palettes.

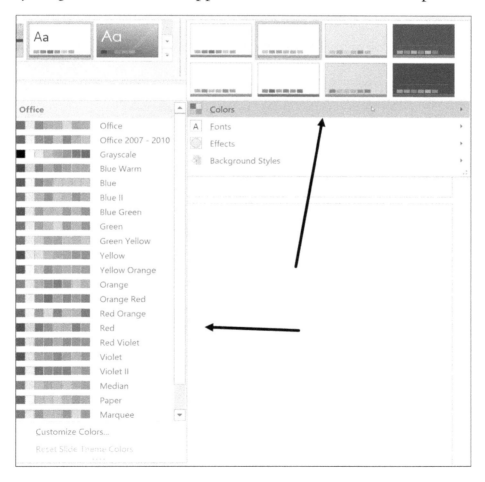

Just like with the theme and variant thumbnails, you can hold your mouse over each color palette to see how it will appear in your presentation. Click on one to permanently apply it.

Changing your theme should definitely not be the last thing you do. Ideally you choose a theme before you start to add your content so that you can adjust as you add your content. But in case it's needed, that's how you do it.

Okay, then. Now let's talk about the various slide layouts that may be available as part of each theme.

Slide Layouts

There are a variety of slide layouts available to you in PowerPoint. Probably more than you'll actually need. But I wanted to run through a handful of the most common ones before we go any farther because I'm going to occasionally refer to a slide layout and I want you to know what I'm talking about when I do.

The images below use the Facet theme with a customized color palette applied.

As mentioned above, to add a new slide into your presentation, right-click in the left-hand task pane and choose New Slide from the dropdown menu.

Or you can go to the Insert tab and choose New Slide from the Slides section. If you click on the dropdown arrow, you can then choose your layout before you insert the slide.

To change the layout of a slide you've already added to your presentation, right-click on the slide, go to Layout, and choose a new layout from the secondary dropdown menu.

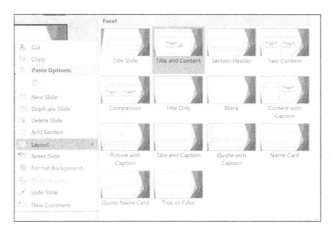

You can also select a slide or slides, go to the Slides section of the Home tab, click on the dropdown arrow next to Layout, and choose your layout from there.

Not all themes or templates will have all layouts. And different themes may have the elements (such as text boxes) of a layout in different locations on the slide. For example, the Slice theme puts the title section of each slide at the bottom of the page instead of the top.

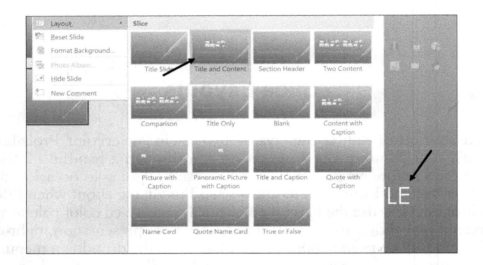

This is why you should definitely look at where the elements are in a presentation theme before you decide to use it.

* * *

Now let's walk through your slide layout choices. In my opinion, you can put together a perfectly adequate presentation with just the Title and Title and Content slides, although there are many more choices than that.

Title Slide

The Title slide is the default first slide for a presentation. It has a section for adding a title and a subtitle and, if you choose one of the templates provided in PowerPoint, a background or design elements that match the chosen theme.

Section Header

If you are going to have sections within your presentation, then you'll want to separate them using a Section Header slide.

This slide has an appearance that is close to that of the title slide, but usually the text or design elements are in a different position. It may also use different colors, fonts, or font colors.

In this theme you can see that the design element on the left-hand side is slightly different from the one used for the title slide. The text is also located in a different location and is a smaller font size.

Title and Content Slide

The Title and Content slide is the one I use for most of my presentations. For a basic presentation with a bulleted set of talking points, this is the slide that you'll probably use the most often.

It has a text box where you can give a high-level title for the slide and then a larger text box that takes up most of the rest of the space on the slide where you can add text or a data table, chart, picture, video, etc.

The design elements on this slide are generally less pronounced than on the title and section slides, but not always.

Here you can see that the design elements are the same as were used on the section slide but that the amount of space for text is much larger and the title is at the top.

Be careful when moving between themes to check your titles on your slides. Some themes use all caps in the title section and some do not. If you're switching between a theme that uses all caps to one that doesn't, you may find that you need to retype your entries because only half of your words are capitalized the way they should be.

Two Content

The Two Content slide is another content slide. This slide has a section for a title and then two separate content boxes. It can be a good choice for when you want to either have two separate bulleted lists side by side or when you want to have text next to an image, data table, video, or chart.

* * *

It can be hard to see the difference between the different slide types when they don't have content in them, so here's a snapshot from the left-hand task pane of the first four slide types we've discussed with content added to them using the Facet theme and then using the Ion Boardroom theme.

The content is exactly the same for both:

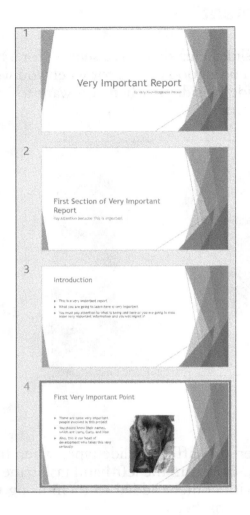
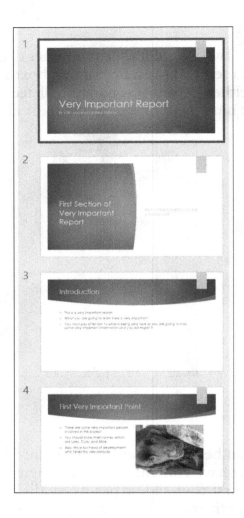

Note that when I changed the theme over to Ion Boardroom it changed the orientation of the image I'd placed on the fourth slide. If you move between themes you need to always go back through your presentation and make sure that all of your text, bullet points, images, etc. still work with the new theme.

* * *

Okay, then. Next slide type.

Comparison

The Comparison slide is a content slide much like the Two Content slide except it has added sections directly above each of the two main text boxes where you can put header text to describe the contents of each of the boxes.

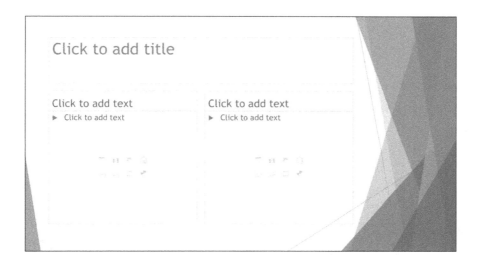

This is especially good for situations where you maybe have side-by-side charts, data tables, videos, or images and you want to be able to label each one.

Title Only

The Title Only slide is a content slide that just has the title section and nothing else. You would generally use this slide when you wanted to add elements to the body of the slide yourself or when you wanted to separate sections and didn't want to use the section header slide.

Blank

The Blank slide has the design elements common to all of the content slides but there are no text boxes on the slide at all.

Content With Caption

The Content With Caption slide is a content slide where the title section covers half of the screen and there are two text boxes where you can add text, images, etc. One of the text boxes is below the title and the other takes up the other half of the slide.

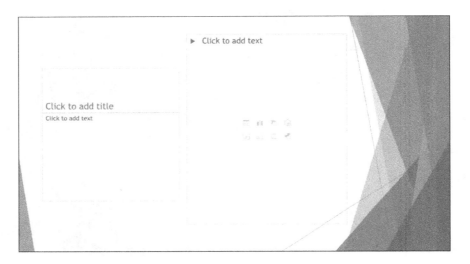

Picture With Caption

The Picture With Caption slide has a large section for a picture and then a text box below it where you can add a title and description of the picture.

Title And Caption

The Title And Caption slide has a large section for a title with a smaller section for text. It would make a good section separator if you wanted a different appearance for a new section such as an Appendix.

Quote With Caption

The Quote With Caption slide is a slide that has quote marks around the main text section and then a smaller text box immediately under that for an attribution of who said the quote. There's also another text box for comments related to the quote.

Other

Some themes will have even more pre-formatted slide types you can use. For example, the Ion Boardroom theme has a three-column slide type and this theme had a Name Card option.

Some themes won't have this many. In that case you can either create what you need by adding on to the Blank or Title Only slides or you can find a theme that better suits your needs.

As I said before, I can put together a perfectly good presentation using the Title and Title and Content slides alone, but it is nice to have more options than that to work with. A presentation where every single slide looks the same can become monotonous and that can lose you the attention of your audience. Although, as always, you need to balance that out against making your presentation more interesting than what you're saying.

Alright, now let's cover how to add content to a slide.

Add and Format Text

Add Text

Adding text to an existing slide is very easy. You simply click and type. For example, here, is a Title slide:

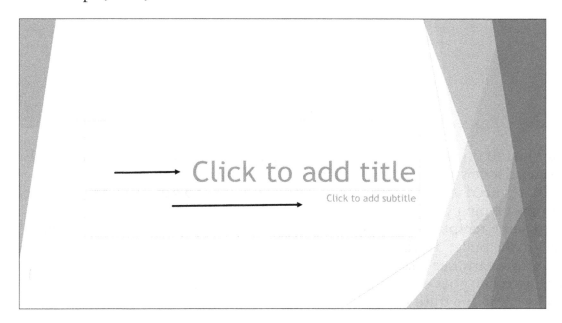

See where it says "Click to add title" and "Click to add subtitle"? Those are both text boxes that are already set up for you to add your text. All you have to do is click on either one and start typing.

When you're done typing in one text box you can click in the other or click elsewhere on the slide.

It works the same for content-style slides. The main Title and Content slide has a text box where it says "Click to add title" and a text box where it says "Click to add text". With this particular theme, the main text is shown as a bulleted list, so you'll see the first bullet is already there and a new bullet will appear each time you hit Enter..

Here is one of those slides completed with three rows of talking points:

All I had to do was click into the text box and start typing. Each time I hit Enter it started a new line for me that already had a bullet point.

If you need to create subpoints you can use the tab key to indent a line before you start typing your text.

In some templates that will also change the type of bullet used or change the size of the bullet. It will often also change the size of the text. In this next image you can clearly see that the third-level of text is smaller than the first level. In fact, each line goes down by 2 pts in this theme. So the first line is 18 pt, the next is 16 pt, and the third is 14 pt.

To remove an indent, use Shift + Tab before your start typing.

For lines that have already been added where you need to adjust the indent, click to the left of the first letter in that line and then use Tab or Shift + Tab to adjust the indent.

You can also use the Decrease List Level and Increase List Level options in the Paragraph section of the Home tab. They're the ones with lines with an arrow pointing either left or right in the middle of the top row of that section. You can click anywhere on that paragraph to use the option; you don't have to click at the start of the text.

If you want complete control over your indent, you can right-click and choose Paragraph from the dropdown menu. This will bring up the Paragraph dialogue box where you can specify an exact indent amount.

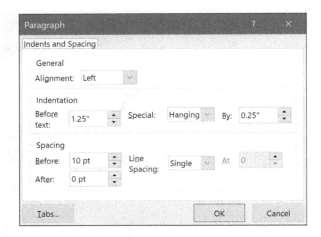

By default the PowerPoint themes use fonts and font sizes that are legible for a presentation given on a projector. That's true for probably the first three levels of indents. But past that point the text may become too small to be legible from a distance.

I wouldn't go below about 14 point for any text on a slide that's meant to be used in a presentation. (As opposed to printed out.) I believe that most of the pre-formatted presentations stop decreasing the font size at 12 point, which may be workable but is just on the edge for me.

Also, sometimes PowerPoint will adjust your text dynamically to make it fit into the text box. So if you use too much text it will make that text smaller than the default in order to get the text to fit.

Because this can happen on a slide-by-slide basis it creates a disjointed presentation when it happens. If one slide has bullet points in a 20 point size and another has bullet points in a 14 point size and another has them in an 11 point size, even if the font and colors are consistent across slides, it can be distracting to a viewer.

Which is why I try when I can to make the font size consistent across slides. The easiest way to do so is to keep your entries short and sweet.

In other words, don't have one slide with a title of "Introduction" and another with a title of "Discussion of the Philosophical Aspects of Polar Ionization and Government Regulatory Structures". Chances are that second slide will automatically be converted to a smaller font size (and may have text that runs outside of the provided text box to boot.)

With bullet points try to keep it to three levels or less. If you can't do that, consider manually adjusting the font size for the fourth-level and beyond bullet points.

And if you absolutely can't avoid lengthy text, then adjust the rest of your slides to the size of the lengthiest text entries. For example, with the Facet theme I've been using here, the default title size is 36 point, but when I put in a very lengthy title it is reduced to 32 point. So to create consistency throughout the presentation I'd change any 36 point titles to 32 point.

(Obviously, it's easier to simplify the language instead, but that's not always an option when working on group projects or with a boss who has certain unmovable notions of what should be said.)

Move Text

If you need to cut, copy, or paste text from within a slide, it works much the same way as it did for the slides in the left-hand pane.

To cut text, highlight the text you want to cut and then use Ctrl + X or go to the Clipboard section of the Home tab and choose Cut from there. You can also right-click and choose Cut from the dropdown menu.

As you'll recall, cutting text removes it from its current location but still allows you to paste that text elsewhere.

To copy text, highlight the text you want to copy and then use Ctrl + C or to go to the Clipboard section of the Home tab and choose Copy from there. You can also right-click and choose Copy from the dropdown menu.

Copying keeps the text in its current location but also allows you to paste that text elsewhere.

To paste text, click on the location where you want to place the text you copied or cut and then use Ctrl + V. If you paste text this way it will take on the formatting of the location where you paste it.

Your other options are to click where you want to paste the text and then either go to the Clipboard section of the Home tab and click on the arrow under Paste or right-click and choose one of the paste options from the dropdown menu.

The paste option with the lower case a in the bottom right corner (Use Destination Theme) will use the formatting of the location where you are pasting your text. So font, etc., but it might still keep the font size.

The option with the paintbrush in the bottom right corner (Keep Source Formatting) will keep the formatting the text already had.

The option with the small picture in the bottom right corner (Picture) will paste the selected text in as an image. (You will not be able to edit this text after it's pasted because it will no longer be considered text.)

The option with the large A in the bottom right corner (Keep Text Only), will paste the text into the presentation but use the formatting that would apply to any text you typed into that specific location.

Here I have taken the word Introduction from the title section of a slide and I have pasted it into four separate bullet points that were formatted to use 12 pt Algerian for the font. (So basically a different font, different font size, and different color.)

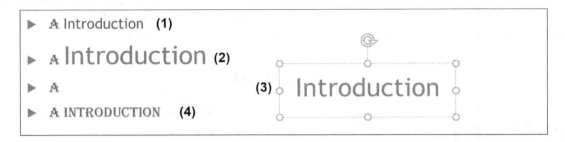

You can see that for Use Destination Theme (1) it changed the font size and color but not the font. For Keep Source Formatting (2) nothing changed. For Picture (3) it inserted the text exactly as it existed originally but as a picture. And for Keep Text Only (4) the font, font size, and font color all changed.

Ctrl + V gives the same result as the first line (1), so change of color and size but not font.

Basically, if you're moving text around you may need to do some formatting once it moves unless you remember to Paste – Keep Text Only.

Alright. That's copy/cut and paste. There are more specialized paste options available under the Clipboard option, but for a beginner level I don't think they're worth discussing here. If you want to look at them click on Paste Special from the dropdown to bring up the Paste Special dialogue box.

Delete Text

If you need to remove text you can either cut that text or you can use the Delete or Backspace keys. Backspace will delete text to the left of the cursor. Delete will delete text to the right of the cursor.

If you've highlighted the text you want to delete then either one will work.

Delete and Backspace can also delete bullet points or the numbers or letters in a numbered list.

Change Font Size

To adjust font size, you have a few options.

First, whichever option you use will require you to make the change before you start typing or to highlight any text you have already typed that you want to change. So do that.

Next, your first option is to go to the Font section of the Home tab and use the font size dropdown to choose a new font size. The current font size should appear in that box unless you've selected text that is more than one size. If that happens, the value will show the smallest font size with a plus sign next to it. So for me just now when I selected four levels of bullet points it showed as 12+ but when I then only selected the top two levels it showed as 16+.

You can either click on the dropdown arrow and select one of the listed font sizes or you can type in your own value.

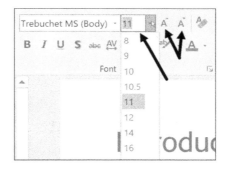

Another way to change the font size is located to the right of the dropdown. There are two capital A's with an arrow in the top right corner. One is to increase font size and the other is to decrease font size. Using those options will increase the font size or decrease it by one spot on the dropdown menu.

So if you have a 10 point font and use the increase font size option it will go up to 10.5 because that's the next available font size in the dropdown. But if you're at 14 it will take you to 16 and 36 will go to 40.

Another option you have is to right-click in the main workspace and use what I refer to as the mini formatting menu. It appears either directly above or directly below the dropdown menu and is a miniature version of the Font section of the Home tab. It has both the font size dropdown menu as well as the increase and decrease font options.

Finally, you can right-click in the main workspace and choose Font from the dropdown menu. This will bring up the Font dialogue box which has a Size option. You can either type in the value you want or use the up and down arrows to change the font size. The size will change by .1 with each use of the up or down arrows. So 14 will go to 14.1, for example.

Which means it'll generally be easier to just type in the value you want.

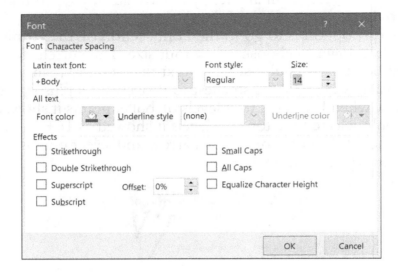

Change Font

In general I wouldn't recommend changing the font because the templates are built to work well with their assigned fonts. But it does sometimes need to be done. For example, a number of my corporate consulting clients have had fonts that they wanted used for all communications to create consistent branding.

As before, you either need to change the font choice before you start typing or you need to select the text you want to change.

Once you've done that, you have a few options for changing your font.

The first is in the Font section of the Home tab. There is a font dropdown menu which is to the left of the font size dropdown menu. In this example the font that's currently in use is Trebuchet MS. To change that font, click on the arrow for the dropdown menu and then click on the font you'd like to use.

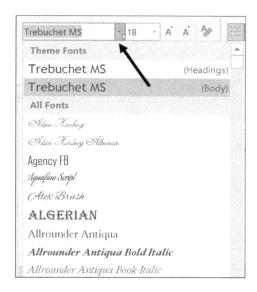

The name of each font in the dropdown menu is written in that font which should help give you an idea of which font to use. I would caution you against using a script (like Aquafina) or a stylized font (like Algerian) for the main text in a presentation slide. A presentation should be about conveying information and the text you use to do that shouldn't get in the way of your communication. Using an overly-ornate font distracts from the text and also from the speaker because your audience is too busy trying to read your slides instead of listen to you.

If you already know the font you want, you can click into the field that shows the current font and start typing the name of the font you'd like. As you type, PowerPoint will auto-complete the field. If you click on the dropdown arrow first and then click into that field and start typing the dropdown list of fonts will move to that part of the alphabet, which comes in handy when the font you want is later in the alphabet.

The mini formatting menu is another available option and works the same way as the Font section of the Home tab.

Or you can right-click and choose Font from the dropdown menu and then change the font choice in the Latin Text Font dropdown menu.

Change Font Color

Another adjustment you might need to make to your text is to change the color of the text. For example, when we discussed the Paste options above some of the options kept the original text color when what would've looked best is changing the font color to black to match the rest of the text in the main body of the slide.

As with all other font choices you either need to make this change before you start typing or you need to select the text you want to change.

Once you've done so click on the arrow next to the A that by default has a red underline in either the Font section of the Home tab or the mini formatting bar.

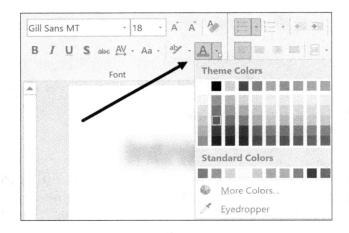

(That line may not always be red. It changes as you change your font color. So the first time you use it, the underline color will change to whatever the last color you used was. This can be useful because then you can just click on the A and apply that color again instead of having to use the dropdown menu each time.)

That initial dropdown menu allows you to choose from one of seventy available colors. Just click on the square for the color you want to use. If you're not sure how a color will look in your presentation, you can hold your mouse over it and your selected text will change to show the color. To apply it, though, you need to click on it.

The Theme Colors section will actually change what colors are shown to you based upon which theme and theme color palette you've chosen. Remember those six colors I mentioned at the bottom of each theme that don't seem to actually get used much? This is where you can find them and apply them yourself as well as shades of each color.

The Standard Colors will not change, however. And if you need a different or a custom color, you can click on the More Colors option which brings up the Colors dialogue box. Within that dialogue box, on the Standard tab you can choose from the honeycomb of colors available by clicking on any of the colored tiles. Or on the Custom tab you can input your own RGB or HSL values.

You can also click into the rainbow of colors above that to select a color or move the black and white slider for different shades of the current color.

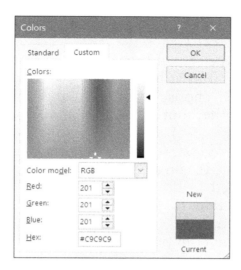

For either the Custom or Standard tab, the color you've selected will show under New in the bottom right corner of the Colors dialogue box and the color you were using previously will show under Current so you can compare them.

When I have corporate clients who have a specified color palette being able to apply the exact right shade of a color using the RGB values is incredibly helpful.

Another option available to you in PowerPoint is the eyedropper. This is for when you already have that color somewhere in your presentation and need to grab it for use elsewhere. For example, I've brought in a cover from a book into a PowerPoint slide so that I could grab the color I need from that cover so that my presentation is consistent with the book it's about.

To use the eyedropper click on the dropdown arrow for Font Color and then choose Eyedropper from the bottom of the dropdown menu. Next, click on the color you want to use from within your presentation. This will change any selected text to that color and will also add the color as a choice under Recent Colors in the Font Color dropdown menu.

Another option for changing your font color is to right-click on your presentation slide and choose Font from the dropdown menu to open the Font dialogue box. On the Font tab you can then click on the dropdown arrow for the Font Color option. It's identical to the other two choices except that it won't have the eyedropper option.

Bold Text

To bold text either select the text you want to bold or make your choice before you start typing.

The easiest option is to use Ctrl + B.

You can also click on the capital B in the bottom row of the Font section of the Home tab or the mini formatting menu.

Or you can right-click, choose Font from the dropdown menu, and then change the Font Style in the Font dialogue box to Bold. Use Bold Italic if you want both bold and italic.

To remove bolding from text, select the text and either click on the capital B or use Ctrl + B once more. If you select text that is partially bolded and partially not bolded, you may need to do this twice because the first time may apply bolding to the entire selection. If that happens then the second time will remove it from the entire selection.

You can also change the Font Style back to Regular in the Font dialogue box.

Italicize Text

To italicize text either select the text you want to italicize or make your choice before you start typing.

The easiest option is to use Ctrl + I.

You can also click on the slanted capital I in the bottom row of the Font section of the Home tab or the mini formatting menu.

Or you can right-click, choose Font from the dropdown menu, and then change the Font Style in the Font dialogue box to Italic. As above, use Bold Italic if you want both bold and italic.

To remove italics from text, select the text and either click on the slanted capital I or use Ctrl + I once more. If you select text that is partially italicized and partially not, you may need to do this twice.

You can also change the Font Style back to Regular in the Font dialogue box.

Underline Text

To underline text either select the text you want to underline or make your choice before you start typing.

The easiest option is to use Ctrl + U. This will place a single underline under your text.

You can also click on the underlined U in the bottom row of the Font section of the Home tab or the mini formatting menu.

If you want a wider variety of choices for how to underline your text, right-click and choose Font from the dropdown menu. You can then click on the arrow for the Underline Style dropdown and choose from a variety of underline styles including a double underline, a darker underline, as well as dashed, dotted, and wavy lines.

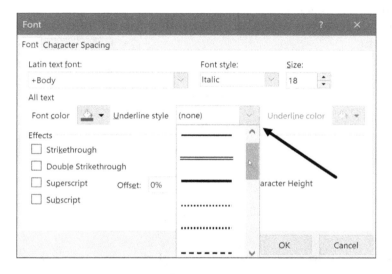

To remove underlining from text, select the text and either click on the capital U with a line under it or use Ctrl + U once more. If you select text that is partially underlined and partially not, you may need to do this twice. If the type of underline was a specialized underline and not the basic single-line style, you will also need to do this twice because the first time you use Ctrl + U or click on the U in the Font section it will convert the specialized underline to a standard single-line underline.

You can also go to the Font dialogue box and change the Underline Style to none, which is the first option.

Change Case

If you want your text to be in all caps or if you have text that is already in all caps that you want to change to normal case, then you will need to change the case of that text.

For this one you have to type the text first and then select it and make the change.

The change case option shows as a capital A followed by a lower-case a, so Aa, and is located in the bottom row of the Font section of the Home tab. It is not an option in the mini formatting menu.

Click on the dropdown arrow to see your available choices and then click on the one you want.

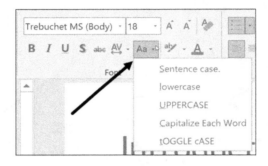

Each choice is written in that style. You can choose between sentence case, lower case, upper case, capitalize each word, and toggle case. (For a presentation unless you have a very good reason for doing so, do not use toggle case.)

Sentence case will capitalize the first letter of the first word in each sentence or text string.

Lower case will put all of the letters in lower case.

Upper case will put all of the letters in upper case.

Capitalize each word will capitalize the first letter of each word.

Toggle case will put the first letter of each word in lower case and all other letters in upper case.

Another option you have is to right-click and choose Font from the dropdown menu but that will only let you apply the upper case option. (By checking the box for all caps).

It does, however, also include an option for small caps which sometimes looks better than using upper case. See here for an example:

> ► ALL CAPS
>
> ► SMALL CAPS

Clear Text Formatting

If you've edited a text selection and want to return it to the default for that theme, you can select the text and then click on the small A with an eraser in the top right corner of the Font section. (If you hold your mouse over it, it will show as Clear All Formatting.)

This will change the selection to whatever font, font size, and font formatting would be appropriate for that location within that theme. It does not change the case of the letters if you used the dropdown menu in the Font section, but it will revert the font, font color, font size, and any bold, italics or underline back to the default for the theme.

Other

You'll note that there were a few other options available in the Font section of the Home tab (text shadowing, strikethrough, and character spacing) as well as additional options in the Font dialogue box.

I've chosen not to cover them here because I want to keep this guide focused on a basic level of PowerPoint presentation and those are ones I expect you wouldn't use as often.

But if there's a text effect you want to apply in a PowerPoint slide that I didn't cover, the Font section of the Home tab or right-clicking and choosing Font to bring up the Font dialogue box are generally where you'll find them.

For more advanced text formatting look to the Drawing Tools Format tab which will appear when you click on any text box in your presentation. There you can apply WordArt styles, text fills, text outlines, and text effects.

Okay. Now let's talk about paragraph-level formatting.

Format Paragraphs

What we just talked about are formatting changes that you can make at the level of an individual word. But there are other changes you can make at the paragraph level. These are generally available through the Paragraph section of the Home tab but some of them are also available in the mini formatting menu or by right-clicking and choosing Paragraph from the dropdown menu.

With the paragraph formatting options you don't have to highlight all of the text you want to change, you just need to be clicked somewhere into the paragraph or section you want to change.

Let's start with one we already covered earlier, Decrease List Level and Increase List Level.

Decrease List Level/Increase List Level

A lot of PowerPoint presentations rely on using bulleted lists. And when you use a bulleted list you will often want to either indent the next line or decrease the indent of the next line.

To indent the next line, you can either click at the beginning of the line and use the Tab key, or you can click anywhere on the line and use the Increase List Level option in the Paragraph section of the Home tab. It's the one that has an arrow pointing to the right at a series of lines.

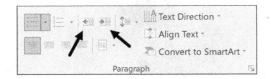

To decrease the indent on a line you can either click at the beginning of the line and use Shift + Tab (so hold down the Shift key and the Tab key at the same time) or you can click anywhere on the line and use the Decease List Level option in the Paragraph section of the Home tab. This is the one with a left-pointing arrow embedded in a series of lines.

If either option is grayed out that's because you can't increase or decrease that indent any further.

These options may or may not be available with plain text that isn't already bulleted or numbered. It will depend on where the text is located within the presentation slide. For example, you generally won't have an indent option in the title section of a slide.

If you have to use very specific placement for your text, you can also right-click and choose Paragraph from the dropdown menu and then use the Paragraph dialogue box to set your indent. It's the value for Before Text in the Indentation section.

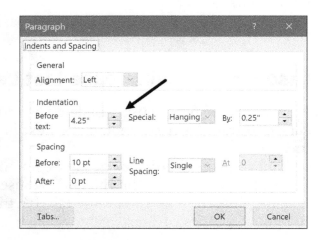

Hanging Indent

Next let's talk about setting a hanging indent or removing one since that's a visible option there in the Paragraph dialogue box and it can be useful to know. (Although keep in mind that if you're working with one of the pre-formatted themes it will likely already have these settings applied and the less you mess with them the better.)

A hanging indent has to do with where your lines of text will start when you have more than one line of text. This is generally used for bulleted and numbered items.

Here is an example where the paragraph is set to have a hanging indent so that the text on all of the lines starts at the same spot. See how the words "also", "development", and "seriously" line up?

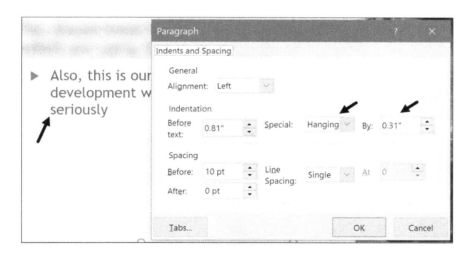

The amount of the indent required to make that happen will be driven by the font and font size. Also by the value you have for "before text".

For each bulleted level on this page the values in the "before text" and "by" fields is different. (This is why it's best not to mess with this and just let PowerPoint do all of it for you.)

If you remove a hanging indent for a bulleted item, it will look like this:

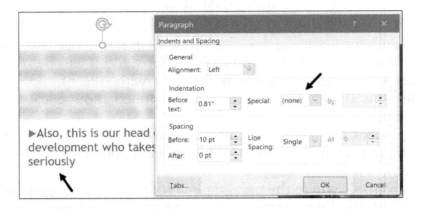

And if you change it to have a first line indent (depending on the value you use), it will look like this:

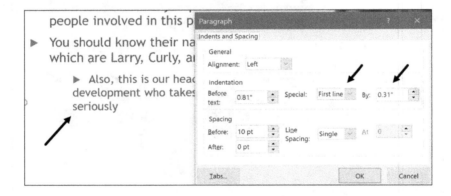

As I said before, I'd generally leave these settings alone, but I have had at least one employer who hadn't created a template for their staff to use, but insisted on very specific indenting for each bulleted item, and the only way to get what they wanted was to adjust these indentation settings.

Okay, then. On to paragraph alignment.

Paragraph Alignment

Your next option is to change the alignment of the text in your paragraph. You have four options.

You can have left-aligned text, meaning that the lines in your paragraph are aligned along the left-hand side.

You can have centered text, meaning each line is aligned along the center.

You can have right-aligned text, meaning each line is aligned along the right-hand side.

Or you can have justified text meaning your text will be spread out across the text box so that it's aligned along both the left- and right-hand side.

Here are examples using the same text where I've copied and pasted it four times and only changed the alignment and the descriptor (left-aligned, centered, etc.)

> ► This is to show you what **left-aligned** text looks like. We need enough text for you to really see how it works.
>
> ► This is to show you what **centered** text looks like. We need enough text for you to really see how it works.
>
> ► This is to show you what **right-aligned** text looks like. We need enough text for you to really see how it works.
>
> ► This is to show you what **justified** text looks like. We need enough text for you to really see how it works.

For bulleted points in the main body of the presentation you can see that left-aligned is generally going to be the choice you want, although justified can work as well. Centered is usually best for headers or titles.

To change the alignment of a paragraph, you can go to the Paragraph section of the Home tab and click on one of the alignment options in the bottom row. Each one is a series of lines that shows its alignment type. Click on the one you want to apply it.

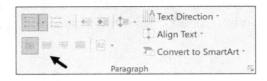

The left, center, and right alignment options are also available in the mini formatting menu.

Or you can right-click, choose Paragraph, and change the alignment using the dropdown menu in the General section. That dropdown has one more option, Distributed which will stretch your line of text across the entire space. I generally don't recommend that for a normal paragraph because the last line won't look good.

Depending on where your text is and what type of text box it is, your selected alignment will either apply to just that paragraph or to all of the contents of the text box. So if you want to use more than one alignment type on a slide (which I generally wouldn't recommend) you may need to use more than one text box to make that happen.

Text Alignment

In addition to setting your paragraph alignment you can also set how the text in a text box will align itself with respect to that text box. Your choices are top, middle, or bottom. Here are examples of each. I've clicked into the middle text box so you can see the outlines of the box. All three paragraphs are in identical text boxes that I've just copied and pasted side-by-side and then changed the alignment to top, middle, and bottom.

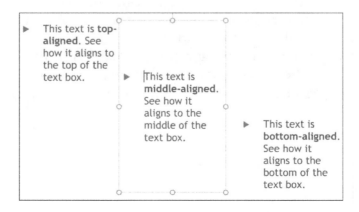

To choose which alignment option you want, go to the Paragraph section of the Home tab and click on the arrow next to Align Text on the right-hand side of the section. This will give you a dropdown menu where you can then click on either Top, Middle, or Bottom.

Your choice will apply to all text within that text box.

If you click on More Options that will open a Format Shape task pane where you can also choose to center the text at the same time.

Using Multiple Columns

If you want your text displayed on a slide in multiple columns you have two choices.

First, you can choose a slide layout that has two equally sized sections like the Two Content slide format and then input your text into both of those boxes, split evenly across the two boxes.

Or, you can use the multiple column formatting option. To split text into multiple columns, simply click anywhere within that text and then go to the Paragraph section of the Home tab and click on the arrow next to the Add or Remove Columns option. (This is the one in the center of the bottom row of that section that shows two sets of lines side by side with a dropdown arrow on the right-hand side.) It is directly to the right of the left, center, right, and justify paragraph options.

You can choose between One Column, Two Columns, Three Columns, or More Columns.

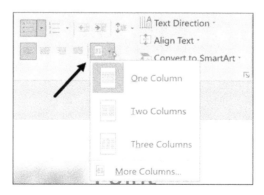

If you click on More Columns you can specify not only the number of columns, but the spacing between them.

The way multiple columns work is that PowerPoint will fill the first column completely before it moves on to putting text into the second column. It does not try to balance across your columns, nor does it make an effort to break a column at a bulleted or numbered point.

Since PowerPoint does not have column breaks like Word does, if you want a specific line to start your second column you have to manually make that happen by using Enter to move that line down far enough that it will move over to the second column.

Also, when you add multiple columns they will appear within that designated text box which can sometimes not look great if the text box is too narrow to really support multiple columns.

In some respects adding multiple text boxes to your slide is a better way to have the appearance of multiple columns while being able to better control the appearance of the text on your slide.

Change Spacing Between Lines of Text

If you want to change the amount of space that appears between lines of text, you can do so by clicking into the paragraph you want to change and then going to the Paragraph section of the Home tab and clicking on the arrow next to the Line Spacing option which is in the top row to the right of the increase list level option. It has arrows pointing upward and downward next to a set of lines.

Click on the dropdown arrow to see the available options. As you hold your mouse over each one you'll see what it looks like in the presentation itself. Click on one to select it.

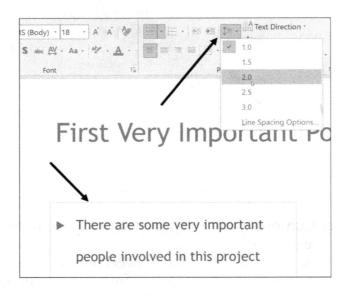

If you choose Line Spacing Options that will bring up the Paragraph dialogue box which can also be opened by right-clicking in the main workspace and choosing Paragraph from the dropdown menu there.

The line spacing options are available in a dropdown in the Spacing section of the dialogue box. In that section of the Paragraph dialogue box you can also change the values for Before and After to place space between your paragraphs.

Here, for example, I've changed the After value to 18 to place a large space between each of these items:

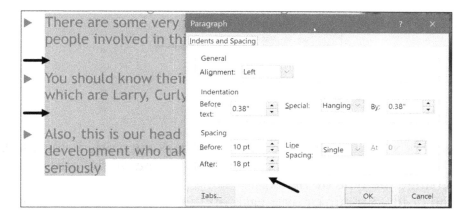

Bulleted Lists

By default, most of the templates include bullets within the main body of each presentation slide. If you want to change the type of bullet, turn off bullets for a specific line, add a bullet to a specific line, or change the bullets to numbers, then you can do so with the Bullets and Numbering options in the top left corner of the Paragraph section of the Home tab.

To change the type of bullet, click on the row you want to change or highlight all of your rows if there's more than one, and then go to the Bullets option (the one with dots next to lines in the top left corner of the Paragraph section of the Home tab) and click on the dropdown arrow.

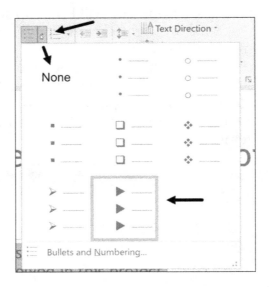

You'll see a box around the type of bullet that's currently being used. Click on None if you don't want a bulleted list. Click on one of the other options if you want to change the type of bullet.

You can hold your cursor over each option to see what it will look like before you make your selection.

Clicking on Bullets and Numbering at the bottom of that list will let you specify the size of the bullet relative to the text as well as the color of the bullet.

If you click on Customize that will let you choose any symbol from the Symbol dialogue box which gives you access to all of the symbols used in fonts like Wingdings which have a number of various shapes available. For example, I was able to change my bullets to a three-leaf clover just now.

The Picture option lets you insert a picture for your bullet.

(But remember that the more you customize things, the more work you have to do throughout your presentation to keep everything uniform and, also, that the you don't want to do something with the formatting of your presentation that distracts from the actual presentation. So, yes, I can in fact make bullets that are pictures of my dog, but that doesn't mean I should.)

Numbered Lists

If you want a numbered or lettered list instead (e.g., 1, 2, 3 or A, B, C) then click on the Numbering dropdown. There you can see a list of available numbered list options to choose from.

If you need to start at a number other than 1 or a letter other than A, click on Bullets and Numbering at the bottom of the list and then choose your starting point using the Start At box in the bottom right.

For lettered lists (A, B, C) when you change that numeric value for Start At it will change the letter. So a 1 equals A, a 2 equals B, etc.

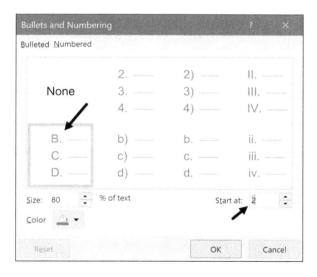

As with the bulleted list, you can also change the relative size of the number or letter compared to the list and change the color of the letter or number using this dialogue box.

Another option for changing both bullets or numbering is to right-click and go to either Bullets or Numbering in the dropdown menu. There is a secondary dropdown that is identical to the one you'll find for each in the Paragraph section of the Home tab.

Format Painter

If you ever find yourself in a situation where the formatting on one section of your presentation or your slide doesn't match another and you don't want to be bothered trying to figure out exactly what the differences are, you can use the Format Painter to copy the formatting from one block of text to another.

This tool can be a lifesaver if someone has done weird things in a presentation you're trying to fix.

To use it, first highlight the text that's formatted the way you want. Next, click on the Format Painter option in the Clipboard section of the Home tab. Then highlight the text that you want to transfer the formatting to.

Font, font size, font color, line spacing, and type of bulleting/numbering should all copy over to the selected text.

You will know that the format painter is on when you see a small paint brush next to your cursor. It will normally turn off the next time you click on text in your presentation, so be sure to go directly to the text you want to transfer the formatting to and highlight all of the text when you do so.

If you have more than one place you want to transfer formatting to, you can double-click on the Format Painter tool and then it will remain on until you turn it back off. To turn it off use the Esc key or click on Format Painter in the Clipboard section of the Home tab once more.

If the result isn't what you wanted or expected use Ctrl + Z to undo it and try again. Sometimes with paragraphs of text it can matter whether you selected the initial paragraph from the top or from the bottom. Same with the paragraph you're transferring the formatting to.

Also, if I want spacing between paragraphs to transfer I always try to select more than one paragraph before I click on the Format Painter.

Add Other Items To a Presentation Slide

Now that we've covered how to add and format text in your presentation let's discuss what other options you have.

If you look at a blank content slide that hasn't had any text added to it yet, you'll see in the center of the text box that there's usually a series of faded images. For example, this is from a text box in a Two Content slide:

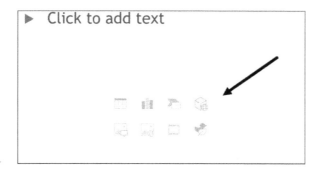

These are the options you have other than just typing text into that box. Your options are Insert Table, Insert Chart, Insert a SmartArt Graphic, 3D Models, Pictures, Online Pictures, Insert Video, and Insert an Icon.

Once you choose one of these options you can't then place text in that area. It's one or the other. (Although you could add a text box to the slide and put in text that way if you wanted. That's intermediate-level so we're not going to cover it here but the option can be found in the Text section of the Insert tab.)

We're not going to cover all of those options in this guide, just adding a table and inserting a picture, but they all work on the same principle and it's good to know they exist.

Alright, then. On to adding a table.

Tables

The first option in that set of images is Insert Table.

   Click on it and you'll see the Insert Table dialogue box. It lets you specify the number of columns and rows you want in your table. Below you can see the dialogue box as well as the table that was inserted into the slide using five columns and five rows after I clicked on OK.

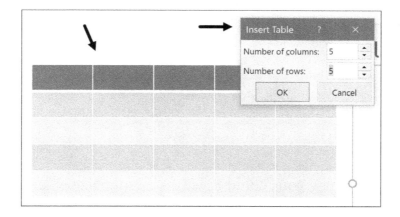

Background Color

By default for this theme, the first row is in a different color because it's a header row for the table. The remaining rows are in alternating colors.

   The colors used are consistent with the presentation theme. You can change the colors used in your table under the Table Tools Design tab.

The Table Styles options provide various layouts that use the color palette of the presentation theme. Or you can select all of the cells in the table or a subset of cells, like a row, and use the Shading option to choose a new background color that way.

The Shape Fill option in the mini formatting menu can also be used to change the background color of selected cells.

Font Color

Font color should be set to work with the original background colors. For example on this table the header row uses a white font color but the main body of the table uses a black font color.

That color can be changed on the Home tab or via the mini formatting menu just like any other text. Either select the text you want to change first or make the color change after you click into a cell but before you start typing.

Add Text or Numbers to Your Table

To add information to the table, click into any of the cells in the table and start typing. If you enter text that is wider than the width of the column, it will automatically flow down to another line and the row height will change to make sure all of the text is visible. Like so:

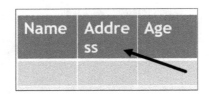

You may need to change your column widths or font size when this happens to better display the text since, as you can see above, having the word "Address" break across that line is not ideal.

If you have your information in an existing table in Word or Excel, you can copy the information from that table into PowerPoint by highlighting the cells in Word or Excel, using copy (Ctrl + C), and then clicking into the first cell in the PowerPoint table where you want to place that information and using paste (Ctrl + V).

If the data you want to paste into your presentation has more columns than the table, PowerPoint will add additional columns. Same with the number of rows. The text in the table will resize to fit on the slide, so it's best to bring in your information first and then format from there.

If you have fewer columns or rows, PowerPoint will just paste your data into the number of columns or rows needed for the data.

PowerPoint is not set up to format numbers well, so I find that it is easier when dealing with numeric data to do that in Excel.

Align Text Within Cells

If after you've entered text into your table you want to change the alignment of the text so that it's centered or left-aligned, etc. you can do this by highlighting the cells you want to change, going to the Table Tools Layout tab, and going to the Alignment section.

The top row where you see the three options with lines is where you can choose to left-align, center, or right-align text. The second row where you see the three boxes with lines in them is where you can choose to place text at the top, center, or bottom of each cell.

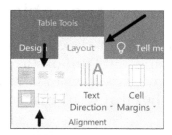

Add Rows or Columns

If you need additional rows in your table, simply use the tab key from the last cell in the last row of the table and PowerPoint will add a new line.

You can also highlight a row, go to the Rows & Columns section of the Table Tools Layout tab, and choose Insert Above or Insert Below.

To add a column, highlight an existing column and choose Insert Left or Insert Right.

You can also highlight a row or column and right-click to bring up the mini formatting menu which has an Insert dropdown with all four choices.

Delete Rows or Columns

To delete a row or column from a table, you can highlight the row or column and use the backspace key. You can also highlight the row or column and then right-click and choose Cut or use the Delete dropdown menu on the mini formatting menu.

Another option is to click into a cell in that row or column, go to the Table Tools Layout tab, and under the Rows & Columns section click on the dropdown arrow under Delete. From there you can choose Delete Columns, Delete Rows, or Delete Table.

Delete the Table

To delete the entire table, right-click on the table and use the Delete option in the mini formatting menu to choose Delete Table.

Or right-click on the table and choose Select Table from the dropdown and then use the Delete or Backspace key.

Or click on the table and then use the Delete dropdown in the Rows & Columns section of the Table Tools Layout tab.

Move the Table

Click on the table to select it. Or right-click and choose Select Table. Hold your mouse over the edge of the table until it looks like a four-sided arrow and then left-click and drag the table to where you want it. Keep in mind that you can drag it on top of another text box but that won't make it part of that text box.

Column Width

To change the width of a column, click on a cell in the column and go to the Cell Size section of the Table Tools Layout tab and change the value for Width. This will change the overall width of the table.

You can also hold your mouse over the right-hand side of the column in the table itself until the cursor looks like two parallel lines with arrows pointing off to the sides and then left-click and drag to your desired width. This will change the width of that column and the one to its right, but not the overall size of the table unless you were resizing the final column in the table.

You can also double-left click along that edge to get the column to automatically resize to the width of the text that's currently in the column. This will also change the width of the table at the same time.

Row Height

To change the height of a row, click on a cell in the row and go to the Cell Size section of Table Tools Layout tab and change the value for Height. You cannot change a row height to a value that would hide any text in that row.

Another option is to hold your mouse over the bottom edge of the row in the table itself until the cursor looks like two parallel lines with arrows pointing up and down and then left-click and drag to your desired height. Once again, you will be limited in how short you can make the row by any existing text in that row and also by the font size for text in that row.

With both methods, only the height of that row will change which means the table height will also change.

Resize the Table

To change the dimensions of an entire table, you can click on the table and then left-click and drag from any of the white circles around the edge of the table. Be sure that you have a white double-sided arrow when you do so or you may just end up moving the table around.

Clicking on one of the white circles in the corner will allow you to resize the table proportionately as long as you click and drag at an angle.

You can also click on the table and go to the Table Tools Layout tab and change the dimensions for the table in the Table Size section.

If you want to resize the table and have the relative height and width of the table stay the same, click the Lock Aspect Ratio box first. When you do that PowerPoint will adjust both measurements at once to keep the ratio of height to width for the table constant.

Split Cells in a Table

You can take one or more cells in a table and split them into multiple cells. To do this, highlight the cell or cells you want to split, go to the Table Tools Layout tab, and click on Split Cells in the Merge section.

This will bring up the Split Cells dialogue box which lets you specify how many columns and rows you want each cell split into.

The choice you make will apply to each cell you selected. So if you select four cells and tell it to split them into two columns and one row, each of those four cells will be split into two columns and one row giving you eight cells total.

You can also bring up the Split Cells dialogue box by right-clicking and choosing Split Cells from the dropdown menu.

Merge Cells in a Table

You can also merge cells in a table which combines the selected cells into one.

In this case, highlight the cells that you want to merge, go to the Table Tools Layout tab, and choose Merge Cells from the Merge section. All of the cells will be combined into one and any text that was in those cells will be shown in the newly-merged cell with one row per line of text working from left to right and top to bottom of the old cell range.

Another option is to select the cells you want to merge, right-click, and choose Merge Cells from the dropdown menu.

Table Design

We already touched on this a bit, but the Table Tools Design tab will let you control the appearance of your table.

You can change the borders around and within your table using the Borders dropdown. Before you apply a border be sure to change the line width, style, and color in the Draw Borders section if you want those settings to be different from the default settings..

Also, the Table Style Options section will let you turn on or off banded rows in your table. (This is where each row of the table has an alternating color.)

You can also turn on or off banded columns which applies alternating colors to each column.

I do not recommend having alternating rows and alternating columns on at the same time.

In the Table Style Options section you can also adjust the settings so that the last row (total row), first column, or last column are formatted differently by checking the boxes for those options.

Pictures

The option directly below Insert Table is Pictures. Click on it and you'll see the Insert Picture dialogue box. By default it will open in your Pictures folder on your computer, but you can navigate from there to any location where the picture you want is stored.

If you click on the All Pictures dropdown option next to the File Name box you can see the picture file types that PowerPoint will accept. (Which looks to be pretty much any type you can image.)

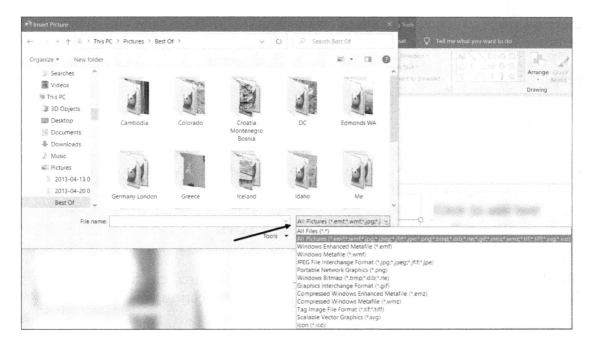

Navigate to where the picture you want is saved, click on the picture, and then choose Insert. This will insert that picture into that text box. It will be centered.

You can also click on the arrow next to Insert and choose to link your photo instead, but I'd generally advise against that because it's far too easy to break a link like that. For example, you link to an image and then copy your presentation to a thumb drive so you can use it on the provided laptop at the conference center and suddenly there are no images in your presentation and you're standing in front of five hundred people not knowing why. (Or knowing why but also knowing it's too late to fix it.)

Better usually to just put the image into your presentation. The reasons to link instead of insert are if you think the image may be updated at some point outside of PowerPoint or if you are using a large number of images and need to keep the file size down. For a printed presentation it won't be a problem. For a presentation you're presenting be sure you have access to those images at the time of your presentation.

Okay, then.

The image you chose will insert into your slide at a size that fits within the text box where you chose to insert it. If the image is smaller than the active area it will insert at its current size, but if it's larger than the active area it will be scaled down.

(This is for when you use the Pictures icon to insert an image into a text box. You can also go to the Insert tab and choose Pictures from the Images section there to insert a picture on a blank slide. In that case the image you insert will be centered in the presentation slide and may fit the entire slide if it's large enough.)

Now let's discuss what you can do with a picture you've inserted into your presentation.

Move a Picture

To move your image, left-click on it and drag it to the location you want. (It will take the text box it was inserted into with it, but if you then delete the image, the text box will reappear in its original location.)

Resize a Picture

You can also resize a picture after you insert it into your slide. If you have specific dimensions that you want to use, click on the image and go to the Picture Tools Format tab. At the far end you'll see the Size section.

Change either the height or the width and the image will resize proportionately, meaning that PowerPoint will adjust the other measurement to keep the height to width ratio the same. This is a good thing because it prevents the image from becoming distorted or skewed.

You can also click onto the image and then left-click on any of the white circles around the perimeter and drag until the image is the size you want. This will not resize the image proportionately, so you can easily end up with a distorted image if you do it this way. But if you click on a corner and drag at an angle that usually will keep the height and width proportional because you are resizing the image on both dimensions at once. (If you don't like the result, use Ctrl + Z to undo.)

Another option is to right-click on the image and choose Size and Position. This will open a Format Picture task pane on the right-hand side of your workspace, which includes fields for Height and Width. You can uncheck the Lock Aspect Ratio box if you want to change one measure independent of the other.

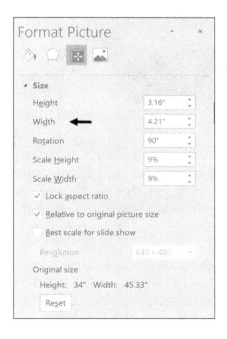

Also, you can reset the image to its original appearance from here, but be careful because that will remove the settings PowerPoint applied to the image as well. So if it resized it to fit that text box or changed the image orientation, that will be lost too.

The Format Picture task pane can also be accessed by clicking on the expansion arrow in the Size section of the Picture Tools Format tab.

Rotate a Picture

If you want to rotate the picture that you inserted, click on the image and then click on the little white outline of an arrow circling to the right that will be visible along the edge or top of the image.

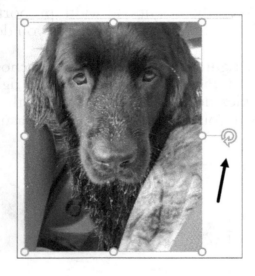

Click and hold this while you move your cursor in the direction you want to rotate the image and it will rotate along with your mouse.

Your other option is to click on the image and then go to the Picture Tools Format tab and click on the dropdown arrow next to Rotate in the Arrange section.

You can choose from there to rotate the image 90 degrees right or left or flip the image vertically or horizontally.

If you need more options than that, click on More Rotation Options to bring up the Format Picture task pane on the right-hand side of the screen. Rotation is the third option in the Size section. You can click into the box there and set the rotation to any value you want from 1 degree to 360 degrees.

(Technically it lets you set a value from -3600 degrees to 3600 degrees, but a circle is only 360 degrees, so...)

Crop a Picture

Sometimes I'll drop a picture into a presentation and then realize that I didn't want the entire picture, I just wanted a section of it. (This is especially true when I take screenshots of Excel using Print Screen and then want to just keep a small section of that screenshot for my presentation.) In those cases, I need to crop the image to only show the portion I care about.

To crop an image, right-click on the image and choose Crop from the mini formatting bar. You should then see small black bars on each side of the image and at the corners. Be sure when you click and drag that the cursor looks like a bar, because otherwise you might end up resizing the image instead. (If so, Ctrl + Z to undo and try again.)

Left-click on those bars and drag until only the portion of the image that you want to keep is fully visible. (The area that will be cropped away will be grayed out but still partially visible like bottom portion of the image below.)

To permanently apply the crop to your image, click away or hit Esc.

If you start to crop your image and realize that you want a different portion of the image in the visible area, you can click and drag on the image to move it around. The part that will remain after you finish will still be fully visible but the rest will be grayed out.

This is especially useful if you insert an image and PowerPoint crops the image for you, because it doesn't always know what part of the image you want visible. Choosing to crop but not actually doing so will let you move that image around until the portion of the image you want visible is in the active area.

Your other option for cropping is to go to the Picture Tools Format tab and choose Crop from the Size section. The first option in the dropdown is a simple crop.

For an image that's already been cropped, the full image will appear with the cropped space already marked. This makes it relatively easy to fix the cropping of an image if you get it wrong the first time since you can just choose to crop again and then drag the image or the bars to the correct location.

In the Crop dropdown in the Picture Tools Format tab you also have the option to crop to a shape or crop to a specific aspect ratio but those are more advanced options that we're not going to cover here.

Bring Forward/Send Backward

If you are ever in a situation where you have images or text boxes that overlap (which if you're using a standard template would only happen if you moved something around), you may need to use the bring forward or send backward options.

Visualize the layers of text and images in your presentation as a stack of playing cards. You're only going to see what's visible from the top of the stack. Which means if you shuffle those cards into a different order, you will see something different.

So, for example, if you have a layer with a picture that you want to be in the background of a layer with text, then you would want to place the picture layer behind the text layer. You could do this by using one of the Send Backward options to position the layer with the picture behind the layer with text.

You could get the same result by using one of the Bring Forward options on the text layer.

The Bring Forward and Send Backward options are available in the Arrange section of the Picture Tools Format tab. There is a dropdown for each one.

Send Backward has the choice to Send Backward, which will move a layer back one spot, or to Send to Back, which will make that layer the bottom layer.

Bring Forward has the option to Bring Forward, which will move a layer up one spot, or Bring to Front, which will make it the topmost layer.

The Bring Forward and Send Backward options are also available by right-clicking on an image and choosing them from the dropdown menu.

I should note here that sometimes Bring Forward and Send Backward didn't perform the way I expected them to, but Bring to Front and Send to Back always did. So if you get stuck with that issue as well, you should be able to stack your layers in any order you want by strategically applying the Bring to Front and Send to Back options. Not as easy, but it works.

Alignment

You can align images to one another or you can align them with respect to the presentation slide itself. If you're using a template and bringing in images as part of a text box, you shouldn't really need to use this, but the option does exist under the Align option in the Arrange section of the Picture Tools Format tab.

You can choose to align left (place the image along the left-hand side of the slide), align center (place the image in the center of the slide as judged from left to right), align right (place the image along the right-hand side of the slide), align top (place the image along the top edge of the slide), align middle (place the image in the center of the slide as judged from top to bottom), or align bottom (place the image along the bottom edge of the slide).

Distribute horizontally will center the image judged from left to right. Distribute vertically will center the image judged from top to bottom. Where this one matters is when you have multiple images selected at once. If you have multiple images selected at once then it will take those images and distribute them either across the width of the slide (horizontally) or from top to bottom (vertically) so that there is equal space between the images and the edges of the slide.

If you do have multiple images, you can select those images, and then under Align choose Align Selected Objects and instead of aligning the objects to the presentation slide it will align them to one another. So, for example, align right would move the left-hand object into alignment with the right-hand object.

Picture Styles

There is a Picture Styles section in the Picture Tools Format tab. Most of the styles involve placing a frame around the image, but some of them also involve skewing the image or adding a shadow to the image so that it looks three-dimensional.

To apply a picture style, click on your image and go the Picture Styles section of the Picture Tools Format tab. Hold your mouse over each style to see what it will look like when applied to your image. Click on one if you want to actually apply it.

Adjust a Picture

PowerPoint provides a number of options for adjusting an image. As with most things, I will advise you against getting too out of control with the special effects. There are industries where that may be warranted, but most times you want to present your information in as clear and succinct a way as possible.

Having said that, click on an image and then go to the Picture Tools Format tab and you'll see on the far left-hand side that there is a section called Adjust.

The Corrections option will allow you to sharpen or soften an image as well as adjust the brightness/contrast of the image.

The Color option will allow you to change the saturation or tone of your image as well as recolor your image.

Artistic Effects allows you to adjust your image so that it looks like a marker drawing, pencil sketch, etc.

For all three options, click on the dropdown arrow to see how each choice will impact your image.

(As a side note, if you really need to do something like this I'd recommend using an image software program instead and then bringing in the already-edited image but I do know that some people do design work in PowerPoint itself. This is where you'd go to do so.)

Animations

If you have a presentation slide with multiple bullet points it's often very useful to have those bullet points appear one at a time. This way people listen to what you're saying instead of trying to read ahead on the slide and see what you're going to say next.

To do this, first go to the slide where you want to add animation. Next, click on the first line of text that you want to have appear and go to the Animations tab. Click on one of the options in the Animation section.

I recommend using Appear. It simply shows the line without any fancy tricks which can be distracting.

Once you apply animation to one bulleted point in your slide, PowerPoint will apply it to the remainder of the items in your slide.

The order in which those items will appear is shown by the way they are numbered. All items numbered 1 will appear first, then all items numbered 2, then all items numbered 3, etc.

So in the example below we have three bulleted items, each of which will appear one at a time starting with the top bullet.

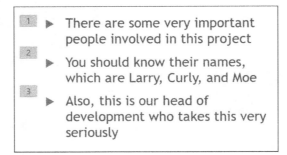

The appearance of the next item is usually triggered by hitting Enter, using the down arrow on your keyboard, or left-clicking to advance through the slide as you present.

If you have indented lines of text, so sub-bullets, you will probably need to fix their numbering because by default they will appear at the same time as their "parent" line.

This is probably best understood visually. See below:

All three lines of text in the image above have a 1 next to them. That means they're all going to appear together which I generally do not want because that means my audience will be reading ahead instead of listening to me.

To fix this, click into the slide, go to the Animations tab and click on the expansion arrow for the Animation section.

This will bring up the Appear dialogue box.

In that dialogue box, click on the Text Animation tab, which is the third one. There will be a dropdown option at the top labeled Group Text. Click on that and choose one of the other grouping levels.

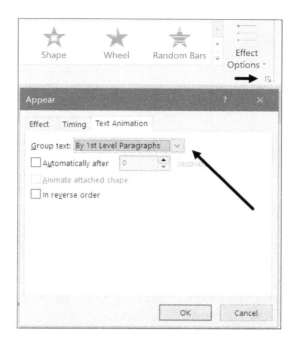

Depending on how many levels of bullets you have on the slide you will probably need the "By 2nd Level Paragraphs" or the "By 3rd Level Paragraphs" option to get all lines of text to appear individually. Once you've made your choice, click on OK.

The slide will now show adjusted numbering based upon your choice. With 3rd Level Paragraphs that means the first three level of bullets are treated as separate lines that appear one at a time instead of grouped together.

By default, a picture will appear when the slide appears. If instead you want your picture to appear after your text, then you need to also apply animation to the picture. You do so the same way you would with your text by clicking on an animation choice in the Animation tab.

If the picture is the first item you applied animation to it will be numbered 1. If you apply animation to it after you apply animation to your text, it will be set to appear after all of your text.

To change the order in which your different elements appear on the slide, go to the Animations tab and click on Animation Pane in the Advanced Animation section.

This will bring up the Animation Pane task pane, which will show all of your elements and the order in which they appear.

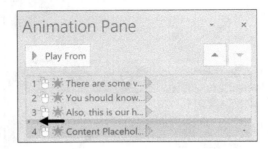

(You may have to click on the small double arrow under a numbered section to see all of your numbered options from your slide. In the image above I've already done that so clicking on it again would hide them.)

To change the order of your elements, click on one of the elements listed and then use the up and down arrows at the top to move that element up or down.

You can also change the level at which your text is grouped in this pane by clicking on the arrow next to one of the text elements and then choosing Effect Options from the dropdown menu.

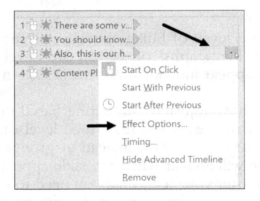

That will bring up the Appear dialogue box.

If you want to have some of your bullet points appear together but others appear separately, the best way I know to do this is to set up the slide as if everything will appear separately and then highlight the rows you want to have appear together and click on your chosen animation option once more. This will change the numbering of those items so that they all are grouped together.

There are other things you can do with animation that we're not going to cover here, such as have each bullet point appear on its own on a timed schedule. But for this beginner guide I just wanted you to know how to structure your slides so that each point you want to make appears separately.

If you click on the downward-pointing arrow with a line under it to expand the animations box you'll see that there is actually a variety of animation choices. Some animations are for bringing in text or images, some are for emphasizing what's already there, and some are for taking it away. The different categories are color-coded with green for entrance, yellow for emphasis, and red for exit.

You can see what each animation will look like by applying it. It will automatically run once when you do so. If it doesn't or you want to see it again later, click on the Preview option in the left-hand corner of the Animations tab and your animations for that slide should re-run.

I know it's tempting to try to make a presentation more interesting with things like this, but if you can't engage your audience with what you're saying then fix what you're saying instead.

I would strongly urge you to keep to just using Appear as your animation option. You can absolutely have your bullet points fly in or even bounce in (please, no), but ask yourself if that's appropriate for your audience.

If you're presenting to first graders, sure, have a bullet point bounce in. But a potential business client? Eh. Or a group of your professional peers? Uh-uh. Don't do it. Don't fall for the temptation.

Okay since we're talking about how to make a presentation "professional", let's talk about a few design principles to keep in mind as well while we're at it.

Design Principles

I've touched on this a few times, but I think it's good to take a chapter and discuss some basic design principles to keep in mind as you're preparing your presentation. I'm going to assume here that you're actually intending to use your PowerPoint presentation as a presentation. Meaning, you're going to talk through it and not expect it to talk for you, and that the slides are going to be presented on a projector of some sort to a live audience.

(In other words, I'm not addressing the consulting model of using PowerPoint where you put together a weekly client presentation on a series of slides that you hand out to your client and pack full of information and then walk through even though the client could just read the darned things themselves without paying you thousands of dollars for you to be there while they do it.)

Font Size

Make sure that all of the text on your slide will be visible to anyone in the room. I'd try to have all of the text be 14 point or larger if you can manage it.

Font Type

As with all other design elements it can be tempting to use a fancy font. Resist the temptation. You want a basic, clear, easy-to-read font for your presentation elements. This means using something like Arial or Calibri or Times New Roman instead of something like Algerian.

Summaries Instead of Explanations

The text on your slide should be there as a general outline of what you're going to say, not contain the full text of what you want to say. Think of each bullet point as a prompt that you can look at to trigger your recollection.

The reason you do it this way is because people will try to read whatever you put in front of them. So if you give them a slide full of text they will be busy reading that text rather than listening to what you have to say.

Also, if it's all on the slide, why listen to you at all?

So use the text on your slide as a high-level summary of your next point instead of as an explanation.

For example, I might have a slide titled "The Three Stages of Money Laundering" and then list on that slide three bullet points, "Placement", "Layering", and "Integration". As I show each bullet point I'll discuss what each of those stages is and how it works. If I feel a need to really go into detail then I'll have a separate slide for each one where I provide further information in small bite-sized chunks.

Contrast

You want your text to be visible. Which means you have to think about contrast. If you have a dark background, then use a light-colored text. For example, dark blue background, white text. If you have a light background, use a dark-colored text. For example, white background, black text.

And beware of anything that could trip up someone with color-blindness. So no red on green or green on red and no blue on yellow or yellow on blue.

Also, and this may be more of a personal preference, but I try to use the slide templates that have white for the background behind the text portions of my slides. I'm fine with colorful borders and colorful header sections, but where the meat of the presentation is I prefer to have a white background often with black text. (That's the easiest combination to read.)

So I'll choose the Ion Boardroom theme before I'll choose the Ion theme, for example.

Don't Get Cute

PowerPoint has a lot of bells and whistles. You can have lines of text that fly in and slide in and fade away. Or slides that flash in or appear through bars. And some of the templates it provides are downright garish.

Resist the urge to overdo it.

Ask yourself every time you're tempted to add some special effect if adding it will improve the effectiveness of your presentation. And ask yourself what your boss's boss's boss would think of your presentation. I've worked in banking and regulatory environments and I will tell you there is little appreciation in those environments for overly-bright colors and flashy special effects. (Whereas some tech company environment where the CEO wears jeans and t-shirts to work may be all for that kind of thing. Know your audience.)

I do think that using the animation option to have one bullet point appear at a time is a good idea. But you can do that with the Appear option. You don't need Fade, Fly In, Float In, Split, Wipe, etc.

And, yes, it can sometimes feel boring to use the same animation for a hundred slides in a row. But remember the point of your presentation is to convey information to your audience. Anything that doesn't help you do that should go.

Other Tips and Tricks

Now that we've walked through the basics of creating your presentation, let's cover a few other things you might want to do, starting with adding notes to your slides.

Add Notes To A Slide

If you add notes to your slides you can then print a notes version of those slides that lets you see not just the slide that your audience sees but any additional comments. So if you're worried about forgetting something but don't want too much text on your slide? Put it in a note.

There is also a display option that lets you see the notes on your screen but not have them appear to the audience. Either one is a great option when you have points you want to be sure to make but don't want to clutter up your slides.

To use notes, though, you first have to add them.

The Notes portion of the presentation is not visible by default, but if you look at the bottom middle of your workspace you should see a little item that says Notes. Click on that and a task pane that says "Click to add notes" will open below your slide.

Click there and start typing to add your notes.

The other option to open or close the Notes task pane is to go to the Show section of the View tab and click on Notes. If the task pane was already open it will close, if it wasn't it will appear.

Spellcheck

It's always a good idea to run spellcheck on anything you create for an audience. To check the spelling in your document, go to the Proofing section of the Review tab and click on Spelling. (It's on the far left-hand side.)

PowerPoint will then walk through your entire document flagging spelling errors and repeated words.

If there are no errors you'll see a dialogue box that tells you the spell check is complete. Click OK to close it.

If there are errors, the Spelling task pane will open and for each one PowerPoint will show a suggested change and highlight the word it flagged in the slide itself. For example, here I had the word "is" twice in a row:

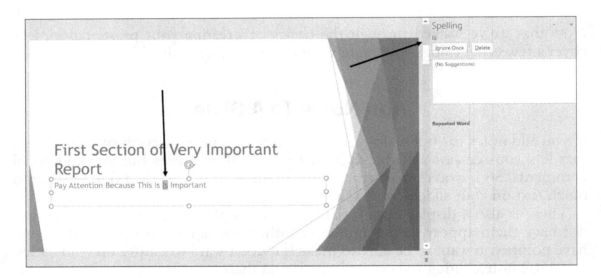

If you don't want to make the suggested change, click on Ignore.

For spelling errors PowerPoint will give you the choice to Ignore All or to Ignore Once. Ignore Once when you just want it to skip this one instance; Ignore All when you want it to skip the word everywhere it occurs in the presentation. For example, I often have to tell Office programs to ignore my first name because it almost always flags it as a spelling error.

That does bring up the third option you'll get with a spelling error which is Add. This will add the word to your version of PowerPoint's dictionary so that the word is never flagged as a spelling error again. So if there's some term that's common to your industry but not in the PowerPoint dictionary you can add the word and then it won't be flagged in any of your presentations. In contrast, Ignore All just applies to the current presentation.

For any issues it flags, PowerPoint will suggest solutions, like above where it gave the option to delete the duplicate word. Click on that option to apply the solution.

With spelling errors, if it can identify a close enough word it will suggest alternatives like here where I misspelled "regret" as "regert" and it suggested four possible words I might have meant.

Spelling
regert

Ignore Once   Ignore All   Add

regret
revert
regent
regrets

Change   Change All

regret
• remorse
• disappointment
• be sorry

To replace the current word with one of the suggestions, click on the suggested word and then click on Change to change this one instance or Change All to change all uses of the misspelled word in the document.

Be careful with Change All and Ignore All. It's possible to miss an error by using one of those options. Also, spellcheck is not infallible. There are times when I've spelled a word wrong but it created another word that was in the dictionary and so PowerPoint didn't flag it. (I really do wish they had spellcheck for certain lowkey cusswords since at least one seems to be pretty easy to use inadvertently.) A good reminder to always read your presentation when you're done. Technology can only do so much.

Find

If you need to find a specific reference in your slides you can use Find to do so. The Find option is in the Editing section of the Home tab (on the far right-hand side). Click on Find and the Find dialogue box will appear.

You can also open the Find dialogue box by using Ctrl + F.

Type the word you want into the white text box under "Find What" and then click on Find Next. PowerPoint will walk you through the entire document moving to the next instance of that word each time you click on Find Next.

You can sometimes save time by choosing to just search for whole words only or to just search for words with the same capitalization (match case). For example, in my industry CAT is a term that is used at times for consolidated audit trail. When I want to find that term in a presentation I match case and find whole words only so I don't have to wade through words like catastrophe or catalog.

Replace Text

If you need to replace text within your slides you can use Replace. This essentially pairs the Find option with an option that takes the word you were searching for and replaces it with another. You can either launch the Replace dialogue box by using Ctrl + H or by going to the Editing section of the Home tab and clicking on Replace.

When you do this you'll see the Replace dialogue box.

The "Find what" box is what you are looking for. The "Replace with" box is what you want to put in its place.

The match case and find whole words only options are helpful when using Find but essential when using Replace. I have seen more than one very awkward instance of replace that went wrong. For example, I mentioned above that CAT is a term I might search for. Think what would happen if I replaced all instances of "cat" with "consolidated audit trail" including in the word catalog.

For replace you can replace your instances of a word one at a time by using the Replace option or you can replace them all at once using Replace All. Be careful with this. And be sure to read the whole presentation if you use Replace All.

Replacing text is easy to do and easy to mess up.

Replace Font

If you go to the Editing section of the Home tab and click on the dropdown arrow next to Replace you'll see that there is an option there to Replace Fonts.

Click on that option to bring up the Replace Font dialogue box. It will show you two dropdown menus.

The first dropdown is where you select the font that is in your presentation that you want to replace. It should only show the fonts used in your presentation. (But don't worry if it shows one or two you didn't think you were using. They may be used somewhere you can't see.)

The second dropdown is where you choose the font you want to replace it with.

Once you've selected both fonts, click on Replace and every usage of the first font will be replaced with the second font. This can come in very handy if you have a corporate requirement to use a specific font that wasn't followed when the presentation was created. (Ask me how I know…)

Just be sure to then look back through your presentation and make sure everything looks "right", because different fonts take up different amounts of space. It's possible that changing over the font could impact the appearance of your slides.

Presentation Size

PowerPoint gives you the choice between two presentation sizes. The standard size is 4:3 and the widescreen size is 16:9. You can also choose a custom slide size.

All of these choices are available in the Customize section of the Design tab on the far right side where it says Slide Size. Click on the dropdown arrow to make your choice.

(If you click on the Custom Slide Size option you can even make a presentation that is in portrait orientation, so like a normal printed report, rather than in landscape orientation. Although, if you're going to do this do it before you start putting together your slides or you'll have a complete mess to fix up. This would not be a good choice for a presentation that's going to be projected on a screen, but could be an interesting idea for a printed presentation.)

Present Your Slides

When it comes time to do your presentation, chances are someone will hook up a laptop with your presentation on it to a projector. By default that will show your computer screen. But you don't want someone to see what you've been seeing this whole time as you built your presentation. You just want them to see the slides and nothing else.

Which means you need to go into presentation mode.

To do this, go to the Slide Show tab. On the left-hand side you have the Start Slide Show section. If you click on From Beginning, this will start a presentation at the first slide in your PowerPoint presentation. If you click on From Current Slide it will start the presentation at the slide that's currently visible.

F5 will also start your presentation from the beginning. And Shift + F5 will start your presentation from your current slide.

Either choice will launch the slides you've created as a full-screen presentation.

There are a number of ways to navigate through your presentation. You can use Enter, left-click, page down, or the down arrow to move to the next slide or bullet point. You can use page up or the up arrow to move to the previous slide or bullet point.

You can also right-click and choose Next or Previous from the dropdown menu.

The PowerPoint screen you've been working in will still be there and open behind the scenes. You can reach it using Alt + Tab to move through your active windows or you can use Esc to close the presentation.

Before you enter presentation mode, I'd recommend having any additional windows you're going to want open already so you can easily access them using Alt + Tab.

And it's always a good idea to run through your presentation slides before you present to anyone so you can check and make sure that all the animations, etc. are working.

There is an option to view your slides in Presenter View. What this does is show on your computer screen the slide the audience can currently see as well as your slide notes and the next slide, but on the presentation screen only the presentation slide will show.

Because I'm currently using both an external monitor and my laptop, when I launch a presentation this happens automatically.

If you don't want that, you can go to the presenter screen and in Display settings change it to Duplicate Slide View. This will make it so both screens just show the presentation

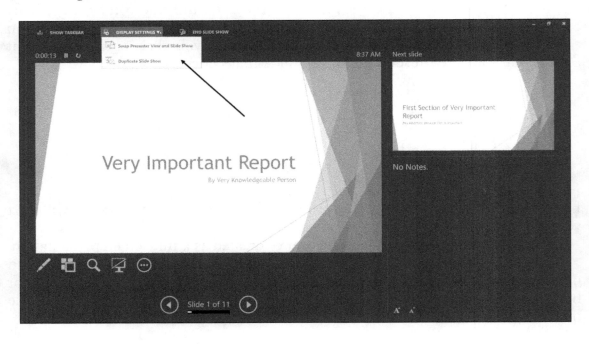

If you need to switch which screen shows which information, choose Swap Presenter View and Slide Show. (Just be aware that if you do this in front of a live audience and you're using notes that they will see any notes you have.)

You can also show and hide presenter view by right-clicking on your presentation and choosing that option from the dropdown.

To close a presentation, hit Esc. Or, right-click and choose End Show from the dropdown menu.

That's the basics of presenting. There are more advanced options, like setting up your slides to advance on a schedule, that are more advanced topics.

Print Your Presentation

You have the option to print your presentation slides, your presentation slides as handouts (so with room for people to take notes), or your presentation slides with your notes.

To do any of these, type Ctrl + P or go to the File tab and then choose Print on the left-hand side.

Both choices will bring you to the Print screen.

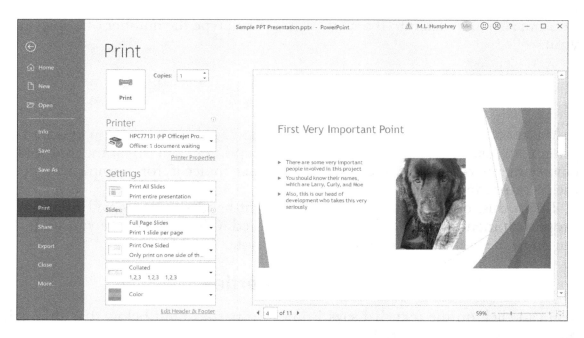

On the left-hand side are your File tab choices, next you'll see a printer icon with a number of setting choices below that, and then on the right-hand side will be a preview of the current slide. You can use the numbers and arrows below that to navigate between your slides.

The default is to print all of your slides and in full-page format and that's what your preview will show. But let's walk through everything you can see on this page and your other possible print options.

Print

Right at the top of the page under the Print header is the printer icon. It shows a printer and says Print under it. This is what you click when you're ready to print your document.

Copies

Next to that is where you specify the number of copies to print. By default the number to print is 1, but you can use the arrows on the right-hand side of the text box to increase that number. (Or decrease it if you've already increased it.) You can also just click into the white text box and type the number of copies you want.

Printer

Below those two options is the Printer section. This is where you specify the printer to use. It should be your default printer, but in some corporate environments you'll want to change your printer choice if, for example, you need the color printer.

To do this, click on the arrow on the right-hand side. This will bring up a dropdown menu with all of your printers listed. Click on the one you want. If the one you want isn't listed then use Add Printer to add it.

Printer Properties

You can click on the text that says Printer Properties right below that although most of the options covered there will also be covered in the Settings section on the main page. If you do click, the Paper/Quality tab this is where you can choose the type of paper, its source, and the quality of your print job.

Print All Slides/Print Selection/Print Current Slide/ Custom Range

Your next option is what to print. By default, you'll print all the slides in the presentation.

If you were clicked onto a specific slide in the presentation and want to just print it then you can choose Print Current Slide. (When you choose this the print preview should change to show just that one slide.)

If you had selected more than one slide in the presentation and then chose to print, you can choose Print Selection to print those slides. (You'd do that in the left-hand task pane.)

Your other option is to print a custom range. The easiest way to use this one is to type the slide numbers you want into the Slides text box directly below the dropdown. This will automatically change the dropdown selection to Custom Range. Your preview will also change to just show the slides you've listed.

You can list numbers either individually or as ranges. If you list a range you use a dash between the first and last number. So 1-10 would print slides 1 through 10. You can also use commas to separate numbers or ranges. So 1, 2, 5-12 would print slides 1, 2 and 5 through 12.

Full Page Slides/Notes Pages/Outline/Handouts

The next choice is what you want to print.

In the top section you can choose to print full page slides, notes pages, or an outline.

Full page slides will put one slide on each page you print and nothing else.

Notes pages will put one slide per page on the top half of the page and your notes on the bottom half of the page. Each page will be in portrait orientation. (Short edge on the top.)

The Outline option will take all of the text from your slides and list it out in the same way it's listed on the slides. So if there are bullet points, the outline will have them, too. If there aren't, it won't. Each printed page will contain multiple slides' worth of information. No images are included.

If you want to provide handout slides the next section gives you a number of options to choose from.

The one slide option will center each presentation slide in the middle of a page in portrait orientation. (Not recommended.) The two slide option will put two slides on each page in portrait orientation. (This is a good choice for handouts because it's still visible but doesn't waste paper the way the one-slide option does.)

You can put as many as nine slides on the page, but before you do that think about how legible that will be for the end-user. If you have a lot of slides with images it might be fine, but if they have a lot of text on them or if people will need/want to take a lot of notes, no one is going to thank you for putting nine slides on a page.

The horizontal and vertical choices determine whether the slides are ordered across and then down (horizontal) or down and then across (vertical). I think, at least in the U.S., that most people would expect horizontal.

Print One Sided/Print On Both Sides

If you want to print on both sides of the page this is where you would specify that. The default is to just print on one side of the page, but you can choose to print on both sides and either flip on the short edge or the long edge of the page.

If the paper orientation is Portrait, choose Flip on Long Edge. If the paper orientation is Landscape, choose Flip on Short Edge. For presentation slides you'll generally be working in landscape and want to flip on the short edge, but if you're printing handouts or with notes you'll generally want portrait and to flip on the long edge.

Collated/Uncollated

This only matters if you're printing more than one copy of the presentation. In that case, you need to decide if you want to print one full copy at a time x number of times (collated) or if you want to print x copies of page 1 and then x copies of page 2 and then x copies of page 3 and so on until you've printed all pages of your document (uncollated).

In general, I would recommend collated, which is also the default. In most situations I've been in the audience is given the entire presentation at the start. But if you're handing out the presentation slides one at a time then uncollated will make that easier to do.

Portrait Orientation/Landscape Orientation

This determines whether what you've chosen to print prints with the long edge of the page at the top (landscape) or the short end of the page at the top (portrait).

In general, PowerPoint chooses this for you and does a good job of it. For example, outline should be portrait and full page slides should be landscape and PowerPoint makes that adjustment for you.

However, you might want to change this for the handout slides. For one slide, four slide, and nine slide printing, I think landscape is a better choice than portrait. You can judge for yourself by looking at the preview and seeing how large the slides are and how much white space is taken up with each orientation.

Color/Grayscale/Pure Black and White

This option lets you choose whether to print your slides in color or not. The choice you make will probably depend on your available print resources. When you change the option you'll see in the print preview what each one looks like.

The Color option will look just like your slides:

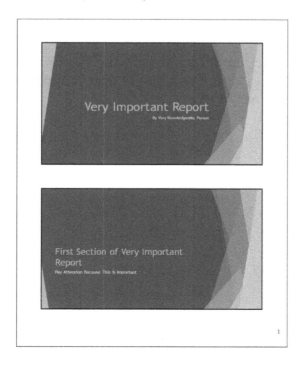

The Grayscale option will print your background elements but strips out any solid background color and converts any colors on the page and any images to grayscale.

The pure black and white one looks to strip the background color as well as the color from most of the design elements. It does appear to leave images in the main body of the presentation in grayscale.

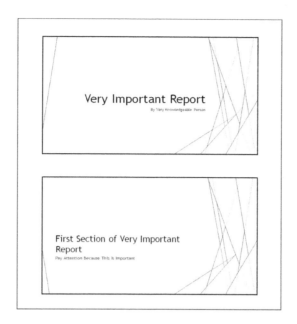

Edit Header & Footer

At the very bottom of the list you can click on the Edit Header & Footer text to bring up the Header and Footer dialogue box where you can choose to add headers or footers to your printed document. The choices available to you will depend on what you're printing.

There are separate tabs for Slides and for Notes and Handouts.

For Slides you can add the date and time, a slide number, and a footer. There is an option to not show this information for the title slide.

For Notes and Handouts you can add the date and time, page number, a header, and a footer.

Some templates will include headers and footers by default.

Once you make your choices, you can see how it will look in the print preview.

Where to Look For Other Answers

Okay, so that's what we're going to cover in this introductory guide.

My goal was to give you a solid understanding of how PowerPoint works and to lead you through the basics of creating a presentation.

There are a number of topics I didn't cover in this guide, such as how to change a presentation slide background color, creating a custom design template, adding timing to your presentation slides, adding objects or text boxes to a slide, adding charts, etc.

At some point you'll probably want to learn about one of those things.

So how do you do it? Where do you get these answers?

First, in PowerPoint itself you have a few options. You can hold your cursor over the choices in any of the tabs and you'll usually see a brief explanation of what that choice can do.

If that brief description isn't enough, a lot of the options have a Tell Me More option below that, like here for the New Slide option in the Insert tab.

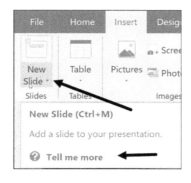

Click on Tell Me More and the built-in Help function in PowerPoint will open a task pane that provides a more detailed discussion of that option. In this example it opens a help topic titled "Add, rearrange, duplicate, and delete slides in PowerPoint" that includes a video as well as written instructions.

Another option is to go directly to the built-in Help function. You do this by clicking on the Help tab and then choosing Help again. You can also press F1.

This will open the Help task pane and you can either search for what you need or navigate through the menu options from there.

I sometimes need more information than this so turn to the internet. (More so with Word and Excel than PowerPoint, but it happens sometimes.)

If I need to know the mechanics of how something works, the Microsoft website is the best option. For example, if I wanted to understand more about the colors used in each theme in PowerPoint I might search for "colors powerpoint theme microsoft 2019".

It's key that you add the powerpoint, microsoft, and your version year in your search so that the result is relevant to your situation.

When I get my search results, I then look for a search result that goes to support.office.com. There will usually be one in the top three or four search results.

If that doesn't work or I need to know something that isn't about how things work but whether something is possible, then I will do an internet search to find a blog or user forum where someone else had the same question. Often there are good tutorials out there that you can read or watch to find your answer.

And, of course, you can also just reach out to me at mlhumphreywriter@gmail.com and I'll try to help if I can.

I'm happy to track down an answer for you or point you in the right direction. Although don't ask me to do your presentation for you. That I won't do. Or I'll do it, but I'll bill you for it.

Conclusion

So there you have it. We've covered the basics of PowerPoint and at this point in time you should be able to create your own nicely polished basic presentation.

Knowing how to create a presentation like this is a valuable skill. I've used PowerPoint presentations for small groups all the way up to rooms full of five hundred people. When you're suddenly standing in front of an audience a presentation like this can help keep you organized and focused on what you wanted to say. It also keeps you from forgetting some vital point as everyone in the room stares at you.

And having a presentation to refer to will in general make you a better presenter because you won't be staring down at a pile of notes the entire time. It also gives your audience something to look at other than you.

Just a final reminder, keep your audience in mind when creating a presentation. Most of my presentations have been given in corporate or regulatory settings, some in more creative settings. But I always live by the motto that the presentation is there to support me not distract from what I'm saying which is why I keep all the crazy shapes and garish color combinations to a minimum. (Although, even I have my weaknesses as you saw with me using the picture of my dog in this book.)

Anyway. Good luck with it. And reach out if you get stuck.

And if you want to continue to learn more about PowerPoint, check out *PowerPoint 2019 Intermediate*.

INDEX

ABOUT THE AUTHOR

M.L. Humphrey is a former stockbroker with a degree in Economics from Stanford and an MBA from Wharton who has spent close to twenty years as a regulator and consultant in the financial services industry.

You can reach M.L. at mlhumphreywriter@gmail.com or at mlhumphrey.com.

www.ingramcontent.com/pod-product-compliance
Lightning Source LLC
Chambersburg PA
CBHW062057050326
40690CB00016B/3119